Praise fu
Antarctic Pioneer: The Trailblazing Life of Jackie Ronne

Joanna Kafarowski's biography of Edith (Jackie) Ronne is an important addition to the tapestry of Antarctic history. All too often, women's voices and contributions are muted or absent altogether. As the first all-women's group across the ice to the South Pole in 1992–93, starting from the Ronne Ice Shelf, we had a sense of pride of the small sisterhood on this vast and remarkable continent.

— ANN BANCROFT, first woman to reach both
the North and South Poles across the ice

It is long overdue that Jackie Ronne gets the acknowledgement she deserves. Her husband, explorer Finn Ronne, would never have reached his goals without her. What contributions to science and Antarctica!

— LIV ARNESEN, first woman to ski solo
and unsupported to the South Pole

An important book for ensuring women explorers like Jackie Ronne are given the recognition they are due, and that future generations may be duly inspired. A much-needed reminder of the work that needs to be done to correct the prejudices of the past.

— FELICITY ASTON, first woman to ski solo across Antarctica

Kafarowski deftly chronicles and celebrates Jackie Ronne's little-known contributions to Antarctic history that helped shatter the "ice ceiling" for women. Told with empathy, indignation, and humour, this fresh and honest account of a determined young woman who overcame a troubled childhood and staunch opposition from the Antarctic establishment to become an explorer and leader in polar circles is set against the backdrop of the struggle for women's rights in twentieth-century America.

— CAROL DEVINE, polar explorer, artist, and co-author of
The Antarctic Book of Cooking and Cleaning

At last! A proper book on Jackie Ronne, a glorious Antarctic pioneer who, for too long, has remained in the shadows. As Joanna Kafarowski writes in these pages, "the history of women in Antarctica has been marginalized," and I am thrilled that she has written this absorbing book to give Jackie the credit she deserves seventy years after her tumultuous expedition. This biography deserves widespread attention.

— SARA WHEELER, author of *Cherry: A Life of Apsley Cherry-Garrard* and *Terra Incognita: Travels in Antarctica*

An inspiring and well-researched book. The story of courageous Jackie Ronne and her experiences in Antarctica in the 1940s is a gift to all women dreaming of adventures in faraway places.

— MONICA KRISTENSEN SOLÅS, Antarctic explorer and author

An engrossing read about a forgotten female explorer. With impeccable research and style, Kafarowski's protagonist is freed from her former trivialized status as merely the supportive wife of expedition leader Finn Ronne.

— LAURIE GWEN SHAPIRO, author of *The Stowaway: A Young Man's Extraordinary Adventure to Antarctica*

Kafarowski's book is an outstanding addition to recent literature celebrating the contributions of overlooked women explorers.

— JAYNE ZANGLEIN, author of *The Girl Explorers*

Smooth, effortless storytelling about a woman's coming of age through adventure and supporting other women to do the same. The stories of women are often left untold — mere afterthoughts in polar exploration. Here, Joanna opens up a life well lived. Well done!

— AMY GIGI ALEXANDER, writer, publisher, cultural explorer

Joanna Kafarowski's scholarly biography is a gripping portrayal of Jackie Ronne — Antarctica's First Lady. Her contributions to polar history are reflected in this well-written and riveting book.

— MARLENE WAGMAN-GELLER, author of *Women of Means:*
Fascinating Biographies of Royals, Heiresses, Eccentrics
and Other Poor Little Rich Girls

A well-researched book on the life and work of Jackie Ronne, shedding light on the pioneering role she played in changing Antarctica from a site of male-only expeditions to one of permanent scientific bases where male and female experts work side by side.

— ANNE STRATHIE, author of *Herbert Ponting: Scott's Antarctic*
Photographer and Pioneer Filmmaker

This book reminds us just how often the Antarctic dreams of great men were accomplished by the support and sacrifice of their wives, at home and on the ice. An inspiring exploration of a pioneering woman in Antarctica and the challenges she faced, both on the frozen continent and on the home front.

— DANIELLE CLODE, author of *In Search of the*
Woman Who Sailed the World

Praise for
The Polar Adventures of a Rich American Dame:
A Life of Louise Arner Boyd

The very first authoritative biography of this shamefully ignored polar explorer.

— *Geographical Magazine*

Like translucent layers over Louise's Arctic exploration maps, Kafarowski weaves threads of Boyd's tenacity, drive, commitment and resilience into the rich tapestry of her biography. Avid readers of Arctic exploration and the lure of polar science will find jewels in these pages.

— *The Northern Review*

Both scholarly and readable … the book is a welcome addition to the annals of Arctic exploration. Kafarowski's narrative brings to life the brave spirit, tenacity, and pure joy of a woman who made the Arctic her life's work at a time when a woman was a rare player in polar exploration.

— *Polar Geography*

A portrait of a brilliant, eccentric woman who was well ahead of her time. Kafarowski vividly transports readers into her subject's northern expeditions. Arctic aficionados, history buffs, and feminists will all be intrigued by this story of an adventurous life.

— *Publishers Weekly*

Thanks to Joanna Kafarowski's biography, Louise Arner Boyd can no longer be ignored in accounts of the history of polar research.

— *Arctic Journal*

ANTARCTIC
Pioneer

Also by Joanna Kafarowski

The Polar Adventures of a Rich American Dame:
A Life of Louise Arner Boyd

Gender, Culture and Northern Fisheries (ed.)

ANTARCTIC
Pioneer

The Trailblazing Life of Jackie Ronne

JOANNA KAFAROWSKI

DUNDURN
PRESS

Publisher: Scott Fraser | Acquiring editor: Kathryn Lane | Editor: Dominic Farrell
Cover designer: Karen Alexiou
Cover image: Jackie Ronne: William R. Latady. Courtesy of the Latady family; Map: American Geographical Society. Courtesy of Karen Ronne Tupek; Icebergs: Anne Dirkse; back cover: Tom Barrett on Unsplash

Library and Archives Canada Cataloguing in Publication

Title: Antarctic pioneer : the trailblazing life of Jackie Ronne / Joanna Kafarowski.
Names: Kafarowski, Joanna, 1962- author.
Description: Includes bibliographical references and index.
Identifiers: Canadiana (print) 20210388463 | Canadiana (ebook) 20210388501 | ISBN 9781459749535 (softcover) | ISBN 9781459749542 (PDF) | ISBN 9781459749559 (EPUB)
Subjects: LCSH: Ronne, Edith M. (Edith Maslin), 1919-2009. | LCSH: Ronne, Edith M. (Edith Maslin), 1919-2009—Travel—Antarctica. | LCSH: Ronne Antarctic Research Expedition (1946-1948) | LCSH: Antarctica—Discovery and exploration. | LCSH: Antarctica—Discovery and exploration—American. | LCSH: Women explorers—United States—Biography. | LCSH: Explorers—United States—Biography. | LCGFT: Biographies.
Classification: LCC G875.R66 K34 2022 | DDC 919.8904092—dc23

We acknowledge the support of the Canada Council for the Arts and the Ontario Arts Council for our publishing program. We also acknowledge the financial support of the Government of Ontario, through the Ontario Book Publishing Tax Credit and Ontario Creates, and the Government of Canada.

Dundurn Press
1382 Queen Street East
Toronto, Ontario, Canada M4L 1C9
dundurn.com, @dundurnpress

To Duncan
for sharing the journey
xoxo

There are some things women don't do.
They don't become Pope or President or go down to the Antarctic.
— Harry Darlington, 1947

I think the presence of women would wreck the illusion of the frontiersman
— the illusion of being a hero…. Women will not be allowed in the
Antarctic until we can provide one woman for every man.
— Rear Admiral George Dufek, 1957

Antarctica [will] remain the womanless white continent of peace.
— Admiral Fred Bakutis,
U.S. Naval Support Force to Antarctica, 1965

I'm glad … that both Jackie and Jennie were good-looking young chicks. It
would have been awful if the first two women to winter over on the ice had
been ugly old hags.
— Paul Dalrymple, 1989

CONTENTS

PROLOGUE

None of us want to be in calm waters all our lives.
— JANE AUSTEN

YOU WOULDN'T THINK that writing a biography of a female Antarctic pioneer would be a hazardous endeavour. Amazingly though, over the course of researching and writing this book, I have been threatened by Ronne supporters and opponents alike, stonewalled, deliberately misdirected, and ignored. It's been seventy-plus years since the daring Ronne Antarctic Research Expedition (1946–1948) mapped and photographed nearly 1.2 million square kilometres of virgin Antarctic coastline, proved that Antarctica was one land mass, and contributed significant scientific findings — all on a shoestring budget. Yet, there have been no published authoritative historical accounts and no biographies of either expedition member Edith "Jackie" Ronne or her controversial husband, explorer, and team leader Finn Ronne.[1] In part, I can see why.

Finn Ronne — and, by association, his fiercely loyal wife, Jackie — continues, even today, to elicit powerful feelings in Antarctican circles. Those privileged enough to work in or explore Antarctica (rather than merely visit as a tourist) are members of an elite circle and are sometimes wary of "outsiders." Dominated by older white men, this group has been profoundly affected by the mythic image of Antarctica and their personal experiences there, no matter how long ago they took place. In their minds, Ernest Shackleton, Roald Amundsen, Robert Falcon Scott, Douglas Mawson, and, more recently, Hubert Wilkins, Richard Byrd, Vivian Fuchs, Edmund Hillary, and Ranulph Fiennes are hallowed names, never to be forgotten. But invoking the name of Ronne stirs a pot that some people wish left undisturbed.

As an Antarctic explorer, Finn is a polarizing figure. Over time, personal opinions about him have been accepted as truths and adopted into the narrative of Antarctic exploration. Jackie's story cannot easily be teased out from Finn's, nor should it be. Jackie and Finn Ronne shared a deep and abiding love for each other and for that loneliest continent at the bottom of the world. As a biographer committed to unearthing and sharing the lives of forgotten intrepid women, I have found it frustrating trying to write Jackie's story, eclipsed as it is by the pervasive influence of her husband. But the woman who started life as plain Edith Maslin in a rundown two-storey apartment house in Baltimore and who became the glamorous, globe-trotting adventurer Jackie Ronne was an enterprising pioneer and deserves to be celebrated for her own achievements. It is time for this woman to step out from the shadow of her husband and have her own extraordinary life story added to the annals of Antarctic exploration history.

There's a faded and peeling 1957 map of the vast continent of Antarctica hanging on the wall. Starting from Little America, the site of the original 1929 Byrd encampment on the Ross Ice Shelf, the eye sweeps in a north-westerly direction past the frigid Amundsen and Bellingshausen Seas and across the expanse of the Ellsworth Highlands, named after American explorer and aviator Lincoln Ellsworth, who led a 1935 trans-Antarctic expedition. Each name on the map commemorates the valour and achievement of a great Antarctic explorer. Just west of the Pensacola Mountains is Edith Ronne Land, named for Edith "Jackie" Ronne, a leading member of the Ronne Antarctic Research Expedition (RARE) and wife of Norwegian-American explorer Finn Ronne. Other members of this privately organized expedition to Antarctica are remembered here too: Dodson Peninsula, Gutenko Mountains, Cape Adams, Cape Schlossbach, Lassiter Coast, Cape Fiske, Mount Thompson, Kelsey Cliff, Latady Mountains, Latady Island, Mount Wood, Mount Robertson, Nichols Snowfield, McClary Glacier, Mount Peterson, Mount Hassage, and Mount Owen.

Along with that, there's another Antarctica map tacked to the wall: a more modern one, and while the names of the men who participated in RARE are still prominently displayed, the geographical landmark "Edith Ronne Land" has vanished. Instead, this tribute to the first American woman to be a member of an expedition to Antarctica has been depersonalized, neutered. Despite appearing as a feature on Antarctica maps for twenty years, "Edith Ronne Land" has been summarily erased; her name replaced by the anonymous "Ronne Ice Shelf."

In the late 1960s, the U.S. Board on Geographic Names proposed changing the names of "Edith Ronne Land" and "Marie Byrd Land" in accordance with the recommendation of the Advisory Committee on Antarctic Names to eliminate all first names from geographic features. Despite vigorous opposition, Undersecretary of the Interior Charles F. Luce stated: "What was named Edith Ronne Land at the time of Ronne's expedition has turned out to be not land but a much more significant feature ... [and] there has been general agreement that the Ronne Ice Shelf name will most effectively commemorate American exploration in this area and that it is therefore important for this name to become established in world usage." Thus, when "Edith Ronne Land" was identified as an important and different geographical feature, the name was changed to recognize the Ronne family of explorers as a group, rather than Edith Ronne herself.[2] Luce continued: "Captain Finn Ronne has agreed to the dropping of 'Edith.'" No one asked Edith "Jackie" Ronne herself what *she* thought about the change. This erasure of Jackie's first name and, by extension, her accomplishments, is symbolic of the treatment of women's history in Antarctica.[3]

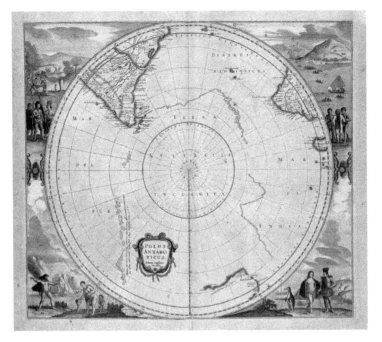

Polus Antarcticus map, 1650.

Women have only come to this frozen continent recently. Historically, Antarctica has been seen as offering the supreme testing ground for a virile, red-blooded male looking to pit himself against an unforgiving environment that often demands the ultimate sacrifice. Famed explorer Captain James Cook was one of the first to document crossing the Antarctic Circle:

> That there may be a Continent or large tract of land near the Pole, I will not deny, on the contrary I am of opinion there is, and it is probable that we have seen a part of it. The excessive cold, the many islands and vast floats of ice all tend to prove that there must be land to the South and that this Southern land must lie or extend farthest to the North opposite the Southern Atlantick and Indian Oceans.

Russia, the United Kingdom, and the United States all claim the distinction of having discovered Antarctica first. In 1820 Russian naval officers Fabian Gottlieb von Bellingshausen and Mikhail Lazarev reported that they had sighted the continent; that same year, British Royal Navy officer Edward Bransfield and mariner William Smith declared the same thing. American sealer Nathaniel Palmer made this claim too. All reported having sighted the Antarctic mainland within months of each other. These momentous sightings spurred on their fellow countrymen, who believed the words of the English poet William Blake that "great things are done when men and mountains meet."

Between the 1820s and the 1840s, daring explorers — including Britons James Weddell, James Clark Ross, and John Biscoe; American Charles Wilkes; Russian von Bellingshausen; and Frenchman Jules Dumont d'Urville — made further discoveries about the islands and coastline of Antarctica. Their discoveries were not met with universal acclaim, however. The approximately twenty-year period following the expeditions of these men was termed "the age of averted interest," by historian H.R. Mill and was characterized by public apathy toward Antarctic exploration. This was due in part to renowned explorer James Clark Ross's widely circulated statement that there were few scientific discoveries left to be made in the region.

Interest was revived in the latter half of the nineteenth century, and this period between about 1897 and 1922 became known as the "Heroic Age of Antarctic Exploration." At the 1895 Sixth International Geographical Congress in London, Resolution Three stated: "the exploration of the Antarctic Regions is the greatest piece of geographical exploration still to be undertaken." Many European countries, including Russia, Germany, France, Sweden, Belgium, and Norway, eagerly joined the race to unlock Antarctica's tantalizing secrets.

These were the years of glory, dominated by expeditions that loom large in Antarctican exploration history, including de Gerlache's Belgian Antarctic Expedition (1897–1899) on the *Belgica*; Borchgrevink's British Antarctic Expedition (1898–1900) on the *Southern Cross*; Charcot's Fourth French Antarctic Expedition (1908–1910) on the *Pourquoi-Pas? IV*; Amundsen's South Pole Expedition (1910–1912) on the *Fram*; Scott's British Antarctic

Expedition (1910–1913) on the *Terra Nova*; Shackleton's Imperial Trans-Antarctic Expedition (1914–1917) on the *Endurance*; and the Shackleton-Rowett Expedition (1921–1922) on the *Quest*.

Antarctica was unashamedly a man's world. Women were not welcome there, and if none were included in the expeditions of the time, it was not due to a lack of trying, as is evidenced by this blithe 1914 letter to Ernest Shackleton.

> We are three strong healthy girls and also gay and bright, and willing to undergo any hardships, that you yourselves under-go. If our feminine garb is inconvenient, we should just love to don masculine attire. We have been reading all books and articles that have been written on dangerous expeditions by brave men to the Polar regions, and we do not see why men should have all the glory, and women none, especially when there are women just as brave and capable as there are men.

The famous advocate for women's rights and contraception (and noted paleobotanist) Marie Stopes applied to Robert Falcon Scott for a position on his ill-fated *Terra Nova* expedition. She was summarily rejected, despite her impressive scientific qualifications. Australian explorer Sir Douglas Mawson received a letter from a Marjorie Collier, who wished to work as his cabin "boy." She declared boldly: "You will find the nimbleness of youth, combined with the knowledge of a woman a very useful factor."

From the 1920s onwards, women demonstrated their willingness to take on the daunting risks and applied regularly as team members of Antarctic expeditions. For example, over twenty-five women made clear that they wished to join the British Australian and New Zealand Antarctic Research Expedition (BANZARE) of 1929–1931. Mawson, in common with other Antarctic expedition leaders of this period, remained unmoved by their supplicating letters. Not all men of the time agreed with this conservative position. In a farewell speech to Mawson, J.G. Turner of the Hobart Marine Board championed the cause of women: "One thing disappoints me a little — that no women are accompanying the expedition. In these

Terres Australes et Antarctiques Françaises
postage stamp showing Abby Jane Morrell.

enlightened times, women have invaded all professions and all businesses, with credit to themselves and to the advantages of the businesses and professions." His protestations fell on deaf ears.

The modest literature on the history of women in Antarctica is inconclusive, contradictory, or, in some cases, inaccurate. While little is known about her, Louise Séguin is regarded as the first European woman to travel to the subantarctic region, which she did on board the *Roland* as part of the 1773–1774 voyage to the Kerguelen Islands with Yves-Joseph de Kerguelen-Trémarec.[4] American Abby Jane Morrell sailed there with her husband on board the *Antarctic* between 1829 and 1831. Her *Narrative of a Voyage to the Ethiopic and South Atlantic Ocean, Indian Ocean, Chinese Sea, North and South Pacific Oceans in the Years 1829, 1830, 1831* (published by J. & J. Harper in 1833) is the first account of the subantarctic region from a woman's perspective.

Ingrid Christensen (l) and Mathilde Wegger (r) on board the M/S *Thorshavn*, 1931.

The Kerguelen Islands, also known as the Desolation Islands, were visited by Elizabeth Morgan and her husband, American whaler Captain Ebenezer "Rattler" Morgan, on the *Julius Caesar* between 1851 and 1853 and by Jane Robinson and her husband, Captain James William Robinson, on the *Offley* in 1858.

While the wives of whaling captains sailing Antarctic waters were likely on board in the early 1900s, credit for being the first woman to sight the Antarctican continent is generally given to thirty-eight-year-old Norwegian Ingrid Christensen (1891–1976).[5] Described as fearless and spirited, Christensen and friend Mathilde Wegger sailed on the M/S *Thorshavn* with Ingrid's wealthy shipping magnate husband, Lars Christensen. It was on this 1931 trip that she viewed Antarctica for the first time. Unable to land due to difficult conditions, Ingrid Christensen returned to Antarctica again with other female companions in 1933 and 1934. During this last voyage, the ship on which she was sailing successfully circumnavigated almost the entire continent.[6]

In 1935 Lars Christensen hired as his captain Norwegian Klarius Mikkelsen, who sailed on the *Thorshavn* to Antarctica with his twenty-eight-year-old wife, Danish-born Caroline Mikkelsen. Encountering favourable conditions, the captain was able to make a successful landing, and Caroline Mikkelsen (1906–1998) became the first woman to set foot on Antarctica on February 20, 1935. Not unsurprisingly, there is no mention of this historic accomplishment in the *Polar Record* account of this expedition. In 1937 Ingrid Christensen returned to Antarctica with her youngest daughter, Augusta Sofie Christensen; a friend, Ingebjørg Lillemor Rachlew; and Solveig Widerøe, wife of the ship's aviator, and the four women set foot on Scullin Monolith in Mac. Robertson Land, Antarctica. Today, the Four Ladies Bank marks this spot, while Mount Caroline Mikkelsen, Ingrid

Caroline Mikkelsen.

Christensen Coast, and Cape Ingrid commemorate other geographic features associated with these adventurous women. On the sixtieth anniversary of Caroline Mikkelsen's first landing, research revealed the exact spot was on the Tryne Islands rather than on the Antarctic mainland itself.

A 2002 notice published in the *Polar Times* that "the title of first woman to land in Antarctica is up for grabs" did not result in a flurry of frenzied speculation as would have been the case if the identity of the first man had been questioned. Today, it is believed that Caroline Mikkelsen was the first woman to land on an Antarctican island and Ingrid Christensen was the first woman to land on the Antarctic mainland during her final trip there in 1937.

Marie Stopes, Marjorie Collier, and so many other unknown, courageous women possessed the burning desire to travel to remote Antarctica, whatever the cost. Ingrid Christensen, Mathilde Wegger, Augusta Sofie Christensen, Ingebjørg Lillemor Rachlew, Solveig Widerøe, and Caroline Mikkelsen were the first to reach the continent and claim this victory for women. Yet their names have slipped into oblivion. This may be, in part, because diaries or letters they may have written about their Antarctic experiences have not survived, or it may be because their achievements have been obscured by that of their better-known seafaring husbands. Another reason is simply that the history of women in Antarctica has been marginalized.[7]

Nine years after Ingrid Christensen and her three female companions clambered triumphantly onto the Antarctic mainland, Edith "Jackie" Ronne did the same and became the first American woman to do so. Like Christensen and Mikkelsen before her, she was there at the behest of her husband. But this time, it was different. By the time she stepped ashore rocky Stonington Island in Marguerite Bay off the west coast of the Palmer Peninsula, Antarctica, in 1947, Jackie Ronne had played a critical role in planning and organizing the mission. She was already a fully fledged member of the Ronne Antarctic Research Expedition (RARE), even though most of the other (male) team members did not approve. Jackie Ronne would become the driving force in maintaining the RARE legacy, and it was her successful participation in this heroic expedition and her work as an Antarctic pioneer that paved the way for other women who would work in, explore, and make policy decisions about Antarctica far into the future.

PART ONE

BEFORE ANTARCTICA

CHAPTER 1

OVERCOMING THE ODDS

Not how you are, but what you make of things.
— NORWEGIAN PROVERB

CHURNING THROUGH THE frigid billowing waves, the battered Zodiac sped straight and true toward tiny Stonington Island in Antarctica. On board, her heart filled with trepidation and her eyes fixed on the approaching shore, was polar icon Jackie Ronne and daughter Karen. Almost fifty years previously, Jackie had been the first American woman to participate in an Antarctic expedition, and one of two daring women to overwinter on the continent. It was now February 1995 and this momentous trip to East Base on Stonington Island was her first visit back in decades. She had never intended to return, but fate had intervened. The thirteen months she had spent there in the company of her husband, famed polar explorer Finn Ronne, and the twenty-two-member expedition team had been challenging, fraught with tension — and the highlight of her life. Years later, her husband

and most of the expedition members were dead and Jackie was beginning to receive the recognition she deserved.

Reaching the pebbled beach, the two excited women and their friend, photographer Ann Hawthorne, were assisted out of the bobbing boat and scrambled awkwardly onshore. The M/V *Explorer*, operated by luxury cruise specialist Abercrombie & Kent, was anchored a kilometre and a half away with ninety-two guests eager for their turn to visit the island. Thankfully, everyone waited respectfully for Jackie to have time there with Karen. It was a laborious, slow climb to East Base, with snowdrifts up to their waist in some areas, but nothing was going to stop them now. Hawthorne remembered how important it was to get Jackie to the base: "It was a walk of discovery back in time." Finally, as skuas dived and careened about their heads, Jackie stood in the clearing of buildings that represented the most momentous part of her life — her time as a member of the 1946–1948 Ronne Antarctic Research Expedition.

The tiny 3.5 x 3.5–metre Ronne Hut in which she and Finn had lived and worked was still there, in a dilapidated state. Jackie had to climb on a pillar of stones to peer through the dirty, streaked window that Finn had installed for her. She was flooded with emotions — excitement at visiting this remote place from her past and sorrow because Finn was not there to share it with her. She and Karen wandered the few steps over to the wooden bunkhouse, with its plaque declaring East Base as a protected heritage site, and then surveyed the foundations of the machine shop, which had been demolished in the intervening years. Lastly, she and Karen entered the science building where the men had conducted their experiments. She was dismayed by the condition — the creeping mould on the wood and the missing panels on the roof. There was evidence of decay everywhere. So much had changed and most of the equipment and furnishings inside the buildings had been stolen, removed, or destroyed.

Karen knew all the exciting stories, but how wonderful to hear them again from her mother in situ, where the historic expedition had taken place. This was where Jackie Ronne's lifelong obsession with Antarctica had come to life and where her role as a pioneer had originated. Karen later commented: "She didn't see herself as a feminist icon who did unusual, difficult things.

She thought she was caught up and swept along by events and ended up becoming famous for going to the Antarctic. She didn't set out to be a rebel."

While her friend Arctic explorer Louise Arner Boyd had yearned to visit the frozen wastelands of the polar pack ice since she was a child, Jackie Ronne (born Edith Maslin) had hardly even heard of Antarctica until she was a teen. History-making in Antarctica — the intense, international competition to be the first to reach the South Pole; the tragedy of the lost lives of desperate heroes; the stark beauty of this desolate continent — was of no real interest to her. It existed in a separate reality from her own. She grew up as an ordinary American girl with a normal, if rather dysfunctional, family. Despite her unremarkable beginnings, Jackie always felt in her bones that she was meant for something extraordinary. Her destiny, to be an Antarctic pioneer, would not be revealed for years to come.

As a cool dawn broke on the morning of October 14, 1919, twenty-three-year-old Elizabeth Parlett Maslin lay in a Maryland General Hospital maternity room in Baltimore, recovering from the travails of birthing her daughter the previous night. A conventional woman of her time, she bestowed two of the most popular names of the year on her daughter: "Edith" and "Anna."

Less than five months earlier, Elizabeth had married strapping twenty-one-year-old Charles Jackson Maslin in a shotgun wedding. Daughter Edith Maslin's first home was in rental accommodations at 1917 Eutaw Place in a genteel Baltimore neighbourhood. While her parents lived there, it was described as "a broad and lovely avenue of fountains and plants and promenades, its twelve blocks from Dolphin Street to Lake Drive a ribbon of elegance." It is still an attractive area today. The community was dominated by towering Victorian mansions originally inhabited by some of the city's colourful characters, including William Van-Lear Black, millionaire publisher, aviator, and sponsor of Richard Byrd's 1926 flight to the North Pole.

Many immigrant families lived in the area nearby, seeking the American dream. The houses there were sprawling, bustling places, frequently inhabited by two or three families. The Maslins' apartment was located in the

Elizabeth Parlett and Charles Jackson Maslin, likely in 1918.

Merriel Pratt Maslin, likely in 1915.

biggest and noisiest house of all: 1917 Eutaw Place was home to six families. In total, nineteen people lived in the house. There was no privacy or quiet time to be had there. Still, if their actual home left something to be desired in terms of peace and tranquility, the proud young parents would have enjoyed the short walk to leafy Druid Hill Park and Druid Lake — the crown jewel of parks in Baltimore, which offered space for recreation and quiet reflection.

Later in life, Edith would learn about other famous Baltimore residents who lived there around the same time. Streets away in Upper Fells Point, a mainly Black neighbourhood, the little girl who grew up to become the smoky-voiced jazz singer "Lady Day" Billie Holiday had spent a troubled childhood being shunted from one reluctant relative to another. One of the greatest American sports heroes of all time, Babe Ruth, was born and attended a reformatory there before he left to join the Boston Red Sox in 1914. Mystery writer Dashiell Hammett of *The Maltese Falcon* and Sam Spade fame probed the seedy underbelly of Baltimore while working for the Pinkerton Detective Agency.

With wavy, dark-brown hair framing a rounded face and wide-set eyes, Elizabeth had a lively rather than a beautiful face. In an early photograph, she looks squarely at the camera with hope and determination. Almost but not quite as tall as her new husband, she had worked as a clerk but gave this up after marriage. Jackie recalled that her mother could be a taskmaster where her homework was concerned and should have been a teacher. Images of Charles Jackson Maslin show him impeccably dressed in a dapper suit and hat. He is boyishly handsome, with a remarkable resemblance to the young writer F. Scott Fitzgerald. Hair slicked smartly back, tie pulled neatly into place, he was a young man with great things ahead of him, or so his young bride must have hoped.

Elizabeth Parlett Maslin was descended from an early Baltimore family that had immigrated from England in the early eighteenth century. There have been generations of Parletts living in Baltimore ever since. The 1901 *R. Polk Directory for Baltimore* lists over fifty Parletts, including a spiritualist, a president of a cigar factory, a horse-shoer, and a tax collector. In the year Elizabeth was born, the list included a munitions worker, a president of a middy blouse manufacturer, and a thirty-four-year-old policeman named Daniel H. Parlett, Elizabeth's father.

Young Elizabeth grew up in a turbulent home, and in 1903, when she was seven years old, her mother sued her father for divorce on the grounds of brutality. This was a dramatic step by a woman with two young children. It would have caused a scandal within her family and community, and was a stigma that Elizabeth struggled with. After the divorce, Elizabeth moved with her mother into the home of her maternal grandmother. As was the case with many divorced women of the time, their quality of life suffered. On the other hand, Daniel Parlett, a fifteen-year veteran of the Baltimore Police Force, started a second family and was financially secure all his life. There is little evidence to suggest that her father or her paternal family ever played a major role in Elizabeth's life.

Elizabeth's young husband, Charles Jackson Maslin, had a distinguished lineage on his mother's side, as he was descended from soldiers who fought in the American Revolution. His parents, Edith Pratt Maslin and Samuel Jackson Maslin, moved from Havre de Grace, Maryland, to Baltimore soon after their marriage. They had two children: a daughter, Merriel Pratt, born in 1895 and a son, Charles Jackson, born two years later. The siblings were close and Merriel always harboured a strong sense of responsibility for her younger brother. The Maslin family played a critical role in the life of young Edith. Edith's paternal grandparents were upstanding Baltimore citizens who took their civic responsibilities seriously. Edith's grandfather worked as a grocer who gave freely of his time to local volunteer organizations. He and his wife were high-minded, steady, and conscientious, and raised their two children to be the same.

Merriel was an unusual woman and became one of the most influential people in Edith's life. Strong-minded and straight as an arrow, Merriel was a Peabody Scholarship recipient and a dedicated physics student at the all-women's Goucher College. At this time, there were few women physicists in the United States and only a handful found jobs in their field. Merriel, however, was determined and became one of the first women physicists to work for the National Bureau of Standards. It is not known if young Merriel was conflicted regarding marrying and starting a family or having a career. Few women scientists were allowed to combine the two. Perhaps she agreed with Florence Watts, who reported that she intended to remain single because "I have other professions open to me in which the hours are shorter, the work more agreeable and the pay possibly better." By the time her niece Edith was born, Merriel had proven herself to be accomplished, hard-working, and successful. Sadly, the same could not be said of Charles, her younger brother and Edith's father.

From the beginning, Charles lacked the steadiness and focus of his sister. By the time he was twenty, he had a questionable employment record. Never keeping a job for long, he shifted between one position and the next. Charles's fallback was always working in his father's grocery, where his father kept an eye on him. When his daughter was born, he worked as an inspector for stove manufacturer Bartlett-Hayward, although this job, too, was short-lived. His lack of ambition and self-discipline would impact on his marriage and the upbringing of Edith. It would also influence the type of man she would later look for as a husband.

As a new wife and mother, Elizabeth Maslin struggled to provide for her child and husband. Strikes were rife across the country — food and coal shortages were the scourge of every household. Food prices skyrocketed. In 1919 Elizabeth would have paid about $660 for her yearly food bill, compared to $380 only three years previously. Having a father-in-law who was a grocer certainly helped.

Growing up a few minutes away from her paternal grandparents in an affluent neighbourhood would have seemed to offer an ideal start to the life of any child. But Edith's world was not as safe and insulated as might be expected. The civil unrest in the United States after the war was experienced in most cities across the country, including Baltimore. Only weeks before she was born, Baltimore residents witnessed a violent race riot. Any young family strolling through Druid Hill Park would know that playgrounds, swimming pools, tennis courts, golf courses, and dance pavilions, in short, anywhere one would want to go in the park, had been racially segregated since the park opened in 1860 and would remain so until the mid-1950s.

Injustice was apparent within other sectors of society, too. Changes in the status of American women were underway. In the summer of 1919, the

United States was in the throes of a divisive battle over the rights of women, provoking strife within households and the community alike. The struggle for a woman's right to vote had been raging for years, but, at long last, the end was finally in sight. In 1916, Alice Paul and Lucy Burns had formed the National Woman's Party as an outgrowth of the National American Woman Suffrage Association. Since that time, relentless pressure on the government had moved the dial. The election of Jeannette Rankin as the first woman member of Congress was a gamechanger. In June 1919, Congress passed the Nineteenth Amendment: "The right of citizens of the United States to vote shall not be denied or abridged by the United States or by any State on account of sex." This amendment was ratified the following year.

Following the passage of the Nineteenth Amendment, women across the country were jubilant, anticipating change across all spheres of life. Politicians feared a "petticoat hierarchy which may at will upset all orderly slates and commit undreamed of executions at the polls." Women reformers were successful in proposing the 1922 Cable Act, which improved the citizenship requirements for married women, and the 1924 Child Labor Amendment addressing the federal regulation of child labour, but this success was diminished when women's groups splintered due to differences regarding strategy and objectives. During the week following Edith's birth, Elizabeth Maslin would have read in the *Baltimore Sun* about the plans for a new Woman's Clinic at the local Johns Hopkins Hospital as well as the nationwide drive on the part of women to support the newly forming League of Nations. Despite all of this, the position of ordinary American women like Elizabeth Maslin did not seem to change much in the household and in the workplace — but the wheels were turning.

The social disquiet that pervaded the country and the city of Baltimore was reflected in the Maslin household. Charles was prone to depression and emotional turmoil, and as a result, he had difficulty holding down a job for any length of time. Needless to say, this resulted in a lot of domestic strife. Elizabeth needed a steady partner and a good provider. Throughout her childhood, Edith's parents fought, the electricity and gas were turned off, and welfare officers visited the home. Edith recalled having to sleep in the same bed as a lodger's daughter, a young woman who would smack her constantly. Edith often informed her grandparents that she was unable to complete her homework or prepare for school tests due to the arguments and tension within the home. The couple separated and reconciled on a regular basis. Clearly, Charles and Elizabeth were not cut out to be parents, and they were never able to form a strong emotional bond with their daughter.[1]

Edith spent more and more time at her aunt's home as she grew older. Although she had a natural tendency toward seriousness, Merriel undertook her role as a substitute mother with exasperated fondness. She wrote to a friend: "This has been the longest morning imaginable. It would have been profitable if it had been spent with Sunday school and church. My small niece has been right at my heels so that it has been jacks, then checkers and then stories. I hope that I have been successful in my persuasions to keep her quiet for a while."

In 1929, by the time Edith turned ten years old, her life began to improve. Merriel married physicist Dr. Irvine C. Gardner, with Edith serving as a bridesmaid. Irvine was a Harvard man six years older than Merriel. The two shared a passion for science. They had met at the National Bureau of Standards where they both worked. His dour appearance belied a mischievous sense of humour that balanced the sterner approach of his new wife. Both the Gardners loved the outdoors and shared this with their young niece. Irvine was a brilliant physicist, balancing his day job with expeditionary work that took him around the world chasing solar eclipses. Merriel accompanied him on most of his exotic travels. Their love of scientific discovery, adventure, and willingness to live life on their own terms had a powerful effect on their impressionable niece.

In her early teens, Edith was shuttled between the homes of her parents, her paternal grandparents, and her aunt and uncle. In the 1930s, she attended the all-girls Eastern High School at which her mother had also been a student. She focused on her studies as best as she could given the challenges at home. Increasingly, Merriel and Irvine Gardner and her grandparents

Dr. Irvine Gardner, likely in the late 1940s.

assumed greater responsibility for her care. By the age of fourteen, Edith lived with her grandparents during the week and Merriel and Irvine on the weekends. She never lived with her parents on a full-time basis again. No formal adoption papers were ever completed, and her parents never challenged the arrangements. By the age of sixteen, Jackie had moved in with her aunt and uncle on a permanent basis.

The transition to living full-time with her aunt and uncle went smoothly. Merriel and Irvine actively pursued their interests in travel, hiking, and expanding the mind. Edith often accompanied them to public talks of scientific interest. In her sixteenth year, Edith attended an event that was to have a lasting impact. Due to Irvine Gardner's participation in National

Edith Maslin as a young woman, in the late 1930s.

Geographic Society–sponsored expeditions, he was often given tickets to their special events in Washington. One evening, Merriel, Irvine, and Edith attended a "Welcome Home" presentation for Admiral Richard Byrd and the members of the 1933–1935 Second Byrd Expedition to Antarctica. Merriel and Irvine would have talked with their niece about the great American hero Byrd who claimed the distinction of being the first to fly to both the North and South Poles. Teenaged Edith was starry-eyed. "I was very impressionable and my eyes were glued to the very handsome and charismatic Admiral Byrd, thinking and hoping some day I would meet a man like that. Little did I know that my future husband was sitting on the platform that night."

The happiest periods of her teenaged years were three carefree summers at Camp May Flather located in rural Virginia. While there, she learned to smoke and acquired the moniker "Jackie" — she and her Girl Scout friends adopted nicknames to aggravate their counsellors. Aunt Merriel and Uncle Irvine continued their global perambulations. In 1936 they travelled to Kazakhstan as part of a joint National Bureau of Standards-National Geographic Society expedition led by Irvine to gather data on a total eclipse of the sun. This was followed by the 1937 National Geographic-U.S. Navy Expedition to the Canton Island in the South Pacific. Edith loved learning about it all. Meanwhile, she graduated from high school in June 1937 and prepared for college.

Wooster College in Wooster, Ohio, was a whole new experience for vivacious Edith. College could not come soon enough for her, especially since she had not been allowed to date during high school. She embraced her new life with gusto. She was active in college sports, joining both the basketball and volleyball teams, and took pleasure in her teams' successes. Her letters home to Merriel and Irvine were breathless accounts of innocent times — lively sorority dances, entertaining movies at the local picture show, and jaunty visits to school friends. Merriel, who was financing her college education, grew increasingly alarmed that Edith was spending too much time socializing.

At the end of December 1937, Edith was dealt a heavy blow. Within a matter of days, she lost both her beloved paternal grandparents, "Ma Ma" and "Nan Dad," to sudden illness. Being close to loved ones became more important than ever. At her aunt's insistence, Jackie transferred to George Washington University (GWU), located in Washington, D.C., which meant that she could return to live with her aunt and uncle. From this point on, Merriel and Irvine Gardner became her adoptive parents — in fact, if not in law.

Moving to Washington from the sleepy backwoods of Wooster, Ohio, meant Edith was introduced to a more cosmopolitan and sophisticated city. Possibilities were much greater for an ambitious young woman. Most importantly, Merriel could monitor her studies.

Edith, now known as "Jackie" to her friends, thrived in this environment. She joined the Beta Alpha Chapter of the Phi Mu Fraternity, serving as both the president and treasurer of her pledge class from 1938 until 1939. Years later, she was remembered as being a tremendous amount of fun, always willing to organize sledding and skating outings in the winter and swimming parties in the summer. This esteemed women's organization provided Jackie with a ready-made network of supportive mentors and close friends, and she valued her status as a Phi Mu sister for the rest of her life.[2]

At George Washington University, she studied history, political science, English, and home economics. She joined the volleyball team and the Cue and Curtain drama club, and began writing for the university newspaper, aptly named the *Hatchet*, which she loved. She became a member of the Columbian Women — a GWU-based charitable women's group that provided scholarships to deserving women and hosted social and artistic events.[3] After such a difficult start in life, Jackie always needed to belong. Finally, feeling settled at George Washington, she made new friends and learned to successfully balance her social and academic lives.

As she grew older, she participated more and more in her aunt's and uncle's lives. Because of their personal and professional interests, Merriel and Irv socialized with other educated women and men of science. This group never minded answering Jackie's inquisitive questions. Their dreams and goals in life were lofty — overcoming challenges, inventing things, visiting far-off destinations. Encouraged by her aunt, Jackie's vision and ideas for her own future broadened. As a pioneering woman physicist, Merriel had broken barriers by entering and succeeding in a non-traditional field for women. She always encouraged her niece to follow her dreams, whatever they might be.

After spending two years at GWU, Jackie graduated in 1940 with an AB degree in history. This was no mean feat, as just over 3 percent of American women in 1940 had completed four or more years of college. But Merriel would accept nothing less. Jackie maintained ties with her alma mater for the rest of her life, and one fellow graduate admiringly recalled her jitterbugging enthusiastically at a GWU reunion.

Jackie began taking shorthand and typing at Lake Secretarial School after graduation. Although she was not actively looking for work, Merriel encouraged her to apply to the National Geographic Society (NGS). She was hired as a general clerk for one of the most prestigious geographical societies

Edith "Jackie" Maslin as a George Washington University
graduate, 1940.

in the world in spite of her questionable secretarial skills. The fact that she
was related to Dr. Irvine Gardner had likely been a benefit. Three years
earlier, the internationally recognized *National Geographic Magazine* had
featured the first natural colour photograph of a solar eclipse on its cover.
This image by Dr. Irvine Gardner had made photographic history.

Jackie worked for the National Geographic Society for almost a year.
She was not in close contact with the movers and shakers who came through
the front doors, but she was exposed to the heady excitement of being part
of something bigger than herself and working for an organization that promoted exploration in unknown regions. It was during her time there that
pioneering archaeologists Marion and Matthew Stirling conducted fieldwork into Olmec culture on an NGS-sponsored expedition to Tres Zapotes,
Mexico; Walter and Foresta Wood carried out aerial photography and mapping of southwest Yukon; and her own uncle Irvine travelled to Brazil to
witness a solar eclipse. In an odd coincidence, Jackie met Marion Stirling

in Panama in March 1948 upon Jackie's return from Antarctica. Jackie and Marion Stirling later became firm friends.

It was also a good time for women explorers. A few years previously, Anne Morrow Lindbergh received the National Geographic Society Hubbard Medal, and Amelia Earhart had received the National Geographic Society Gold Medal for the first solo transatlantic flight by a woman.

It was an amazing first job for twenty-one-year-old Jackie and she enjoyed her work thoroughly. She was popular with co-workers. When Jackie accepted a position with the Civil Service Commission and entered government service, her NGS colleague Ruth Whitman wrote: "You radiate happiness and the joy of living.... You stand out as one of the finest girls I have ever known." Later that year, Jackie transferred to the Department of State where she would stay for the next four years.

Her new position delighted her. Her office was located in the austere Old Executive Office Building, originally known as the State, War, and Navy Building — it has been renamed again and is now called the Eisenhower Executive Office Building. Located on 17th Street NW between Pennsylvania Avenue and State Place, and backing onto West Executive Avenue, Jackie's workplace was a dream come true for the recent history graduate. Theodore Roosevelt, William Howard Taft, and Franklin D. Roosevelt had all had offices there before becoming president. Five secretaries of the navy and four secretaries of war had also worked in the building. Once the country's largest office building, it had 550 offices, 1,572 windows, and almost two and a half kilometres of corridors. Jackie loved the historic building redolent with power and buzzing with intrigue.

Jackie's first job in the Department of State was in the Division of Communications and Records, where she worked as a junior clerk. Soon after starting there, she moved to the Division of the American Republics, which was in charge of U.S. relations with Cuba, Mexico, Haiti, and Central and South America. As often happened in her adult life, she was an ordinary person who became swept up in world events. She joined the department at a momentous point in history. Cordell Hull was the forty-seventh U.S. secretary of state. Tall, charming, and genial, Hull was one of the most highly respected of President Franklin D. Roosevelt's advisors and the longest serving of all the secretaries of state. Although Jackie served in a junior position initially, she would have been aware of the seething undercurrents in the department as Roosevelt and the United States teetered on the brink of war. On the world stage, the Second World War was continuing. Thus far, the United States had remained out of it, but things were heating up.

It was during this tense time that Jackie met a co-worker named Elizabeth "Bettie" Earle. Bettie and Jackie became inseparable friends and remained close for the rest of their lives. Like Jackie, Bettie was smart, well-educated, and ambitious, with a strong interest in international affairs. Jackie remembered huddling with Bettie outside Secretary of State Cordell Hull's office on December 7, 1941, when Hull dismissed Kichisaburo Nomura, the Japanese ambassador to the United States, and Special Envoy Saburo Kurusu after Japan bombed Pearl Harbor.

Working at the Department of State, Jackie was not only privy to historical events, but she also met individuals who loomed large in American history. While Jackie and Bettie worked at the Division of the American Republics, the notorious Alger Hiss worked as assistant to Stanley Hornbeck, advisor on political relations, in the same building. Who knows how often the paths of Jackie Maslin and Alger Hiss may have passed in the corridors of power? Jackie would have heard about him from Bettie, since both Hiss and Earle participated in the 1944 Dumbarton Oaks Conference at which the details of the setting up of the United Nations were hammered out.[4]

Jackie had overcome the odds. She had survived a deprived and emotionally scarring childhood to become a successful and confident woman. Through the intervention of a kind-hearted and spirited aunt and through sheer hard work, Jackie attained a good education and raised herself high. Her job in the Department of State was fulfilling, paid well, and offered ample opportunities for advancement; her home life was stable with a supportive and loving aunt and uncle; her social life was hectic but fun. It seemed that life might always continue this way for her. But things were about to change, and the trajectory of her future was about to be set.

CHAPTER 2

MEETING FINN

One love, one heart, one destiny.
— BOB MARLEY

MANY YOUNG WOMEN of Jackie's generation settled for the secure, comfortable middle-class existence of a 1940s housewife: marrying the high school sweetheart, bearing the requisite 2.5 children, and dutifully volunteering for the Junior League, the Red Cross, or other worthy causes. Fortunately for Jackie, though, she knew that there was more to life than that. The ambitions of her physicist aunt and uncle had exposed her from a young age to the wondrous realm of science and exploration. This world, peopled by clever, thought-provoking friends of the Gardners who sought the unknowable, was the real world for Jackie. It was not confined to the pages of the fabled *National Geographic* as it was for most Americans. Her aunt and uncle lived and breathed stimulating scientific inquiry, and Jackie was part of their remarkable lives.

The National Bureau of Standards (NBS), where Jackie's aunt and uncle worked, served as the national physical laboratory for the country and

Jackie Maslin, early 1940s.

promoted "U.S. innovation and industrial competitiveness by advancing measurement science, standards and technology in ways that enhance economic security and improve our quality of life." During the Second World War, the NBS was engaged in vital war work. Irvine Gardner was a trailblazer and made significant contributions to the field of optics applied to aerial photography.[1] During the war, he worked on gunsights and other optics for the military. His NBS colleagues were engaged in a variety of cutting-edge projects including atomic bomb and new weapons research, designing carbon monoxide indicators for fighter plane cockpits, and testing new plastic products and textiles.

At the Department of State, Jackie was also busy with war work. U.S. foreign policy in Latin America was coordinated by the Division of the American Republics — Jackie's office. This region assumed heightened importance to the United States after the Japanese attack on Pearl Harbor in December 1941. Following the attack, most of Latin America severed ties with Axis countries (i.e., Germany, Italy, and Japan), and became more reliant on the United States for trade opportunities. Keen to protect the Panama Canal and ensure a steady flow of goods, America worked to develop its influence in this region, increasing it dramatically during Jackie's tenure.

She was good at her job and coped well with the high-pressure atmosphere and tight deadlines. Knowing she was doing meaningful work and was a valued member of the team would always be important to her. Throughout her time in the Department of State, the number of female employees steadily increased.[2] For a young woman who had an extensive network of girlfriends and who had delighted in being part of female-centred organizations such as the Girl Scouts, Phi Mu Fraternity, and the Columbian Women, this must have provided a collegial workplace.

In her early twenties, Jackie Maslin was fun-loving, bright, and high-spirited. While not a classic beauty, her wholesome looks and uncanny knack of giving her undivided attention to the person she was with, guaranteed she was always popular with the opposite sex.

There was a steady stream of unassuming, pleasant, and safe young men who paraded through her young life. She would soon meet someone completely different. In late 1942, she agreed to go on a blind date. Bettie Earle had invited Jackie to join her along with Bettie's boyfriend and a navy acquaintance of his named Finn Ronne. Jackie wasn't told much about him beforehand, but, as always, she hoped to meet someone lively and fun. The two young women were giddy with excitement planning a romantic picnic in Rock Creek Park, not far from the National Zoo. It proved to be the perfect setting for Jackie to meet this mystery man.

Sparks flew between them almost immediately. Finn Ronne was well-built, suave, and ruggedly handsome. A man's man. Not tall — Jackie ruefully reported that at 5′8″, he matched her in height — but an attractive man, with penetrating brown eyes that never left Jackie's face. Just shy of his

31

Finn Ronne, late 1930s.

Finn Ronne During Byrd Antarctic Expedition in a Workshop Holding a Model. Painting by D.I. Price.

forty-third birthday, he was twenty years older than Jackie, but this never mattered to either of them. She was charmed by his lilting Norwegian accent and his charismatic personality, which drew people to him effortlessly. The contrast between Finn and the callow young men she was accustomed to could not have been greater. Self-assured and confident — just this side of arrogant — disciplined, driven, ambitious, competitive, he had an enviable career as a lieutenant commander in the U.S. Navy, where he was serving with the Bureau of Ships. As she soon learned, he also had a glamorous past as a hardy Antarctic polar explorer. What girl had a boyfriend who could top that?

It's hard to ignore the possibility that in Finn, a man significantly older than her, she saw the nurturing father figure she had never had. Since moving to Washington years earlier, she had rarely seen her parents, and this estrangement only grew more acute over time. For Jackie, Lieutenant Commander Finn Ronne was no doubt someone who could offer the security and stability she craved throughout her life. As well, there was the thrill of a romance with an alluring older man in uniform. Finn was attracted to her refreshing American girl-next-door good looks, youthful energy, optimism, and intelligence. Her zest for life matched his own.

Things moved quickly between them. They discovered shared interests, including sports, a love of the outdoors, and socializing, and had a common outlook on life. Both were forward-thinking people who just got on with things. It took no time at all for Finn to reveal his heart to Jackie and introduce her to Antarctica, his one true love. A mere two weeks after they first met, Finn invited Jackie over to his cramped F Street apartment to view his stirring black-and-white lecture film documenting the daring U.S. Antarctic Service Expedition (1939–1941) in which he had recently participated. Jackie had never seen anything like it and watched in wonder. She recalled applauding Admiral Byrd onstage years earlier and realized that Finn had been there too. It must have seemed that fate had brought them together.

Any other young couple might have ended up snuggling on the couch. For Finn and Jackie, however, this was a night that altered both of their lives. It introduced Jackie to the explorer's world and to those singular, stout-hearted men who were willing to risk it all to accomplish their goals. She learned about the vast, mysterious continent of Antarctica — a land which she would grow to love as much as Finn. Finn had met the woman who would share his life, support his dreams, and fight by his side to protect his legacy and her own.

From their earliest time together, Finn shared his passion for Antarctica with Jackie and began courting her with determination. As she soon learned, Finn was not a man to recognize obstacles or deviate from his life's path. Once he made up his mind about Jackie — once he was sure that she would make the best life partner for him as a man and that she was committed to his goals as an explorer in Antarctica — there was no stopping him. How could Jackie resist a man who whispered to her not of the loveliness of her cornflower-blue eyes or how he admired her shapely figure, but instead of the towering ice cliffs of Palmer Land, the never-ending raw whiteness of the Ellsworth Mountains, and the colonies of comical waddling Adélie penguins? It was a beguiling love song, crooned by few men (or women) on earth. Jackie was not immune to the persuasive charms of this fascinating man. Antarctica began to weave a spell over Jackie as well. The more she learned about Finn, his exotic Scandinavian heritage, and his attraction to the world's most southerly continent, the more she wanted to know. At this stage in her life, she was ready for a serious relationship, and he was the man for her.

Jackie was thrilled by Finn's adventurous spirit and soon discovered that he was a man obsessed. A journalist later reported that "[a]s soon as he is questioned about Antarctica, the conquest of which has been the dominant goal of his adult life, he turns on like a teenager on LSD at a rock festival. The pale brown eyes come alive like a husky's at feeding time." Finn had once proclaimed that he would never return to Antarctica, and upon returning to the United States from the Byrd expedition, he had told a journalist sharply, "No, I'm not glad to be back. When you are away from civilization for a long time you get used to it and enjoy the peace and quiet."

* ✳ *

Unlike most polar explorers of the time, Ronne was born with impeccable Antarctic credentials. It was a legacy that would inspire him, tantalize him, and drive him relentlessly throughout his life. He was born in 1899 in Horten, Norway, as the fourth child and third son of Maren Gurine Gulliksen and Martin Rønne.[3] Martin Rønne's name is forever associated with the renowned Norwegian Roald Amundsen, considered one of the greatest polar explorers of all times. From 1910 until 1912, Martin Rønne had participated in Amundsen's first expedition to Antarctica.

Martin Rønne, early 1930s.

Between 1918 and 1920, he took part in the traverse of the Northeast Passage in the *Maud*, and between 1925 and 1926 he was part of Amundsen's team at Ny-Ålesund, Svalbard, when Amundsen made the first successful flight over the North Pole in the airship *Norge*. Martin Rønne was responsible for creating one of the most iconic polar historic artifacts: the three-person silk tent taken by Amundsen to the South Pole in 1911 and left there to be found weeks later by the ill-fated Robert Falcon Scott party.

Martin Rønne was also the trusted colleague of another famous polar explorer — a man who would later become Finn's nemesis. Upon Amundsen's personal recommendation, in 1928, Martin Rønne was taken on as a master sailmaker by the American explorer Byrd for the First Byrd Expedition to Antarctica. Martin Rønne's resourcefulness and work ethic were highly valued by Admiral Byrd. Rønne was also the only member of the expedition with any Antarctic experience.

Martin Rønne's bunk in Antarctica with Finn Ronne, late 1930s.

As a true Antarctic pioneer, Martin Rønne was a larger-than-life role model for his son. Finn was spellbound by his father's involvement in polar exploration and was determined to follow in his footsteps. Somehow, Martin knew that Antarctica would be his son's destiny as well. When Martin met an untimely death at the age of sixty-nine, Finn replaced his father as a member of the Second Byrd Expedition (1933–1935). After landing at the Little America base, Finn entered the hut to locate where his father had slept. Years earlier and unbeknownst to Byrd and all other team members, Martin Rønne had scrawled his son Finn's name above his bunk. Finn later reported that it was the draftiest and most uncomfortable bunk there. Still, it was a connection with his father that Finn would always cherish.

As a young boy growing up in the modest traditional port town of Horten, Finn Ronne was raised on epic tales about Roald Amundsen and his accomplishments in the polar world. As a child, he had played on the deck of the *Fram* prior to the Third Fram Expedition (1910–1914) to Antarctica in which Finn's father had taken part. Being a small country that has, historically, wielded relatively little power on the world stage, Norway has not launched as many Antarctic expeditions as have other, richer countries. It was not involved in Antarctican exploration until the early 1890s, but it still proudly boasts a stellar polar heritage. Amundsen was an icon for all Norwegians, including young sports-mad Finn who, like his hero, spent as much time as possible in vigorous outdoor pursuits, including cross-country ski racing and ski jumping. Amundsen's single-mindedness, drive to succeed, and fascination with the polar regions captured Finn's attention. As a proud Norwegian and as the son of Martin Rønne, Finn grew up suffused with pride for the polar heritage of his homeland, and this inspired him all his life.

Soon after their fateful blind date, Jackie and Finn were spending all their spare time together. During the day, Jackie continued to work at the Department of State and Finn worked with the navy. Most evenings found the couple excitedly planning their bright future. Jackie's aunt Merriel was not thrilled with the age difference between her young niece and Finn — he was a mere four years younger than Merriel herself. As a result, the relationship between Merriel and Finn would always be somewhat strained. That Jackie was willing to endure her aunt's disapproval is a testament to her growing feelings for this man. It is unlikely that she shared the information that during their early courting days Finn was separated but not yet divorced from his first wife.[4]

After dating for just over a year, Finn knew what he wanted. He proposed to Jackie and she happily accepted. Their wartime wedding on March 18, 1944, was modest and subdued. Neither of them wanted a fuss. Jackie chose to be married inside the home of her aunt and uncle in Chevy Chase, Maryland, in which she had spent her early years. Her maid of honour was Bettie Earle, while Finn asked Carl Eklund, his co-participant on the Third Byrd Expedition, to be his best man. There were no other attendants. No

Jackie and Finn on their 1944 honeymoon in Stowe, Vermont.

one from Finn's Norwegian family flew over for the occasion, and Jackie's parents, from whom she was now completely estranged, were not invited. After their wedding, they travelled to snowy Stowe, Vermont, for their brief honeymoon. It was to be a grand skiing vacation.

After enjoying a blissful time just focusing on each other, the newlywed couple returned to Washington, and Jackie moved into Finn's apartment on F Street. Although they both returned to their previous work on a full-time basis, Jackie and Finn shared a commitment that would change their lives irrevocably and impact the course of Antarctic exploration history.

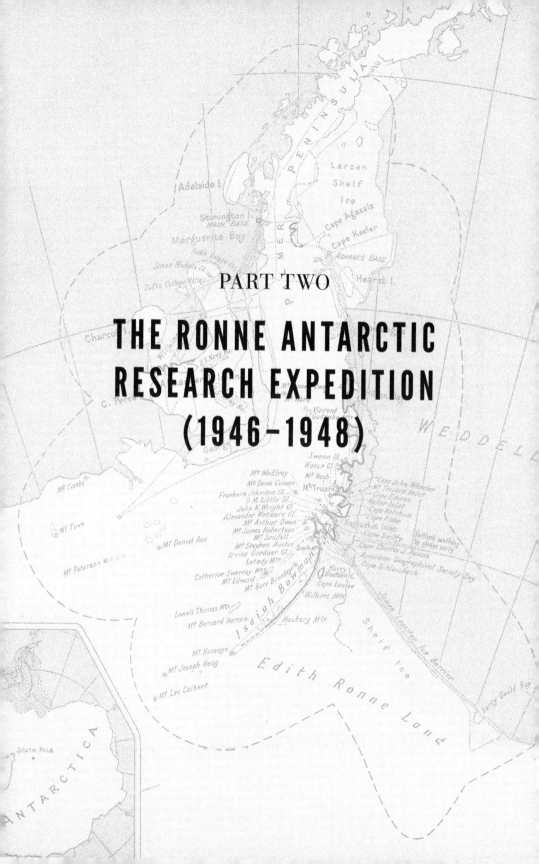

PART TWO

THE RONNE ANTARCTIC RESEARCH EXPEDITION (1946–1948)

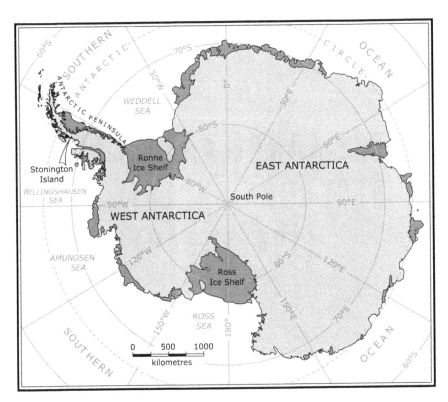

Map of Antarctica.

CHAPTER 3

THE BEGINNING

Antarctica, My Destiny!
— FINN RONNE

JACKIE JOYFULLY BEGAN her new life as a young bride. She moved from the comfort of her aunt and uncle's spacious suburban house into Finn's cramped "efficiency" bachelor apartment. Finn had chosen the apartment himself and furnished it according to his own spartan, masculine tastes. It didn't matter to Jackie; she was resilient. She had survived the turbulence of a childhood home run by irresponsible parents and adapted to life with loving relatives. She took moving into her new husband's apartment in her stride, cheerfully making room for her own belongings. This union brought the peace and order to her life that she had always longed for. In marrying Finn, she became Jackie Ronne, although she would always be known as Edith by her family.

Finn's life changed little in comparison, except that he no longer had to shop, cook, and clean for himself. Of course, Jackie was no traditional

Jackie and Finn early in their marriage, mid-1940s.

1940s housewife. She and Finn may have listened to the new *Adventures of Ozzie and Harriet* radio show that premiered that year, but their marriage did not conform to the stereotypical wife-husband relationship it presented. Unlike many women of the period whose husbands demanded they leave their job after marriage, Jackie remained in her job with the Department of State. There was no expectation from her new husband or her employer that this situation should change. Finn's expectations were of a completely different kind.

Now working in the Office of International Information and Cultural Affairs, she was steadily moving up through the ranks. The year 1944 was a hectic one for employees in the State Department. In July, Jackie was thrilled to be swept up in the excitement of the United Nations Monetary and Financial Conference in Bretton Woods, New Hampshire. She worked with delegates from over forty-four Allied nations that were hammering out postwar financial arrangements. The outcome of this conference would be the creation of the International Monetary Fund. She reported to her aunt Merriel:

> My job is perfect, the people around me so nice, we have had many parties and loads of fun. I have met figures of importance from all over the world and they have stepped on my toes on the dance floor. I have the honor of being the only woman to ... dance with none other than the distinguished Finance Minister of Brazil. My bosses are very excited about the leering gent 'cause they are struggling to put through an office deal with him while he is in the States.

By early 1946, Jackie and Finn had established a comfortable life together with separate work routines. Jackie could not have been prouder when Finn was hired for the top-secret Operation Nanook project led by the U.S. Navy. In July he left Washington and travelled by ship throughout the Canadian Arctic and Greenland for the next three months. Operation Nanook was notable for establishing a radio and weather station at Thule in northwestern Greenland and conducting extensive cartographic work. It was the first time that Jackie and Finn were parted for a period of time, but it would not be the last. Jackie was getting her first taste of what married life would be.

Finn may have enjoyed his work in the Arctic, but he had bigger ideas involving polar exploration. Throughout their life, Jackie said that Finn always had a plan simmering. It isn't clear when the grand plan for launching his own expedition began forming in his imagination or when he first shared this with Jackie. He later confided in his book *Antarctica, My Destiny* that he had been thinking about it while on the Second Byrd Expedition in the 1930s, but likely, the idea had been planted in his mind as a young boy watching his father sail away with Roald Amundsen. Following his trip to Greenland and the Canadian Arctic, he was convinced his time had come. He was "willing to risk everything to be an explorer of the world's unknown." Once a firm plan had formed in his mind, it was all systems go.

After participating in two Byrd expeditions, Finn knew that Antarctica was the place for him: "Only one section of our planet remained a mystery: the Antarctic. Of the continent's thirteen million square kilometres, only one fourth had been explored. There was still much to learn about the vast area at the southern end of the earth." Finn had many questions that needed answering: Was Antarctica one continent or two? Was the Weddell Sea bordering the Atlantic Ocean completely separate from the Ross Sea that bordered the Pacific Ocean? Or did these two bodies of water link and bisect the frozen continent? How could this be proven? Answering these questions remained at the core of the scientific program he was planning.

Choosing the U.S.-owned East Base on tiny Stonington Island adjacent to the Palmer Peninsula as his base camp would help facilitate a rigorous exploration and mapping of the Weddell Sea coastline by air and on foot.[1] Finn had already stayed at East Base as Byrd's second-in-command during the U.S. Antarctic Service Expedition and knew its advantages and shortcomings inside out. He devised a wide-ranging program — encompassing geophysics, geology, meteorology, and seismology — that would be ambitious for a large-scale operation but seemed near impossible for a modest, privately funded expedition. But he always dreamed big. Finn and Jackie had their work cut out for them from the beginning and they both knew it. Jackie's carefully crafted fundraising appeals and Finn's charismatic presentations to potential donors proved to be a potent combination.

The shopping list for the year-long Antarctic expedition was exhaustive and the items expensive. He needed a ship, airplanes, tractors, sledges, skis, coal, radios, film, gasoline, scientific equipment, food, clothing, and dogs. He needed lots of money and reputable sponsorship, the higher the profile the better. And he required a few good men to explore and carry out the scientific program with him.

Initially, Jackie's help consisted only of editing Finn's correspondence and reports — English was still a struggle for him. Finn was the experienced explorer, not Jackie, but she was able to help him communicate his plans

Expedition planning in their Washington, D.C., apartment.

and ideas. Soon, Finn came to realize that Jackie's sharp mind and astute organizational skills were valuable assets to him, and her role broadened from
being a typist and editor to being an equal partner. Jackie recalled, "I too
was closely involved in all of the planning for his new expedition. Evenings
and weekends were consumed with countless plans, lists and endless detail
so necessary to the launching of such a venture." There was no question that
this was Finn's expedition, but the fact that Finn recognized the significant
role played by Jackie in expedition planning emphasized the non-traditional
aspects of their relationship. Of course, it went without saying that she was
also expected to do the housekeeping, cleaning, shopping, and meal preparation on top of her full-time job at the Department of State.

The year 1946 was a challenging one for Jackie and for all American
housewives; they encountered food shortages and skyrocketing post-wartime

prices for consumer goods. On top of that, her new husband was not an average man working a nine to five job who left all his cares at the office. Finn Ronne was a force to be reckoned with, as an explorer and as a man. Life as his wife was surely challenging at the best of times.

During this initial planning year, Finn slept only four to five hours a night, pushing himself hard in order to ready his expedition. He commented in *Antarctic Conquest* that it was "remarkable how much a person can accomplish in a few twenty-four-hour days." He set himself a punishing schedule and Jackie was his equal partner in this as in all things. She advised him regarding his strategy in seeking funding and supplies, consoled him when his requests were denied, and shared his gleeful enthusiasm when he succeeded. Her naturally sunny disposition counterbalanced Finn's despair when the obstacles they faced seemed too great to overcome. When Finn's world darkened, it was Jackie who saved them both.

She reported: "We talked, read and studied the Antarctic for the greater part of our free time." At this stage, there was no plan for women to take part in the expedition so they agreed that Jackie's role while Finn was away would be to manage matters related to the expedition on the domestic front. This itself would be no small undertaking; Jackie prayed she was up to the task.

Given Finn's years of experience in Antarctica and his distinguished naval background, the planning process should have progressed smoothly. Yet, from the initial stages until the ship left for Antarctica, Finn and Jackie encountered obstacles at every step of the way. Richard Light, president of the American Geographical Society outlined these challenges in his article "The Geographical Society and the Explorer":

> The would-be explorer faces a grueling task. By nature, he is, or should be, a field man, able to cope with the raw environment of the area he expects to study, yet he can never reach that area unless he has been successful in coping with another environment, with which all too often he is not in the least bit familiar. I refer to the environment of disinterest, skepticism, even jealousy, that greets him in his round of visits while he is seeking support for his venture. Few explorers are

wealthy. They must beg for the materials, or for the money with which to buy the materials, on which their expeditions depend. It results that many expeditions meet with disaster even before leaving home, and only the lucky few set out on the real adventure.

Jackie's confidence in Finn was supreme and she believed that he would be able to overcome everything. One thing she hadn't reckoned on was the bitter opposition of a man she had admired for years — Admiral Richard Byrd.

Byrd was a renowned, highly respected public figure and the foremost American explorer of Antarctica. By 1946 he already had three Antarctica expeditions under his belt and a fourth, code-named Operation Highjump, was planned for the end of the year. A descendant of one of the First Families of Virginia and married to a member of the Boston Brahmin, a navy admiral, a Freemason, and a close friend of the Roosevelt family, Byrd was supremely well-connected. There was every reason to believe that Byrd would use his influence to support Ronne every step of the way. After all, Byrd had a long-standing relationship with the Ronne family that began with the participation of Finn's father, Martin, in Byrd's first expedition to Antarctica in 1928. That relationship was maintained until Martin's sudden death, and Byrd kept in regular contact with Martin Rønne's widow.

The relationship between Admiral Byrd and Finn Ronne was a complex one, however. For years, the relationship between them was amicable and Byrd adopted a paternal regard for Finn. In 1933, prior to the Second Byrd Expedition, Byrd interceded with Finn's employer to secure a paid leave of absence and found a job for Finn's first wife, Liv. When this marriage broke down, Byrd was first in line to offer his commiserations. Byrd, the famous explorer, offered an inexperienced young man the opportunity of a lifetime — to sail to and work with him in Antarctica. The ties between the two men were strong and personal. Finn worked hard for Byrd during their two expeditions together, but, over time, their relationship subtly changed.

The two men were alike in many ways. Both had an abiding love for Antarctica. Both were passionate, dedicated, charismatic, and driven, with a penchant for self-promotion. In the end, these similarities and their shared

Richard E. Byrd in 1928.

desire to gain glory as Antarctic explorers drove them apart. Over the years, the close-knit relationship between the men became marred by jealousy and suspicion. In society, however, the two men maintained a thinly veiled veneer of courtesy.

In 1946 Finn and Jackie were developing their preliminary plans for the expedition. The fact that Finn wanted to lead his own Antarctic expedition came as no surprise to Byrd. Finn was now an experienced navy man with connections of his own. It soon became clear that Byrd was not happy with the idea. They frequently met casually, as the two lived only a block away from each other. Byrd and Finn even worked in the same building and often bumped into one another as they walked to work.

Sometimes Jackie accompanied them, and she recalled how Byrd encouraged Finn to share his own expeditionary plans while at the same time trying to dissuade him from carrying them out: "Finn, you know I thought the world of your father. He was the salt of the earth. I was sorry he died before my second expedition, but I'm glad you were able to take his place. Now I would very much like you to go along with me again. If you will give up your plans for your own expedition, I will see that you are made a Captain in the Navy."

In *Antarctic Conquest*, Finn remarked how Byrd grilled him about his plans for his upcoming expedition despite Finn's reluctance and his suspicions regarding Byrd's motives. His fears were realized as Finn's goal of photographing the Weddell Sea coast was adopted as part of Byrd's own Operation Highjump plans. Although angry about Byrd's theft of his plan, there was nothing Finn could do about it. From the beginning, Finn Ronne believed that Byrd interfered with his plans.[2]

In her autobiography, Jackie recounted how Byrd called Finn into his office to witness a telephone call in which Byrd appeared to pull rank and give his full support to Finn's expedition, requesting that Finn be given all supplies he asked for: "After the call was over, Byrd turned to Finn and said, 'There, you see, Finn? I am helping you all I can.' After Finn left his office, Byrd called the man back and asked him to ignore his first call and do just the opposite. In complete bewilderment, the man in question later reported both conversations to Finn."

The resistance from Byrd represented a tremendous obstacle to Finn's securing everything he needed to reach his objectives.

Despite Byrd's opposition, the Ronnes pushed on. Finn first approached the navy about obtaining a ship. Because of his experience, he knew which ships would be suitable and available for loan. His insider knowledge was key. Despite offering early support, both the chief of naval operations and the secretary of the navy turned him down. After many trying months, intervention by friends in high places, including General Curtis LeMay, deputy chief of air staff for research and development, resulted in a special congressional bill being passed that allowed the secretary of the navy to lend Finn a ship. LeMay also secured three airplanes for the expedition.

Finn was successful in negotiating a lucrative contract with the North American Newspaper Alliance (NANA) for exclusive rights to all expedition news. Founded in 1922, this newspaper syndicate regularly supported the work of explorers, including Percy Fawcett's ill-fated 1925 search for the Lost City of Z near the Mato Grosso region of Brazil, and Sir Hubert Wilkins's 1926 Detroit Arctic Expedition. Known for hiring the best-known writers of the time, the agency had secured the services of a young Ernest Hemingway to cover the Spanish Civil War. He later turned his experiences there into his famous 1940 novel *For Whom the Bell Tolls*. The North American Newspaper Alliance was to play a significant role in supporting Jackie's work in Antarctica.

Amidst these hectic preparations, Finn was contacted by old school friend Kristian Ostby, who worked for the Norwegian embassy in Washington. Although Finn had become a naturalized U.S. citizen in 1929, his ties to Norway and the Norwegian-American community were always strong. Ostby hoped for Finn's assistance for a young countryman trying to fund his own expedition.

The premise for the expedition sounded crazy, but Finn graciously invited him to his home. Following Norwegian tradition, the meeting between the Ronnes and the ambitious young Norwegian began with coffee and cake. At Finn's invitation, Thor Heyerdahl explained his plan of drifting across the Pacific Ocean from South America to the Polynesian Islands on a balsa raft in order to prove his theory that early South Americans had settled Polynesia in pre-Columbian times.

To the Ronnes' surprise, they learned they already had a connection with the young man. The Ronnes had spent their skiing honeymoon at Strom Lodge in Stowe, Vermont, run by adventurer and fellow Norwegian Erling Strom.[3] Strom Lodge attracted important European dignitaries and politicians, and it was during their honeymoon that Jackie had made the acquaintance of Liv Coucheron-Torp, who turned out to be Thor Heyerdahl's wife. The Heyerdahls had shared a year-long adventure on Fatu Hiva, one of the Marquesas Islands in the South Pacific.

Both Jackie and Finn thought the idea of sailing across the ocean on a balsa raft was ludicrous, but who were they to judge? Finn kindly spent the afternoon reviewing Heyerdahl's plans and provided him with advice on how to secure equipment, supplies, and funding. When the 1947 Kon-Tiki Expedition proved to be wildly successful, Jackie and Finn could not have been prouder of a fellow Norwegian.

A key aspect of expedition planning is identifying exactly the right combination of rugged individuals who can do their respective jobs well and work as solid team players under primitive conditions. This is critical to the success of any expedition but especially in an extreme environment like Antarctica. Overcoming the isolation, plummeting temperatures, endless dark months without sunlight, monotonous diet, lack of privacy, lack of contact with loved ones, and the ever-present danger posed by the remote polar location can only have appeal for a certain gung-ho, risk-taking, hardy sub-section of the population.

Today, the critical task of choosing expedition members only occurs after rigorous and prolonged psychological testing, but during the 1940s no such stringent measures were available. To put it bluntly, ending up with a team that worked as an efficient unit and stayed sane and, most importantly, alive was a crapshoot in the dark. Regrettably, unlike Amundsen and Shackleton, Finn did not possess an innate instinct for choosing a harmonious team. This would always be his fatal flaw and, in due time, would come to cast a long shadow over the work of his expedition and his legacy.

Where was an expedition leader to go to find such a group of idiosyncratic individuals and how would he make his choice? Finn started with men he had worked with before — men he knew and trusted with his life. At the top of the list was polar veteran Isaac "Ike" Schlossbach. At fifty-four, he was the oldest and by far the most experienced of the team, having served as a member of Sir Hubert Wilkins's 1931 expedition by submarine to the Arctic, two Byrd Antarctic expeditions, and the 1937 McGregor Expedition to Greenland.

By the end of his long and colourful career, he had survived four plane crashes and taken part in twelve polar expeditions. Modest, fair-minded, and tolerant, he also had only one good eye. Recalling Ike's hiring, Jackie wrote in her autobiography:

> Finn was in need of a skipper. Although Ike did not have a skipper's licence, he immediately volunteered to enroll in a Merchant Marine school in New York. A well-known polar character, Rear Admiral Edward "Iceberg" Smith gave him his final exam, leaning over Ike's shoulder and shaking his head if Ike marked a wrong answer on the true and false portion. His licence allowed him to take the ship to and from the Antarctic but was invalid after his first port of call in the U.S. upon his return.

Another member of the team hired early on was chief commissary steward Sigmund Gutenko. Like Ike, "Sig" was a veteran of the U.S. Antarctic Service Expedition and had worked on a navy ship to Greenland. Sig was keen to take part in Finn's expedition, but only a year previously he had been flat on his back on a hospital bed encased in plaster, recovering from life-threatening injuries sustained when he was blown out the side of his battleship. A Baltimore native like Jackie, he was the brother of scrappy former bantamweight boxing champion "Kid Williams." Sig and Ike were used to the world of hard knocks, and they never let Finn down.

Finn was on rockier ground when choosing his scientific team, and Jackie's input was invaluable. Although he had a degree in marine engineering, Finn had a limited grasp of other physical sciences and relied on the recommendations of others. Bob Dodson was the son of Finn's boss at the Bureau of Ships and had worked in his office. During the Second World War, he had been an eager messenger boy bedazzled by Finn's Antarctic stories. Now a Harvard graduate, he had kept in touch with Finn and was one of the first scientists to sign up for Ronne's expedition. He was hired as an assistant geologist, was partially responsible for handling the dog team, and planned to conduct cold weather clothing experiments for the government. Tufts College professor Robert "Bob" Nichols accepted the position of chief geologist since it suited his enthusiasm for field-based work to a T. A geology student of his later reported that Bob Nichols was a bit of a showman with a great sense of humour. The two Bobs would make excellent working partners.

Engineer and physicist Harries-Clichy "Harcly" Peterson was another Harvard graduate. As with most of the men, Peterson specialized in one field but had other skills that came in useful later on: he had a private pilot's licence and a sound grasp of instrument design and radio apparatus. Andrew "Andy" Thompson, a Yale man with a degree in physics and philosophy, was hired as the geophysicist. Despite his mild-mannered demeanour, he had earned some repute as a formidable professional boxer. Clarence "Larry" Fiske was hired as the climatologist but became known as an invaluable jack of all trades. William "Bill" Latady was the chief aerial photographer and, like most of the others, was a talented, versatile individual. A president of the Harvard Mountaineering Club who had climbed the 5,500-metre Mount St. Elias in Alaska, Bill was a genius when it came to inventing or fixing anything mechanical. Lawrence "Larry" Kelsey was hired as the radio operator and Donald "Don" McLean as the expedition doctor.

With such a skilled team, Finn and Jackie had high hopes for the success of the mission. Raising sufficient funds was a worry, however, right up to the very end. Team members were exhorted to use their contacts to secure donations either in cash or in-kind. Family members were not exempt, and Jackie's aunt and uncle became sponsors and even Finn's niece Ruth Bugge donated woollen clothing from Norway.

As the ambitious plans for the Ronne Antarctic Research Expedition developed, media attention intensified, and news of the upcoming American expedition flashed around the world. This was a politically sensitive time in Antarctic geopolitical history and the stakes were high. Many countries jostled for power in this great unknown continent, in part because of its potential for mineral resources and possible strategic importance.

As Finn's plans progressed, the volume of diplomatic communiqués between the United States and other interested nations increased. Great Britain was agitated about American plans to use East Base on Stonington Island. Their own British Falkland Islands Dependencies Survey (FIDS) team would be working at British Base E (also on Stonington Island) at the same time. Finn Ronne and the American government were formally

Port of Beaumont being loaded up.

notified that, although Base E had been erected in February 1946, team members had also been staying at East Base without American knowledge or permission. The British government advised that East Base was no longer fit for habitation. Furthermore, vast stores of equipment, including gasoline and coal left behind by the U.S. Antarctic Service Expedition and which Finn had counted on using, were not salvageable.

Finn and Jackie's supporters in the United States government were struck with consternation at this unexpected news. Finn was horrified and angry. Working in the U.S. Department of State, Jackie was well situated to advise her husband regarding the diplomatic ramifications of his expedition and this news. The extensive correspondence between the two nations during the 1946–1947 period reveals the vigorous attempts made by Great Britain to dissuade Finn from launching his expedition. Finn could not be deterred, however. He and Jackie were too far ahead to change their plans now. Months later, when Finn landed at East Base, he would discover that the situation there was even worse than he expected, but there would be no turning back.

At long last, in early January 1947, everything was near to completion and Finn flew to Beaumont, Texas, where the ship he had hired was docked. Finn was to feverishly complete the preparations in Beaumont, and then Jackie planned to take a two-week leave of absence from her work, fly to Texas, and help with last-minute details.

Finn was assisted by his close friend Sir Hubert Wilkins, who enthusiastically supported the endeavour. A native Australian, Wilkins was a consummate explorer who had begun his career on Sir Ernest Shackleton's last (1921–1922) expedition to Antarctica and racked up a series of remarkable polar accomplishments, including pioneering flights in the Arctic in the 1920s and the ill-fated 1931 Nautilus Expedition, in which he attempted to travel under the Arctic ice by submarine. A few years older than Finn, Wilkins had worked with him in Washington and the two adventurers got along famously.

Things seemed to be going well, but Jackie and Finn took nothing for granted. They were not surprised when they encountered a last-minute snag in securing insurance for their vessel. Finn had to pull more strings in Washington in order to obtain this. Only weeks before their ship was due to begin its journey, the roles of Finn and Jackie were clear. The plan was that while Finn was on the expedition in Antarctica, Jackie would remain in Washington, in charge of handling expedition affairs and continuing her full-time job at the Department of State. As time passed, though, Finn became convinced that Jackie's assistance would be critical to him closer at hand.

A lively debate exists in the polar literature about Finn's intentions to invite women on the expedition. Both Finn and Jackie vehemently asserted publicly and privately that this was a last-minute decision. This is corroborated by their formal accounts of the expedition. Still, there is no doubt they were well aware that the official participation of women in the expedition would be a historic event, garnering widespread publicity. But would that publicity be positive or negative? Would it help or hinder the objectives of this serious geographic mission? In a *Milwaukee Journal Sentinel* article, "It's Not the Weather That's Keeping Women from South Pole," published in January 1947, Jackie related candidly that the reason women didn't go to the South Pole was because they were not wanted by men. She diplomatically sidestepped her own personal views, stating instead that male explorers strongly oppose the prospect.

> Women, they say, would be a disturbing element on an expedition with a group of men living at close quarters for 14 or 18 months. It would be completely impractical to worry about the welfare of womenfolk when there are serious aims and objectives to accomplish.... Every member of the party must pull his share of the load. To be a participant, a person must have sound scientific qualifications — not just the urge for glamour to be the first there.

The article hints at Jackie's urge to visit Antarctica as she waxes poetic about "the great Ross Ice Shelf, rising 150 feet from the sea for 400 miles." After all, she had worked as hard as Finn to make sure this expedition came to fruition. Of course, no matter how interested Jackie may have been in seeing the great white continent that she had heard about, talked about, and dreamed about for years, the fact remains that she would not have travelled there without Finn's express desire. In Beaumont, Texas, the frenzied, last-minute expedition plans did not yet include Jackie on the team roster. Those plans were about to change.

Neny Fiord, Antarctica. Painting by Leland Curtis.

VANITY – THOU ART A WOMAN[4]
Harold Merriman Dudley

They say women are vain!
Why not? God made them that way.
Here's to the dash of them,
Suspected trash of them,
Eternal clash of them,
Lip-stick and all.

Ah, there goes a neat ankle!
Why not? I like them that way.
Here's to the rule of it,
Passionate school of it,
Wicked who fool with it,
Kicked like a mule by it,
Garters and all.

Now, did you ever see anything to match that?
Why not? The race lives on that way.
Here's to the roll of it,
Rhythmical stroll of it,
Dynamite soul of it,
Each part and whole of it,
Ribbons and all.

Dedicated to Captain Finn Ronne, the Antarctic explorer who took two women with him to the unknown icy dangers of the South Pole.

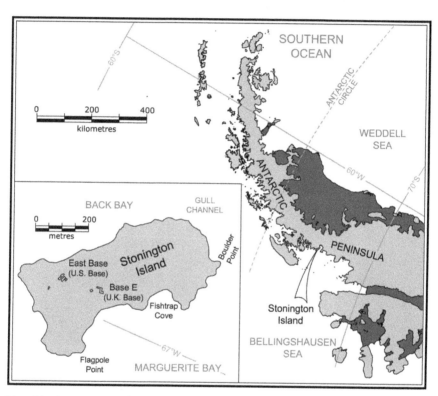

Map of the Antarctic Peninsula and Stonington Island. In 1946, the Antarctic Peninsula was known as the Palmer Peninsula.

CHAPTER 4

GETTING THERE

The greater the obstacle, the more glory in overcoming it.
— Molière

IF FINN EXPECTED things to go easier once his departure for Antarctica was imminent, he couldn't have been more wrong. At the dock in Beaumont, Texas, there was a desperate flurry of last-minute activities, including loading up the ship with a mountainous pile of heavy equipment, battered crates, and sloshing gasoline drums; building sturdy pens for the dog team; finalizing the crew; arranging media coverage; and finishing the complicated paperwork. The heavily laden vessel would make short stops along the way in Panama, and Valparaíso and Punta Arenas in Chile, but the bulk of the work was to be completed in Beaumont. Finn was in charge, but he couldn't be everywhere at once.

Almost from the start, the expedition seemed in peril. Newly returned from Washington, where he had finally obtained ship insurance, Finn joined the men who were labouring hard in the Pennsylvania Shipyards where *Port*

The damaged Beechcraft in Beaumont, Texas.

of Beaumont was berthed. On this January day in 1947, Finn had a feeling of dread, as there were so many things that could go amiss. The planes were about to be loaded on board and some tricky manoeuvres were required. As Finn and others held their breath, the twin-engine Beechcraft was slowly and carefully hoisted up and into the air. Suddenly, and without warning, one of the lugs on the plane failed. As onlookers gasped in horror, unable to assist, the plane lurched and twisted at a perilous angle and then abruptly gave way under the pressure.

Plunging dramatically to the ground, the Beechcraft landed upside down with gasoline pouring from its engines.

Finn recalled the situation: "Here we were almost ready to leave, and our main airplane, the only one that could carry the trimetrogon camera installation for photographing the Antarctic, lay draped over the heater crates, with its wheels in the air and twisted structural members sticking out through tattered metal sheeting." There was nothing to be done to save the plane. Finn raced to keep the dumbstruck crowds back as firefighters arrived to contain and remove the hazardous material. This event threw a

Jennie and Harry Darlington on board *Port of Beaumont.*

pall over the anxious men. Finn remarked ruefully: "The Ronne Antarctic Research Expedition of 1946–48 seemed to show all the earmarks of a hard-luck expedition."

Finn's chief pilot and third-in-command, twenty-nine-year-old Harry Darlington III, was furious and blamed Finn for the accident.[1] Tall, lanky, and of a brooding disposition, Harry had been a junior member of the Third Byrd Expedition, so Finn had some idea of what to expect of him. Harry was now an experienced naval pilot and Finn had initially been pleased when Harry joined his team. Misgivings began surfacing, however, after he was contacted by Harry's mother who suggested that all was not well with her son. She implored Finn to look out for Harry during the expedition. He dismissed Mrs. Garrett's letter as the work of an overwrought parent, but Harry's explosive blow-up after the accident should have made him think twice. He seemed to be a loose cannon. Things were moving quickly now, though, and it was too late in the game for second thoughts. At this stage, Finn was more concerned with saving the fate of the expedition. He would come to regret not heeding these early signs about Harry.

Finn feared that the expedition was in jeopardy and scrambled in order to secure another plane. He knew this wouldn't be easy since he and Jackie had fought tooth and nail for every dollar raised for the expedition. It was a shoestring operation as it was. And this was no ordinary plane, as the Beechcraft was specially outfitted with trimetrogon cameras for photographing the Antarctic — one of the most critical jobs of the expedition. This equipment would enable the team to take oblique and vertical images simultaneously, something necessary for topographical mapping. By this time, Jackie had reluctantly taken a leave of absence from her job and joined Finn in Beaumont so that he would not have to face these problems alone.

Jennie Darlington rolling a gas drum.

Luckily, he had confidence in the technical crew he had hired: Nelson "Mac" McClary was first mate and supply officer, Walter "Smitty" Smith was second mate and navigator, James "Jimmy" Robertson was hired as airplane mechanic, and Ernest "Woody" Wood as assistant engineer. The aviation team was made up of two swaggering hotshot test pilots, James "Jim" Lassiter and Charles "Chuck" Adams, both recently seconded from the navy. Charles "Chuck" Hassage (chief engineer) and young Eagle Scout Arthur "Art" Owen were last-minute additions to the team in Beaumont. With the exception of teenaged Art Owen, all of these men were in their twenties.

Newspaper article about the expedition's' wives (clockwise: Jackie Ronne, Jennie Darlington, Helen Fiske, and Harriet Swadell).

In the final days, the pace was frenetic. It was all hands on deck, with everyone pitching in as best they could — from the scientists to the pilots, mechanics, engineers, and any wives of the expeditioners who happened to be around.

This included Jackie; Jennie, wife of Harry Darlington; Helen, wife of Larry Fiske; and Harriet, wife of Carl Swadell, an early RARE team member who was asked to leave the venture at the last moment. Everyone scrambled to meet the pressing deadline and prepare the ship for Antarctic weather conditions ahead.

While they were still docked in Texas, Finn asked Jackie to accompany the ship as far as Panama, their next port of call. There were still so many details that needed her attention, and he trusted her as he trusted no one else. Jackie had been working full out as Finn's partner in this mission. As time passed, he realized how truly indispensable she was to the expedition. He must have wondered if he could have got that far without her writing and editing skills, superb organizational abilities, and her steadying influence. Grudgingly, she agreed to his entreaties. But when the ship finally sailed, Jackie was not the only woman on board. She had convinced Jennie Darlington to come along as well. This was unplanned and unexpected, but the women and the entire crew firmly believed the women would be leaving the ship shortly.

It was a day off for the whole town on January 25, 1947, and buzzing crowds thronged the Beaumont harbour to glimpse the daring explorers and wave off the great ship. The endless packing and loading, rearranging and rechecking was over, and it was time for the expedition to begin. Speeches by local dignitaries were made, and the local band played with enthusiastic vigour. While the Pennsylvania Shipyards, the Chamber of Commerce, and other companies and individuals made substantial donations to RARE, it was the presentation by the Port Neches Elementary School, whose students had collected nickels and dimes totalling $15.86, that tugged at the team's heartstrings. The Lone Star flag was presented by the local chapter of the

Jackie on board the *Port of Beaumont.*

Daughters of the Republic of Texas, and then Jackie stepped forward and proudly christened the ship the *Port of Beaumont.* As the vessel moved away from the dock, Jackie was thrilled that the expedition had started at last. Finn mused to himself that "considering the obstacles and accidents that had befallen us, it was a miracle that we ever got away at all." Nothing could stop them now.

Jackie described their progress as they set out: "After months of planning and weeks of hectic last-minute work, the blue waters of the Gulf of Mexico now surround us. We are under-way — and land cannot be seen in any direction. With both Diesel engines now going all out, we are making about 11 knots against the current. We need to make good time in our race against the Antarctic's winter ice."

Sailing out through the Gulf of Mexico, with the Mexican and Central American coasts to starboard, the crew found their sea legs, got to know each other, and began getting accustomed to the ship's routine. Finn had quietly left the ship for a few days to pick up the replacement aircraft but rejoined them in Panama. Meanwhile, the scientific program was underway. Early on, Bob Nichols and Bob Dodson had been tasked with collecting plankton samples for Dr. Mary Sears of Woods Hole Oceanographic Institution. Later rising to the rank of commander of the U.S. Naval Reserve, Sears was the highly decorated first oceanographer of the navy and a pioneering planktonologist.

At first, Jackie just tried to enjoy herself, but she soon learned that Finn had an ulterior motive in asking her to remain on board. Jackie knew that something was brewing, and, upon his return to Panama, Finn asked her to join the expedition on a full-time basis and continue with him to Antarctica. This was not done for sentimental reasons, as Finn's focus was always on his expedition. The account of his decision is short and no-nonsense: "While no woman had spent a winter in the Antarctic before, that was no reason for believing that it could not be done." Jackie opposed this from the start, but when Finn had a plan, he was relentless. Eventually he wore her down and she agreed to go to Antarctica with him.

Jackie did not make this decision lightly. What woman would have? She loved her high-powered job as an information officer at the Department of State and wondered how they would get on without her. At least it would be waiting for her when she got back. She worried about leaving her aging aunt and uncle in the lurch. After all, they would be responsible for the tremendous amount of work required to close up the Ronnes' apartment; store their furniture and belongings; and handle all correspondence and financial and administrative matters over the coming year. That was assuming that nothing went wrong, and their Antarctic stay was not extended due to unforeseen circumstances. And it easily could be. Jackie knew that she could rely on them to handle any concerns she might have, but it was a tall order indeed, especially at short notice. And she thought of the likely dangers in Antarctica — the perilous crevasses and the swirling blizzards that could trick the mind and easily lead a man — or a woman — far from the safety of camp.

Finn stood his ground and convinced Jackie that her skills were critical to the mission. Ensuring the success of the expedition meant everything to

Jackie and Finn. Her decision to accompany Finn is a testament to Jackie's courage, her commitment to the expedition, and her love for Antarctica. It is true that she trusted Finn, but few women would have agreed to undergo an arduous year in Antarctica just to please their husbands. Remote and dangerous even today, in the 1940s Antarctica was truly forbidding.

Of course, there was another side to this as well. It is almost certain that the interests of the North American Newspaper Alliance, with whom Finn and Jackie had a lucrative contract for exclusive coverage of the expedition, were also a factor. From a media perspective, having the first female Antarctic expedition member along was better than gold dust.

Jackie agreed to join the expedition as a full-time participant as long as Jennie Darlington, the wife of pilot Harry Darlington, would come along as well. Since the Darlingtons had only been married a few months earlier, Jennie thought this would make a marvellous honeymoon!

The decision to take women to Antarctica was made solely by Jackie and Finn, without consulting the rest of the team. The news had an electrifying effect on the male crew members. In public, Jackie and Finn downplayed the furor that erupted, but it precipitated the first crisis in leadership that Finn faced and did not bode well for the rest of the journey. Instead of rallying behind their commander and welcoming the women on board, the crew split into bitter factions. No one spoke out in support of the idea. Jennie Darlington's husband was dead set against it and was part of a small but vocal group that circulated a petition in an effort to prevent the women from coming along. Jennie included that note in the book she later wrote about her experiences during the expedition:

> We, the undersigned, feel that it would jeopardize our physical condition and mental balance if the Ronne expedition consisting of twenty men were to be accompanied by one or more females for that period of time spent in the Antarctic. Therefore, we agree to form a united front to block that possibility. We are all prepared to leave the expedition in Valpo as a group if one or more women accompany it.

Almost all of the men had joined RARE shortly after serving during the Second World War, and they were keen as mustard to extend their "boy's own" experience. Surely just the presence of women in Antarctica meant there would be fewer opportunities for proving their manhood. The distractions would be greater, and the frisson of expedition life would be diluted. Most of the men were aggrieved that women in general should take part, but for some, it was personal. In later years, the children of climatologist Larry Fiske contended that he had wanted his wife to come along as well. Helen Unterecker Fiske, sister of noted biographer and poet John Unterecker, was a cartographer and journalist who had written for *National Geographic* and the *Explorers Club Journal* and could have easily held her own.

Jackie later confided her own misgivings to a journalist, stating that even she wasn't sure she had made the right decision. "[The men] were acting macho and chauvinistic, but the threats were idle. They would never have given up the opportunity to go on this history-making expedition."

The men's opposition was not well received by Finn, who was adamant that this was his decision to make as leader.

The expedition team weren't the only ones to object. After sharing the news with friends and family, Jackie met fierce opposition. Her aunt Merriel sent her a long list of reasons why she should not go, including that Jackie might ruin her complexion. Unexpectedly, Jackie's best friend and Department of State colleague Bettie Earle agreed.

> Please come to your senses and realize that this is a most foolhardy plan — where in heaven's name is your common sense, good judgement and clear thinking. Let Finn do this job — why do you want to detract from whatever publicity may be forthcoming — don't you realize that the expedition's worth would be sunk in the mere fact that you, as a beautiful, glamorous woman had done a daring feat? I cannot believe that you, above all people, would even stop to consider such an idea. Why not reconsider the whole plan as a sensible woman — please gather yourself together.

Dr. Don McLean and Andy Thompson were part of the group that opposed the inclusion of women on the expedition.

Her Phi Mu sisters in Washington gave her their full support, however, stating: "That's just like our Jackie…. She was a live wire and it isn't surprising that she has taken to exploring with her husband."

Finn and Jackie did not revisit the decision. Once he had made his mind up, Finn was inflexible. It was not a quality that endeared him to his team.

Soon after the momentous decision was made, the *Port of Beaumont* sailed along the South American coast. The next stop was the town of Valparaíso, Chile, but they were there for a few days only. Young Jorge di Giorgio joined the crew there, and this brought the full crew complement up to twenty-three. As Jackie and Finn had suspected, the men's reaction to the women joining the expedition had been all bluster. No one wanted to give up this once-in-a-lifetime opportunity of going to Antarctica.

One can only imagine the desperate consternation experienced by Jackie and Jennie after deciding they were going to Antarctica for a year. The fact that the two women joined the expedition was proof of their mettle, particularly in the face of the men's disapproval. Jackie had been preparing for this trip for years and would be travelling in the privileged position of the leader's wife, but Jennie Darlington's situation was different. Unlike the men who had had months to obtain specially designed equipment and clothing, as well as choose personal items that would provide comfort and diversion over the coming year, the women were under pressure and had to scramble at the last minute. Jackie always joked that the staple items in the suitcase she brought from home were a good suit, her high-heeled shoes, and nylon stockings — none of which she would need in Antarctica.

At least Jackie and Jennie had each other, and the two formed a solid friendship from the beginning despite their differences. Jennie Darlington was an unexpected choice of a wife for Harry. Because Harry came from a wealthy family and had attended exclusive prep schools, newspaper articles assumed that Jennie's antecedents were the same. The *Star Press*, a small paper published in Muncie, Indiana, referred to her as "Jennie Russell — that blonde and glamorous New York belle." In fact, twenty-two-year-old Jennie Orval Zobrist was the daughter of a road construction foreman descended from Swiss-German immigrants. Only a few years earlier, she had been working as a dance instructor. Unlike Jackie, who was well educated, had a good job, and a secure position within the expedition, Jennie Darlington had to overcome challenges at every turn. She faced the shortcomings of her modest background compared to Harry's, she was learning to live with a newly minted husband, and she was about to embark on an expedition on which she was not wanted, not even by her own husband. Harry had insisted on bringing his beloved husky, Chinook, along with them, and Jennie always contended that Harry cared more for Chinook than he did for her.

Leaving Valparaíso, the ship sailed through rough, choppy seas for several days on its way to Punta Arenas, the last stop before Antarctica. This

Jackie helping to feed the dog team.

was a dangerous stretch of water, and everyone on board suffered unhappily with recurring bouts of seasickness. Located at the northern tip of Tierra del Fuego, Punta Arenas was the southernmost city on the continent and their last chance to obtain supplies.

It had not been the smoothest of sailings so far. Morale was lowered by a mysterious ailment sweeping their husky population. Eventually identified as distemper, the disease killed over half of the forty-three dogs during the journey, to the great dismay of the canine-loving crew.

Finally, in the early morning of March 8, *Port of Beaumont* left Punta Arenas and entered the treacherous Drake Passage on their final leg of the journey. Located between Cape Horn at the southern tip of South America and the South Shetland Islands, it marks the convergence between the Atlantic, Pacific, and Southern Oceans. Almost one thousand kilometres wide, with near-cyclonic winds and icy temperatures, the Drake is a perilous body of water, and crossing it was a two-day experience that none of them ever forgot. When the unpredictable weather and the huge swells subsided, everyone was treated to the sight of majestic humpback whales swimming nearby, feasting on the abundant plankton. Squawking seabirds, including sooty shearwaters, black-browed albatrosses, and southern giant petrels, wheeled overhead, following the ship on her journey. The appearance of the first iceberg on the horizon was cause for great celebration.

On board, the men took bets on when the actual arrival day might be. The prize was a meagre tin of sardines, which was of little interest to the eventual winner, cook Sig Gutenko. For Finn, this was a completely different sailing experience than his last approach on the Third Byrd Expedition eight years earlier. At that time, the impenetrable pack ice had extended so far that the ship's entry was severely limited. This time, the seas were a deep blue with open water most of the way in.

Finn was relentless in keeping watch on the bridge. As the *Port of Beaumont* eased her way forward, Jackie was thrilled beyond belief. She

Aerial view of Stonington Island.

stood on deck gazing in awe as Antarctica drew ever closer. Finn pointed out the landmarks: Black Thumb Mountain, Red Rock Ridge, and, finally, the opening to the Neny Fjord. Everyone was on deck marvelling at the dramatic landscape. "It appears out of the fog and low clouds like a white comet in the twilight. To enter Greater Antarctica is to be drawn into a slow maelstrom of ice. Ice is the beginning of Antarctica and ice is its end." Finn's eyes strained to catch sight of tiny Stonington Island, which would be their home for the duration of their Antarctic stay. And finally, there it was.

> No words can do justice to the grandeur of the great snowy mountains that tower up all around the island, the massive glaciers ... always cracking, grumbling and roaring, the vast sapphire icebergs growling their way like huge animals through the smaller ice of the bay, the long Antarctic sunsets turning the snowfields pink, the bare rock, and the whistling winds.

Located northeast of Neny Island in the eastern part of Marguerite Bay, Stonington Island was a sight for the weary crew to behold. It was less than a kilometre in length, half a kilometre in width, and only took ten minutes to cross by foot. As *Port of Beaumont* sailed closer, Jackie marvelled at the small islets, reefs, and icebergs of varying shapes passing the decks. Connected to the Antarctic mainland by Northeast Glacier, this neck of ice would provide a secure place for a working trail party to access the plateau, making Stonington Island an attractive location for a base. It later became Jackie's ski hill. Finn immediately noticed that the glacier had significantly decreased by 120 metres in width since his stay in 1941. Although it was covered in deep snow when they arrived, as it was for most of the year, it was partly exposed during the brief summer season.

Finn could not quite make out East Base, but the British Base E and several men from the British team could be seen in the distance. As *Port of Beaumont* anchored about a kilometre from the beach near Fishtrap Cove, they could see a solitary individual making his way down to the beach. Finn, Harry, McClary, and Latady climbed into a small boat and rowed to shore.

Finn made sure that Jackie (but not Jennie) was on board as well to mark the historic occasion. On March 12, 1947, Jackie Ronne became the first American woman to set foot on Antarctica and the first female member of a scientific expedition there. She was thrilled with her achievement. In an article, "Mrs. Ronne Describes Role of Women on Antarctic Expedition," published in the *Washington Star*, she wrote that "it was an exciting honor to be the first woman to set foot on the south polar continent, let alone to be the first to live there but it meant living a man's life."

Their daughter, Karen, stated:

> Even though Jennie Darlington was along, my father made sure that my mother was the first with everything. She was the first to step onto Stonington Island. The first woman to fly in an airplane there. It may sound petty in a way, but he did want to lock down my mother's legacy. Even though he downplayed it later. Of course, he gave her the big honour of naming the area "Edith Ronne Land." He was very proud of my mother and all she accomplished.

The British team had been on Stonington Island since February 1946. As with the Ronne Antarctic Research Expedition, their reason for being there was, at least in part, to support their government's polar objectives. In 1943, and in response to political jostling for territory in Antarctica, the U.K. government had initiated Operation Tabarin. This secret mission was designed to protect Antarctic waters and strengthen British claims to the sovereignty of the Falkland Islands Dependencies, which included the British Antarctic Territory and South Georgia Island. The first bases were Base A at Port Lockroy on Goudier Island and Base B on Deception Island. Later, the number increased to nineteen, with several being demolished, closed, or removed. At Base E on Stonington Island, the British team developed an impressive scientific agenda, including establishing meteorological stations, performing topographical surveys, geological and biological studies, keeping tidal records, and making sea ice observations.

As the American members reached the shore, the British base commander, Kenelm Pierce-Butler of the Falkland Islands Dependencies Survey, was waiting at the water's edge with his hand extended in greeting. Despite Finn's impatience to see East Base, he accepted Pierce-Butler's invitation to tea. Jackie and Finn were impressed with the trim quarters and homey touches at the British base, which included purple pansies adorning the tables and scarlet gingham curtains in the windows. If Pierce-Butler was surprised to learn there were two female members on the Ronne team, he hid his feelings well.[2]

Compared to the United States, the United Kingdom was far behind in its attitude toward allowing women to work in Antarctica. The first British woman to conduct fieldwork in Antarctica was Janet Thomson in 1976, and the first women to overwinter in Antarctica did not do so until 1993, over forty years after a woman from the United States had accomplished that feat.

The commander welcomed the group to Stonington Island and did his best to prepare Finn for the bad news to come. Finn already knew that East Base had been repeatedly ransacked, with some destruction of the goods left behind by the last American expedition.[3] Still, he was unprepared for what he discovered. As the Americans strode the one hundred metres separating the two bases, Latady took photographs to make sure that all was documented. Jackie was tense with anxiety; Finn was already agitated.

It was hard for Jackie to gain a full sense of what her new home would be like given its appalling condition. She reported that "there was shocking evidence of complete and utter vandalism. It's doubtful that any property could have been ransacked more thoroughly." Finn was livid. He knew exactly the condition East Base had been in when the last American expedition had left. According to Finn, over 80 percent of the items left there had been removed or damaged. While he knew that visiting Chilean and Argentinian ships had been in part responsible, Finn was also suspicious of the British. Not only were certain items left by the Americans in evidence in the British hut, but he soon learned that the British team had lived and worked in the hut for a prolonged period. Thankfully, the buildings themselves were all in reasonable condition and the supplies of aviation fuel, coal, and diesel oil were still intact.

The main bunkhouse and science building at East Base.

Despite the cordial welcome, the relationship between the American and British teams did not start out on a positive footing. Finn complained bitterly to Pierce-Butler about the state of East Base and did not let the matter rest there. Lodging an official complaint with the American government resulted in further posturing between the U.S. and U.K. governments, both on the world stage and on Stonington Island.[4] To the great annoyance of the British team, one of the first actions taken by Finn after formally retaking possession of East Base, was the raising of the American flag. This was done with gusto, particularly on the part of Finn. As Jackie pointed out, like all Norwegians, Finn was an inveterate flag-waver. As Jackie wrote in her book, "Finn saw to it that the American flag flew day and night, through winds, storms and blizzards, month in and month out, as long as our expedition was on Stonington Island." Both the United States and the United Kingdom laid claim to this small island.[5] Official communications were exchanged and then the two camps agreed to disagree.

After arriving on Stonington, Jackie, like all other team members, had to dive right in. In many ways, this was a blessing. When she had made her way up to East Base for the first time, she could not have been more disheartened. While Jackie's autobiography catalogues the flagrant vandalism carried out by previous visitors, she downplays the sheer stinking mess of the place.

Jennie Darlington didn't hold back in *her* memoirs. She was horrified by "the vast agglutination of refuse forming a malodorous aspic by the front door" that she had to walk through to reach the bunkhouse. Decaying food supplies, rusted and leaking oil drums, and discarded medical supplies had all been randomly tossed out the door onto an overflowing garbage pile that had frozen and thawed and frozen again. Conservation policies regarding safe waste disposal would not be in place for several decades. The British had also used East Base as a storage facility for a variety of things, including over sixty reeking seal carcasses used for dog food. The interiors of the buildings were hardly more appealing. Ransacked boxes were strewn about, stacks of unwashed dishes were piled high in the galley, and old clothes hung from washing lines. The men, many of them fresh from doing service in the Second World War, would not have been fazed by this additional hardship. It was, however, hardly an atmosphere that offered comfort to either of the two women. In a gross understatement, Jennie reported that those early weeks were challenging.[6]

There was nothing to do but accept the conditions as they were and start working as quickly as possible. Weather on Stonington Island was unpredictable and unforgiving. It was impossible for the RARE team to move into East Base immediately due to the squalid conditions, so Finn pivoted to Plan B. *Port of Beaumont* was moved from Neny Island through the narrow strait into Back Bay, which was a mere kilometre from their camp. Most of the team, including Jackie and Finn, stayed on the ship and made their base there while a few of the men camped on the island. Half of the party were in charge of cleanup and the other half in charge of unloading the unwieldy supplies. It was a hectic time for all as the work had to be completed before the snow came.

Both Jackie and Jennie were painfully aware that the men had not wanted them to participate in the expedition and thought carefully how to minimize any additional friction they might cause on the basis of their sex. Jennie related:

My job was to be as inconspicuous within the group as possible. I felt that all feminine instincts should be sublimated. I believed that I should ask for no favours nor expect any, not even from my husband. Whereas a woman's natural instincts are to play up to men, I felt it imperative to play down.… Any drawing of attention to myself as female, any gesture or indication that I expected certain courtesies, any show of bossiness or pretence would have been resented.

Jackie, too, was forced to mask her femininity. Finn did not take her for a scenic romantic stroll around Stonington Island, pointing out his special places to his young wife, but she hadn't really expected that. As commander-in-chief of the expedition, Finn could not openly display warmth toward Jackie but maintained a firm, in-control persona whenever they were in public.

Jackie and Jennie displayed resilience and flexibility in responding to these new, unexpected conditions. Life on *Port of Beaumont* with twenty-one

Port of Beaumont in Antarctica.

men and two women; a pack of snarling, continually howling dogs; three airplanes; and hundreds of crates was smelly, uncomfortable, and unpleasant. That was incentive enough for both women to do whatever had to be done. No one wanted to be stranded on the ship if storms blew in early. Living on an Antarctican base was difficult and dangerous enough but living on board was a different matter entirely.

EAST BASE, UNITED STATES ANTARCTIC SERVICE EXPEDITION, 1939–1941
Richard Blackburn Black

The one best answer I can pose
Is that I like the place
In spite of all its trials and woes,
It meets one face to face

With challenges not elsewhere found —
Rewards that lift the soul —
I know that, while atop the ground,
I'll cry "Antarctic, Skoal!"

CHAPTER 5

THE ADVENTURE GETS UNDERWAY

Strive to be the best, however hard the path.
— E.O. WILSON

IT SOON BECAME a race against time. On March 13, the day after the ship anchored in Marguerite Bay, the first snowflakes were glimpsed. It would only get colder, darker, and windier from then on as the brutal Antarctic winter was fast approaching. Finn's plans to settle into East Base right away and begin his ambitious scientific program had been thwarted by the deplorable condition of the buildings. Unfortunately, there is little flexibility in an Antarctic expedition schedule. Time is of the essence and is always subject to the vagaries of fickle weather conditions. With the Arctic terns circling above and dive-bombing at will, the crew worked feverishly to offload the ship and prepare the American base camp on Stonington

Transferring supplies from *Port of Beaumont* to East Base.

Island. It would be another two dreary months until the team moved there permanently.

The conditions were rough, with half the team living in primitive conditions on Stonington and the rest remaining on board. Cook Gutenko operated a makeshift galley on *Port of Beaumont,* but it was hardly three square meals a day. With the constant toing and froing of the crew between the ship and the island, it was often whatever food was closest at hand. Jennie Darlington remembered that break times usually consisted of "tea bags tossed into a cracked cup containing melted-down chunks of iceberg and seven-year-old cookies found on the [East Base] premises."

Until a radio station was assembled at East Base, contact with the United States was made via the ship's radio. As expedition leader, Finn was determined that the flying program and the work of the scientists begin as soon as possible. The Stinson L-5 was the first of the three planes to get offloaded in preparation for early reconnaissance flights along the coast. The mechanic, Robertson, conducted some minor repairs and gave it the once-over and then Darlington and Latady flew off toward George VI Sound to check the route for future trail parties.

Much of the time, Jackie stayed on board. She had assumed her role in charge of communications even before the ship left Beaumont, Texas. Like Finn, Jackie treated her job with the utmost seriousness. Wasting no time, she sent her first Antarctic story to the *New York Times* shortly upon arrival. She made sure that engaged readers around the world participated in the expedition, if only vicariously. Through the thrilling stories that Jackie and other team members wrote, readers could keep abreast of the expedition's activities, celebrate the team's achievements, and commiserate with them over their hardships. And there would be plenty of those. Some articles went out under Jackie's byline, a few were sent by other team members, but the vast majority would be sent under Finn's name, even though they were written by Jackie.

Each day, Jackie worked with Finn to present rousing, well-written material that would capture a reader's imagination. She cared deeply about the expedition, and this was reflected in her work. "I was very pleased with the incoming message from NANA that our British story had made the front page in the *London Daily Telegraph* and that NANA had given it good publicity as well." She became adroit in subtly highlighting certain aspects of RARE activities and accomplishments while downplaying others. By choosing what to focus on and what to leave out, she was helping to shape the expedition's legacy.

Jackie was also fulfilling the terms of the generous contract that Finn had signed with John Wheeler of the North American Newspaper Alliance months before. This provided much-needed funds in return for exclusive rights to expedition highlights. Most twentieth-century polar expeditions sought to establish and nurture such a relationship.[1] Reader interest in expedition stories translated into a later demand for books written by the leader, lucrative lecture tours, and increased opportunities of funding for future work. Part of Jackie's job was to keep the momentum going through feeding the public demand for stories and always keeping them wanting more. It was a delicate balance to maintain. The fact that Finn entrusted this critical job to Jackie demonstrated his understanding of how important this role was as well as the level of trust he accorded his wife. According to Jennie, "The press took precedent over other jobs" and everyone knew it.

RARE insignia.

A few days after their arrival in Antarctica, Jackie and Finn celebrated their third wedding anniversary, but there would be no long-stemmed red roses and chocolates for her. Instead, she was down on her hands and knees vigorously scrubbing the filthy floors and ramshackle cupboards of the vandalized bunkhouse while Finn ferried supplies from the beach to the base camp. For Jackie, spending time away from the cramped quarters and reeking, fetid air of the ship was a welcome respite and allowed her to start familiarizing herself with Stonington Island. Even the grim conditions at East Base could not diminish Jackie's pleasure at having some time to herself. She welcomed the bracing polar air and the opportunity to be doing hard physical work.

The bitter disagreements between the men and ongoing petty pilfering that had started in Beaumont created a tense atmosphere on board. Much-coveted packages of cigarettes, chocolate, and sweets had been disappearing from the ship's stores at an alarming rate. This was a serious matter on a polar expedition, and Finn responded swiftly by firing one expedition

Ronne Hut at East Base.

member before the ship left Valparaíso. He took a dim view of looting and with good reason. But Jennie recalled that Finn's irate lectures and memos on the subject only made things worse.

East Base was a revelation for Jackie. She and Finn had talked excitedly about it for so many years, she felt she knew it intimately. Of course, Finn had described the place he had lived in as part of the 1939–1941 U.S. Antarctic Service Expedition and not the ravaged site it had become. Still, gradually, and with imagination, she could see a proper camp emerging from the squalor.

Walking uphill from the beach at Fishtrap Cove, past the barking Weddell seals, there were five modest structures: the bunkhouse, the science building, the machine shop, a storage hut, and an outbuilding. Constructed of the original 1.25 x 2.5–metre panels, the sturdy buildings had been erected by Finn, so Jackie knew they were designed to last. At seven metres in width and twenty metres in length, the bunkhouse was by far the largest building and dominated the camp. It would provide a home for all expedition members except the Ronnes. During the previous expedition, Finn had constructed a small 3.5 x 3.5–metre hut, and this became the living quarters and offices for Jackie and Finn. Although the Ronnes were to maintain an open door policy, Jackie was relieved that she would have some semblance of privacy. Later, she would be thankful to have a place of her own to which she could escape.

During the early weeks, everyone was working hard setting up the base: lugging over the heavy equipment and machinery, overflowing crates, and yowling dogs from the ship; pulling together as a team; and establishing a professional relationship with their British Falkland Islands Dependencies Survey counterparts. It was tough, dirty work with aches and bruises aplenty and the clock was ticking.

From the start, Finn imposed rigorous safety precautions; he knew very well that Antarctica was a hazardous place to be. Despite everything, the team didn't have long to wait before the first crisis occurred.

The day the men chose to erect the radio station was a miserable one. Regardless of the weather conditions, everyone had to get up and work. There was no avoiding it, except on medical grounds, and no man wanted to be labelled a shirker. Visibility was poor due to the swirling snow, and the men could hardly hear themselves talk over the howling winds. McClary, Nichols, Robertson, Smitty, and McLean assembled and raised an eighteen-metre pole close to the science building and then trudged out to the glacier to erect the other three.

Each man took his position, with McClary stretching out the guy wires to one of the poles. Concentrating on keeping the wire taut, McClary paced steadily backwards toward the precipitous edge of the glacier cliff. Failing to see the bright orange danger flags dug into the snow and misunderstanding the frantic shouts and waving arms of his colleagues, he continued treading past the warning signs. The other men watched in horrified disbelief as McClary reached the glacier edge and then disappeared over it. It had happened in the blink of an eye. The men rushed quickly as close to the edge as they dared and peered over. McClary had plummeted fifteen metres straight downwards into the frigid waters of the bay below.

Miraculously, that part of Marguerite Bay was open water. Gasping for air and flailing about in the waves, he was unharmed, but every second counted. Without a moment to lose, Robertson threw out a heavy climbing rope, which McClary managed to catch hold of and clumsily tie around his waist. Then the team man-hauled him up and over the lip of the cliff. Only eight minutes had elapsed between the time of the accident and the time he was rescued.

On the surface of the glacier, a violently shivering McClary was unceremoniously rolled in rough blankets and then carried quickly to the nearby bunkhouse where he was warmed up and checked over by the doctor. Although he would always be susceptible to exposure, there was no lasting damage. The team had responded swiftly, but it had been a narrow escape. If the accident had happened only a few weeks later, when the ice had completely frozen over, McClary would have been killed outright.

Everyone was relieved when the date was set to move the whole party permanently to East Base. In a way, it would be a new start to the expedition and there was a renewed sense of purpose and camaraderie. It was hoped that this next stage would put an end to the discontented squabbles and divisive rivalry. The men seemed to argue about everything — the food, who they worked with, what tasks they were assigned, Finn's strictness, who had borrowed their tools, who was snoring too loudly, whether they could visit the British base, and how often they could send radio messages. In Antarctica, every single concern whether big or small was magnified.

Already Finn recognized with deep regret that he should have taken more time to vet the potential team members. The men he had chosen fit a certain profile: "Expedition life had an appeal to the young brash restless soul who served duty in the Second World War and who had not been able to settle down yet, who was looking for some excitement before doing so. To a few, it was either the romantic history and/or their desire to contribute to it that was the compelling factor."

Although most of the RARE team had recently served in the military and respected the chain of command, they had not expected to follow it in

Antarctica. Finn, on the other hand, was still on active service with the navy and demanded obedience.

Even at this early stage in the expedition, rumblings of opposition to Finn's leadership were becoming noticeable, and the brash and outspoken Harry Darlington was the most vocal of those complaining. Finn and Harry had nearly come to blows already regarding safety regulations and different approaches to the flight plans, and Harry was censured for calling Finn a "goddamned liar" in front of the team.

Third-in-command and head of the aviation program, Harry expected to have greater input into Finn's decision-making and reacted badly when he didn't. McClary and Dr. McLean supported Harry's position and usually sided with him against Finn, but even McClary was surprised by Harry's lack of self-discipline. McClary wrote about Harry in his diary on May 1, 1947: "Seldom have I seen a man so worked up over a comparative trifle — twice during the discussion [about his problems with Finn] he was agitated literally to the point of tears."[2]

Understandably, the friendship between Jackie and Jennie suffered as a result, since each woman supported her own husband, regardless of what they might have thought privately.

The official move-in day, when the entire crew transferred from the *Port of Beaumont* to the base camp, was cause for celebration. East Base and Stonington Island would be home for the team for the next eleven months, and the bunkhouse would be the centre of it all. And what a home it was. Jennie vividly related: "Inside was a damp, stagnant smell, an unaired man-smell of sweat frozen into old clothes, tobacco and cooking odors." Five crowded cubicles, each with an upper and lower bunk, lined two walls of the bunkhouse, and there was a battered mess table set up in the centre. At one end of the room was a pot-bellied stove and at the other was Gutenko's galley, with the coal range, coal bin, and the counter on which he placed the food at each meal. The range was notoriously temperamental, periodic-ally exploding, billowing smoke, and coating everyone in the vicinity with black soot.

Finn made the unusual decision to assign bunkmates on the basis of their dissimilarity, deciding that this was the best way to avoid cliques forming.

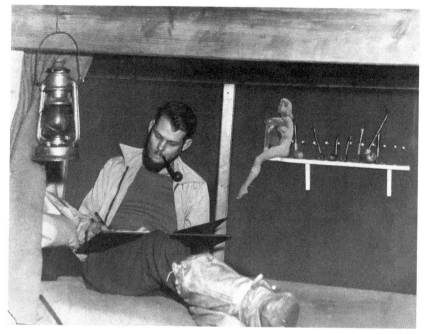

McClary with pin-up decorating his East Base bunk.

This arrangement was not successful, as the disparate pairings of men — one man who liked to read late forced to share a space with another who retired early; a man who snored put together with a man who was a light sleeper; and a man who was neat stuck with the one who was messy — only created dissent in the close quarters. Jennie remarked that "as the months progressed, it became a living, breathing, snoring, cursing exhibit of human nature in all its conflicting, raw, and unvarnished forms."

Each man decorated his bunk according to personal tastes and these "private" quarters reflected the individual. Latady painted a mural of the *Port of Beaumont* in the bay and hung up his ice axe, cameras, and Coleman lantern. McLean's bunk, which became known as Pitcairn Island (a reference to the place of refuge offered to the crew of the British ship HMS *Bounty* who defied their captain, William Bligh), attracted many admirers due to his extensive collection of voluptuous pin-ups, while Ike's bunk was

(Left to right): Ike Schlossbach, Harry Darlington, and Nelson McClary baking in the galley.

only reached through an ever-growing pile of dirty clothes, discarded cigar butts, tools, and the infrequently washed enamel mug that he used for heating soup, melting ice, and storing his dentures. Despite his eccentric habits, he was held in the highest esteem. No one messed with Ike.

The bunkhouse also provided the living quarters for newlyweds Jennie and Harry. To gain some privacy, they moved into what became known as "Darlington's Roost" — a small corner area at the end of the bunkhouse that had previously been occupied by the doctor of the last Byrd expedition. Jennie was mildly perturbed by the eye-popping gallery of women's photos decorating Harry's old bunk,[3] but furtively reading through a stack of his old well-thumbed love letters he had left behind made her feel even worse. Harry protested that he couldn't remember any of the women, but it was an unsettling experience for the recent bride who was still getting to know her husband. Jennie was comforted by the fact that with Jackie close by in the Ronne Hut, the two women could chat and keep each other company. Both

Jackie and Finn at work in the Ronne Hut at East Base.

women were anxious for Finn and Harry to mend the rift that was opening between them. Sadly, Jennie's eager hopes for female companionship would be dashed.

Jackie did her best to soften the primitive qualities of the compact wooden hut and make it comfortable for herself and her husband. "I have tried to decorate just a bit the private quarters that Commander Ronne and I share. Perhaps it's not important. But I can't help feeling that just that little touch of home must help, must ease his spirit when he faces hard decisions, relax him after a hard day of work and planning."

In the Ronne Hut, there was a built-in bunk with a mattress covered by a dark green blanket; a worktable where Finn plotted the flights; another table, with a typewriter, at which Jackie spent much of her day; two chairs; a shortwave radio; a washstand; a coal bin; and coal-burning stove. She pasted maps on the walls and used bright orange aviation tape as a border, bravely remarking that the conditions were crude but very comfortable by Antarctic standards. Finn did his part as well, enlarging the original single bed into a double and installing new double-paned windows that allowed views of the towering mountains. He also constructed a tunnel connecting the Ronne Hut with the bunkhouse. It was always a challenge keeping warm and never more so than in the mornings. Getting up in the morning in Antarctica held special challenges. In an interview published in Washington's *Sunday Star* after her return, Jackie recalled those experiences: "When temperatures are well below zero, we use eiderdown sleeping bags: but otherwise we sleep beneath four or five heavy blankets and in woolen pajamas. During the night, when temperatures drop, frost is apt to form around the opening of the sleeping bag from the breath. This has to be brushed aside before getting up in the morning."

A simple task such as obtaining water for drinking and bathing that would have taken only seconds in the United States took hours in Antarctica. The unlucky crewmen tasked with this job would row out into the bay, lasso a small iceberg, splinter off a small section, and transport it back to the camp. Pieces of it would be broken off, thawed, and run through a jury-rigged filtration system in the galley. Every drop of water was precious.

Clothes cleaning and bathing was not a top priority for many of the men, but Jackie and Jennie worked hard to keep themselves clean, neatly dressed, and attractive in the same way that other 1940s American housewives living thousands of kilometres away would. Most photographs of the women taken during the expedition show them wearing scarlet lipstick and sporting painted nails. Little did the men know the price of beauty, as bottles of nail polish froze and lipstick tubes had to be thawed out each morning. Jennie put her hair in pigtails to avoid the need for excessive washing and styling and used plain lanolin on her face instead of face cream. While Jackie tried to use a clumsily constructed shower, she often reverted to sponge baths in the relative privacy of the Ronne Hut. She was responsible for washing the Ronnes' clothes as well, and visitors entering the Ronnes' private space did so at their peril. The men often found themselves ducking beneath a clothesline filled with Jackie's "unmentionables"! It was up to Jackie to make sure that Finn always looked presentable. Jennie spoke admiringly of the expedition leader's appearance: "Standing very straight, with his chin tipped back in a way that

Jackie washing clothes in the Ronne Hut.

made him seem taller, the commander, who never had a button off his shirt or a whisker on his face, presented an impressive picture of a polar man."

Apart from the bunkhouse and the Ronne Hut, the two other major structures were the science building and the machine shop. These were located next to each other, just steps from the bunkhouse. Much of the geographic work would be conducted in the science building, which included a three-storey tower for meteorological studies. The science building also housed some unlikely guests. Cook Gutenko had smuggled in a flock of chickens, but the only place for them to live was in a corner of the science building. This arrangement was objected to by the working scientists until

Petunia laid her first egg. Once highly prized fresh eggs became available at mealtime, the scientists' tolerance for the noisy inhabitants increased. The machine shop stored the field gear, generators, and engines. There was also the blubber building, which was located some distance away due to the odours generated when seal meat was rendered to feed the dogs.

By the end of May, the sun had set and would not rise again for several months. Throughout May, June, and July, there was heavy snowfall and blizzard conditions were the norm. The men and women were often unable to go outside, doing so only to feed the dogs or use the outhouse on the hill. If the cold and the darkness did not weigh down their spirits, the wind did. The fierce katabatic winds that blew up to 160 kilometres an hour were a constant force in their lives. Finn wrote, "For days at a time the wind would howl and whistle through ventilators and stovepipes until we felt as if we were living in a wind tunnel. If it stopped, it was only to start up again a few seconds later." Jackie described this difficult period in her autobiography:

> The winternight is that long stretch of cold and darkness when the sun never rises above the northern horizon.... Each man must call upon his inner self to provide the stimulus to his interests, which he often may not receive from his associates. During this period, men's dispositions become tender and tempers flare over minor incidents which take on major proportions. It is the time, when the man himself is revealed perhaps for the first time in his life, and it is the most difficult period of an expedition.

This period poses the greatest challenge for any Antarctic expedition leader; he (and, decades later, she) must ensure that everyone in the team is kept physically active and mentally alert and that apathy and despair do not set in. At this time, minor problems can escalate, and mental health concerns become evident.

Harry's frustrations with Finn's decisions were now causing problems on a daily basis, with Harry and Jennie avoiding the Ronnes as much as possible. McClary commented in his diary that engineer Chuck Hassage suffered from a "war neurosis" and was treated with compassion and kindness by Finn especially during the early months. Latady and Kelsey's introspective tendencies were more acute, and even Dr. McLean confided in his medical report that he himself regularly suffered from bouts of depression "precipitated by mental straits." Living in close quarters with twenty-one men and two women during a bleak Antarctic winter was not for the faint-hearted.

Finn made sure that the work of the expedition did not falter during the dark time. The team was engaged in indoor pursuits preparing for the upcoming field programs. Bill Latady established a makeshift darkroom in the science building where he was able to put his creative talents to full use. Jennie remarked:

> Without any proper polar equipment, he improvised, invented, and made do to the extent of photographing hundreds of thousands of miles during the exploratory flights that later took place. For aerial mapping, he invented a drift viewfinder of sheet aluminum and made a lens of ground glass. As his cameras had to be loaded in the dark during the flights, he made a flying darkroom. It was a plywood box with armholes. In it he changed the two-hundred-foot rolls of film for the trimet cameras, kept the shutters from freezing, kept detailed logs from the time of take-off until landing, and saw that the three cameras, covering "horizon to horizon," were in constant operation — all more or less simultaneously.

After RARE, Latady became a noted optical mechanical engineer and would be awarded a Technical Oscar for his design of a snorkel camera used in underwater photography.

Physicist Peterson had started his meteorological work on board *Port of Beaumont*. On Stonington Island he continued to collect and send daily observations to the U.S. Weather Bureau. Nichols and Dodson's geological plans had to wait until the weather improved, but they did what they could in the immediate region. Everyone had their own project to work on.

Finn instructed Wood and McClary on building the wooden trail sleds for the dog team parties, while Dodson, Owen, Lassiter, Adams, and Fiske were kept busy making dog harnesses. Other jobs included the creation of trail flags, testing the cold weather gear, and caring for the rambunctious team of dogs. Men worked in pairs in the blubber shack making dog pemmican for the trail parties. The job required the cooking of seal blubber, something that, understandably, everyone hated. Finn describes it in *Antarctic Conquest*: "The most noticeable part of the job is the smell, a biting, lingering, pervasive stench that penetrates everything in the neighbourhood and saturates human skin, hair and clothes. The blubber shack had few visitors and these did not stay long." When the wind was from the north, the stench would reach the camp and the men would threaten to move back to the ship.

Handmade Acey-Deucey game with Chilean coins, created by Clarence "Larry" Fiske.

Jackie had no trouble keeping busy, but later she would recall longing for sunny skies and a warm climate in the midst of the bone-chilling cold of the polar nights.

Finn did not forget that a man's leisure time in Antarctica had to be planned for as well. This included boxing and other competitive sports; a lecture program in which the men gave presentations in their area of expertise, which included celestial navigation, meteorology, first aid, surveying; movies three nights a week, with cake and ice cream afterward; reading; and playing board games.

Practical jokes were commonplace such as when Peterson hid a water-filled balloon in Kelsey's bunk and Kelsey retaliated by putting a sack of coal in his. It was really only during this precious leisure time that Jackie lowered her guard with the men. As the leader's wife, it was a luxury that she indulged in infrequently.

The men found other ways of letting off steam as well. Unbeknownst to Finn (and against his express orders), Andy Thompson and Dr. McLean had erected a still and hidden it amongst the scientific equipment. Their clandestine bootlegging operation was an ongoing and popular concern throughout the expedition, despite it being repeatedly discovered and shut down. It somehow always managed to get restarted. Not all the men agreed with the Ronnes' insistence on clean, healthy living.

At the very least, they were well fed — although that didn't stop the complaints when the men didn't get their favourites. Sig Gutenko had twenty years' experience as a chief commissary steward, and he provided a diet that was balanced and nutritious. A typical breakfast at East Base included juice, pancakes with butter and syrup, oatmeal, bacon, and coffee. Lunch was usually soup or stew with bread, butter, and tea, and dinner included meat and potatoes, a canned vegetable, a canned fruit, and pie or cake. The cook had discovered that as the weather got colder, the men's desire for sweets increased. Men who never cared for candy before were now eating half a kilogram or more every day. In addition to a small supply of frozen pork, chicken, and ham, the galley was well supplied with nearly three thousand kilograms of frozen filet mignon. Compared to many average Americans in the post-war period, the RARE team ate very well indeed. Still, Jackie reported that the men soon tired of the prime steak and craved a good old-fashioned American hamburger doused with ketchup. And she did too.

As June 1947 drew to a close, Jackie reflected with pride on the work she had contributed so far. She knew she had earned her place as a member of the team. The group had weathered crises, setbacks, and internal conflicts, but she had every reason to believe that, with warmer weather on the horizon and, thus, the opportunity to conduct scientific work in the field, things would improve. Her faith in Finn as commander was absolute, although it was plain to see that his leadership style generated friction with some members of the team. Finn and Jackie together had made sure that the work schedule was maintained despite the challenges caused by the storms and the darkness. Every man and woman there was eager to move forward and continue with their adventure.

CHAPTER 6

STRIVING FOR GLORY

A passion to see and to report truly.
— J.C. BEAGLEHOLE

BY EARLY JULY, the worst of the blustery winter weather was behind them, and Jackie was desperate for the sun to make an appearance in the sky. When it finally did, the team was jubilant. After being confined to quarters for nearly two months, all twenty-three RARE members were bursting to get outside and get going, and Finn was anxious to put the full scientific program into action. It had been a challenge for Jackie to generate exciting stories for NANA while the team remained indoors, so she was delighted when the men went out into the field. And although she had some privacy, sometimes the Ronne Hut must have felt like a gilded cage.

> For the most part, I purposely kept myself isolated in our quarters.... I did not want the men to feel I was spying on them. As the wife of the leader, I was in a difficult position.

I did not want to interfere with their work or butt into their bitching sessions. I never heard a curse word or a dirty joke on the entire expedition and I was always treated with respect. The men knew where I was and if they wanted to see me, they came to our shack to do so, and many did.

For Finn, the primary objective of the scientific program was "to discover and explore the world's last major coastline which lay between Palmer Peninsula and Coats Land four hundred miles away." In order to do this, he planned a continuous series of extended flights and perilous sledging trips that would collect detailed photographs and data about the terrain. The information would be used later in the creation of new Antarctic maps.

One of the first trail parties to be sent out would establish a weather station near the tip of the Palmer Peninsula. This would provide necessary

William "Bill" Latady adjusting the trimetrogon camera equipment on board the Beechcraft.

data about weather conditions that would be used for the team. Finn was determined that the scientific plans would be successful, and he needed as much data as possible to help with his decision-making process. Weather played a critical role in both the flying and trail programs. After initial test flights, Latady worked with Robertson fine-tuning the trimetrogon camera equipment that had been installed on their replacement twin-engine Beechcraft, nicknamed "Edward Sweeney" after a RARE donor and Ronne family friend.

Doing meticulous, outdoor work on the three airplanes was no joke, and the men's frostbitten, blistered hands reflected this. Finn had used the dark time to work on his plans for the reconnaissance flights and trail parties, painstakingly calculating weights and distances and consumption of food and fuel over and over again. The consequences of not doing this correctly were grim. Due to the heavy loss of dogs to distemper on their journey down, the American dog team was not as robust as it should have been but the Americans had superior planes. Finn and Commander Pierce-Butler of the FIDS team decided that collaboration between the British and the Americans on several of these missions would benefit everyone.

As the weather improved, Finn saw an opportunity to conduct a training exercise and size up the men's abilities in the field. The team would erect the weather station at the same time. Not everyone would be given the chance to join a trail party, but each man desperately wanted to. Even today, Antarctic scientists admit that life at a base is more challenging than life in the field. There is greater freedom in the field, more control over one's own time, fewer people, and often, no leaders breathing down their neck.

Finn led Latady, Owen, Adams, Peterson, and Dodson out on the trail with a dog team. After eight days, most of the men returned with Finn, leaving Peterson and Dodson to complete the weather station. Physicist Peterson would also have the opportunity to take some initial sun refraction measurements. Although Finn and his group returned safely without incident, things went downhill from there. A few days later, the pilots were unable to make a scheduled supply drop to the pair due to adverse weather conditions. Sporadic radio contact with the team turned into no contact at all. When the weather cleared, Finn sent out the Beechcraft to find Peterson and

Dodson. Several passes were made. Their tent was located, but the men were nowhere to be found. Finn and the others were growing frantic. The hours of daylight were limited and the whereabouts of the two men unknown.

That night, as Finn finalized plans for a full-scale search to be launched at daybreak, the door to the bunkhouse burst open and a wan, frost-covered Dodson staggered in, shouting hoarsely for Finn. Jennie recorded: "Simultaneously ... all of us were struck by a sense of disaster." Peterson had fallen into a deep crevasse and was trapped. This was one of the most calamitous situations to occur in Antarctica and is dreaded by expeditioners even today.

The RARE team was galvanized into action. A few FIDS members were visiting, so a joint American-British rescue party was hastily assembled. At 11:00 p.m., the group, including the doctors from both camps, set off with rescue apparatus and medical supplies. The remaining team members, including Jackie and Jennie, prepared for the worst. At first light, Harry Darlington took a plane up and reported that the search party had miraculously located Peterson thirteen kilometres from the base in a heavily crevassed area. Despite shock and fatigue, Dodson had managed to leave the area well marked, but it had still taken almost four hours to locate the missing man. Peterson had vanished into a narrow crevasse and was wedged deep inside.

It had already been ten desperate hours since Peterson had disappeared. Finn later confided to Jackie that he and Pierce-Butler believed there was no way that Peterson could have survived. At the crevasse edge, the men shouted down to the afflicted man and shone a bright light into the chasm into which he had fallen. There was no response. Dr. Dick Butson from the FIDS team was the smallest man of the group and valiantly volunteered to rappel down into the crevasse. As he descended deeper, Butson found Peterson wedged into the crevasse, head facing downwards. The good news: he was alive!

Although Butson tugged as hard as he could in the confined space, Peterson did not budge. Precious minutes ticked by. The team lowered a rope harness that Butson tied to Peterson's body.[1] Slowly, the pressure between Peterson and the crevasse wall was released. He was quickly lifted to

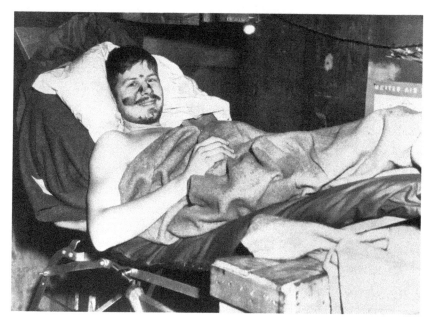

Harries-Clichy Peterson after his accident.

the surface and ministered to. The two doctors methodically checked him over and applied heat and morphine. Jennie Darlington wrote about the incident: "The ice that had broken his fall and trapped him had also saved him. Due to his thick clothing and the stagnant air at the bottom of the crevasse where it was at least 25 degrees warmer than the air at the surface, he was practically unhurt."

He had suffered shock and exhaustion, but only one of his exposed hands and the nerves of his right arm sustained any lasting damage. Once it was safe to do so, the rescue team carried Peterson back to the camp where he spent the next few days recovering from the near-fatal ordeal. Peterson later reported, "It was like torture.... I think I passed out every now and again. I thought: *Well, this is my fate.*"

Peterson's accident shook the team up, but, regrettably, it did not bring them closer together. The personality clashes between the men and fiery outbursts that marred the early months of the expedition only intensified.

Finn's clumsy attempts to unify the team were often rebuffed, and although the tension within the team waxed and waned, it never completely dissipated. Months later, the fractured relationship between Harry and Finn came to a head. While the cause and circumstances of the irrevocable rupture varies according to the narrator, the outcome was the same. Harry challenged Finn's decisions once too often. Harry either rashly offered his resignation without expecting it to be accepted or he was fired outright by Finn. When the end came, it was shocking and dramatic, especially within the claustrophobic confines of East Base. In late October, three-quarters of the way through the expedition, Harry Darlington was relieved of all RARE responsibilities. His duties as a pilot and as third-in-command were taken over by his colleagues.

Once the schism between Finn and Harry had occurred, there was no turning back. The men were either with Finn or against him. There were a few who tried to remain neutral and remain in harmony with both men. But after all, the opinionated, risk-taking men who had signed up for this hazardous Antarctic expedition were not representative of the average American Joe and tempers ran hot. Dr. Don McLean was one of the most vocal supporters of Harry Darlington and openly defied Finn. He later confided: "I never came so close to killing anybody in my life." Indeed, his fury at Finn had barely diminished over fifty years later when McLean shared his memories with a journalist. Everyone at East Base was impacted by Finn's irrevocable decision. Later, his intransigence powerfully affected the legacy of the expedition he had worked so hard for.

In the midst of this bickering and, at times, borderline mutiny, Jackie counselled a beleaguered Finn. She alone understood his ways and his thirst to succeed. She knew that her larger-than-life husband was a man like any other with human frailties and she provided a sounding board when he needed to talk. Whether Finn did the same for Jackie is unknown, although an outlet for her own stress would have been welcomed. Privately, she wrote in her diary, "Living under continuous tension, among men who had rivalries and jealousies between themselves, and who were always looking for some reason to blame Finn for their problems, was a never-ending strain." Although Jackie welcomed chats with the men if they needed to talk, it was clear where her personal allegiance lay. They felt more comfortable sharing their woes with approachable Jennie than they did with the boss's wife. Although it was more difficult than ever to carry on as if nothing had changed, the scientific agenda resumed.

Despite this breakdown within the team, Jackie's work continued. She was incredibly prolific, averaging three stories a week and over 150 in total while at East Base. Over the course of the expedition, Jackie's articles, published in major North American newspapers including the *New York Times*, the *Washington Post*, and the *Boston Globe*, displayed a shrewd understanding and grasp of the heroic narrative.

Early stories filed with the North American Newspaper Alliance — including "Ronne Polar Ship Meets Heavy Seas" (March 6, 1947); "U.S. Antarctic Base Looted" (March 18, 1947); and "Ice Cliff Menaces Polar Expedition" (April 2, 1947) — reflect the difficult conditions encountered during the sea voyage and the vandalized state of East Base. Once the crew was established on Stonington Island, Jackie's articles focused on two major categories that were each designed to evoke a powerful emotional response on the part of the reader. Articles with headlines including "Ronne Plane Saves British Fliers Trekking After Antarctic Crash" (September 25, 1947); "Ronne Sledge Party Delayed as Member Breaks Collarbone" (October 22, 1947); and "Starvation Threatened Ronne Geologists" (January 2, 1948) emphasized the raw courage of the male RARE team members and stirred a reader's sympathy. In "3 British Fliers Down in Antarctic: Ronne Planes Search in Blizzard," Jackie stressed the hazardous conditions undertaken by the search party and emphasized the co-operation provided by the Americans to the British. This was critical, given the overheated political rivalry between the United States and Great Britain toward Antarctica. She wrote: "Although hampered by a fierce blizzard that began the night of the Auster's disappearance and grounded all search planes for forty-eight hours, we put the entire facilities of our group at the disposal of Major K.S. Pierce-Butler."

While Jackie wrote about their hardships, she deliberately avoided topics such as the hostility within the RARE team, the challenges to Finn's leadership, and problems between the American and British camps. Other articles — including "Ronne Party Adds to Antarctic Data" (June 10, 1947); "Ronne Seismographs Recording Quakes in Unstudied Regions" (August 21, 1947); and "Ronne Solves Mystery of Weddell Sea Isles" (November 12, 1947) — focused on their contributions to science and were designed to inspire the admiration and respect of readers. Jackie wrote 90 percent of these articles and either edited or at least assisted with the other 10 percent. The information that she communicated through these articles was accurate, but she was highly selective in what incidents she focused on. By doing so, she satisfied the demands of her editor and protected the RARE legacy and American interests in Antarctica all at the same time.

In comparison, she wrote little about her own and Jennie Darlington's personal experiences, believing it detracted from her husband's accomplishments and the RARE legacy that Jackie helped to construct. The few articles about the two women, which were typically short, factual, and devoid of introspection, were primarily published at the beginning and the end of the expedition. Lacking any analytical content, they focused almost exclusively on the historical aspect of the women's participation: "Mrs. Finn Ronne and Wife of Flier Go to Antarctic" (March 1, 1947); "2 Women Join Icy Expedition" (March 2, 1947); "Mrs. Ronne Makes First Antarctic Flight" (August 20, 1947); and "First Women to Set Foot in Antarctica Thrilled by Scenery" (April 12, 1947). Notably, Jennie's accomplishments are not recognized in Jackie's articles. For example, on board the *Port of Beaumont*, Jennie monitored the gauges on the evaporator that converted salt to fresh water, but this important responsibility is mentioned only in Jennie's own memoir.

All RARE members were required to be versatile and while Jackie fulfilled the primary role of communications, she carried out other responsibilities as well. Equally important as media relations was her job assisting Finn. The couple had planned the expedition for years before the other team members had even heard about it. Finn had talked everything over with Jackie and she was as familiar with his plans as he was himself. The articles and reports she wrote and edited were technical and detail-oriented in nature. Published in newspapers around the world and read by polar specialists and the general public alike, there was no room for error. Quite simply, Jackie knew her stuff and that was enough for Finn. He later confided to a journalist:

Although my wife is not a trained scientist, she was most certainly involved in the expedition's scientific program. Not only did she have sufficient interest, background, and knowledge of the expedition's scientific work to interpret the individual disciplines in laymen's language for syndicated news articles, but she participated in the program as a data collector herself. She was perfectly familiar with the studies being conducted, their terminology and possible future importance.

While the other men understood that the couple worked as a close team, few of them understood just how important Jackie was to Finn until the day he announced to the stunned group that if something should happen to him in Antarctica, Jackie would assume command. In announcing this, he was flouting the hierarchy within the group that he himself had instituted, but his word was law.

Jackie also worked as an assistant to several of the scientists when they went into the field. She had been an eager participant in the lecture program and enjoyed learning how to use scientific instruments along with the men. In particular, she often helped geophysicist Andy Thompson with his seismographic and tidal analyses and found it enormously satisfying. He had already set up several small shacks in which to collect his data. His program involved long-term observations of tidal movements, collecting data on terrestrial magnetism that would be added to similar magnetic studies in Central and South America, and maintaining a daily record of the salinity of the sea water. The seismological studies were of particular interest, and the data was correlated with centres at the U.S. Coast and Geodetic Survey and various universities. In her article "Women in the Antarctic or The Human Side of a Scientific Expedition," Jackie wrote:

> I took over the operation of both the tidal gauge and the seismographic work. I made daily trips down to the tidal shack, checked to see that the tide changes were being automatically recorded, and then wound the clocks. The seismographs took more time and were a bit more complicated. Every twelve

hours I crawled into a dungeon-like room, pulled up the trap door, beneath which the instruments were concealed, and changed the photographic sheets on the revolving drum. The machines were then checked for correct operation and the necessary adjustments made. To ensure their continuous twenty-four-hour-a-day operation, Andy had rigged up a complicated battery system which worked most satisfactorily. When several of the recorded sheets had accumulated, I developed them in the same manner as one would a negative. Then they were washed six times and hung up to dry.

Jackie also wrote articles that appeared in the *New York Times* about this work entitled "Ronne Expert Records Quake in Antarctic Lasting 2 ½ Hours" and "Ronne Party Adds to Antarctic Data."

Following the expedition, Thompson prepared four scientific reports for the Office of Naval Research: *Tidal Work on Marguerite Bay, Antarctica, Antarctic Seismological Bulletin, Establishment of Antarctic Seismological Station*, and *Microseisms and Weather on Palmer Land Peninsula, Antarctica.* Despite the fact that Jackie had regularly assisted Thompson with the fieldwork that formed the basis for these technical reports, her name is glaringly absent from the pages of these reports.

On August 21, 1947, Jackie attained another historical first for women. On that morning, she climbed into the Stinson L-5 with pilot Lassiter and flew on a reconnaissance mission toward the nearly two-thousand-metre-high Palmer Land plateau. This was no pleasure flight, as Jackie acted in an official capacity as observer. Based on her training, she was able to detect the polar phenomenon known as "dark-water skies."[2] The sighting in this case indicated that there was open water northwest of Alexander I Island. Finn was delighted with the valuable data she returned with and authorized additional work. Later she confided to a journalist that plane flights were among her most exciting experiences: "I got in quite a bit of action flying with some of the search planes."

Over the course of the expedition, Jackie flew many times in the Stinson L-5, as well as in the two other planes, the Beechcraft and Norseman. This was a privilege not extended to most of the other expedition members. Her first flight would be the subject of one of the few stories Jackie wrote about herself. In a NANA article entitled "Mrs Ronne First Woman on Antarctic-based Flight," she wrote:

> Captain James Lassiter took off on a reconnaissance flight today in our L-5 single-engined, ski-equipped plane with Mrs. Ronne along. It was the first Antarctic-based flight by a woman. Many years ago, the wife of a Norwegian explorer flew over a portion of the continent with her husband but she did not land there. Today's trip was to check flying approaches to the 6,000-foot plateau, on which we have established a weather station, before flying in additional equipment.

Jackie making pemmican with Sig Gutenko.

Jackie was also the de facto manager of the camp, handling all the administrative tasks. She also helped the cook in the weighing and packing of the trail food and took her turn cooking in the galley. The full scope of Jackie's contributions to the expedition was never formally recognized, even by Jackie herself. Finn did, however, offer nodding acknowledgement of her contributions in his book *Antarctic Conquest*. Finn pushed Jackie as hard as he pushed himself, but he recognized that she pushed herself hard too. Despite all of the work that Jackie already did for the expedition, she "only wished the days were longer so she could work more things into her busy schedule." For Finn and Jackie, the focus remained on the success of the expedition, whatever the personal cost.

The work that Jackie did kept her busy all day every day and she rarely took any time off. At twenty-seven, she was closer in age to most of the men than to her own forty-seven-year-old husband, but she acted more mature than her years. Like Finn, she referred to the team as "the boys" even years

Jennie Darlington at East Base.

later. First and foremost, she bore the burden of her role as the leader's wife and concealed her vivacious, fun-loving side. She took her multiple roles on the expedition — communications expert, administrator, counsellor, and assistant scientist — seriously. The fact that Finn had chosen her as his replacement in a crisis meant that she was second-in-command in all but name.

In contrast, Jennie Darlington had no formal role on the expedition and had much less control over her time and activities than did Jackie. To her credit, Jennie did her best to find useful occupations for herself and to offer assistance where she could, doing such things as helping Latady with photography and organizing the two-thousand-volume base library.[3]

She was in the unenviable position of being married to a man who had an uncontrollable temper, who referred to her regularly using a racial epithet, and who had opposed her even taking part in the expedition. If her husband didn't seem to appreciate her, the other men in the party did. Jennie may have been a married woman, but she was also a beautiful one. The fact that there were only two women in this confined male space for thirteen months meant that sexual tension was palpable, at least for some of them. Certainly, the young Chilean Jorge di Giorgio had an intense crush on Jennie.[4]

Living close to the men in the bunkhouse meant that she was privy to their often coarse locker-room talk and jokes in a way that Jackie never was. Being a newlywed in the testosterone-fuelled environment of East Base made things even more uncomfortable. The rupture between Harry and Finn had created a divide between the women that could not be bridged even in times of crisis. It was a loss for both women. Jennie noted: "I thought of Jackie alone in her quarters.... Now was the time when we should be close together, close as only women can be in times of trouble. Now we should be confiding our fears to each other, drawing strength, the one from the other, but I knew that any overture I made would be rebuffed or would result in further embarrassment."

The tension caused by the conflict between Finn and Harry continued for months as Harry vented his frustration on his teammates. Harry and Jennie even explored ways they could leave East Base early, but these ideas proved impractical. Finn was determined to keep the scientific agenda on

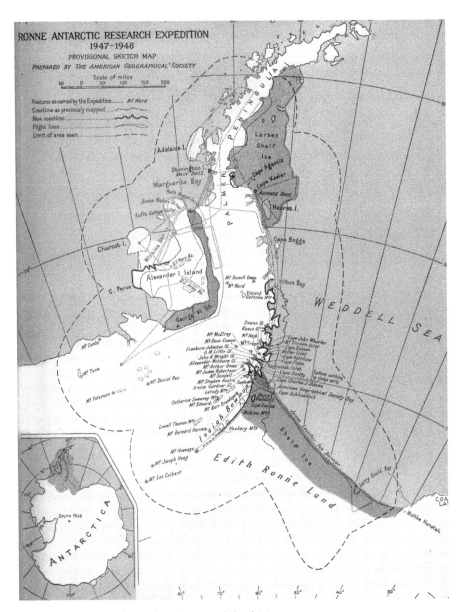

Ronne Antarctic Research Expedition Provisional Sketch Map.

track. For the next several months, the RARE team continued their program photographing the coastline, sending out trail parties, and collecting data. There were plenty of successes to celebrate, including a missing British FIDS aviation crew valiantly rescued by RARE pilots Lassiter and Adams, but there were crises too, like McClary breaking his collarbone. Most notably, Finn now had evidence that Antarctica was one continent. The relationship between the Americans and the British remained cordial with co-operation occurring on several projects.

By January 1948, the bulk of the scientific program had been concluded and the next few weeks were spent preparing for their departure. While the Beechcraft and Norseman were loaded back onto the *Port of Beaumont,* the Stinson L-5 was kept flying. The scientists desperately collected the last of their data and everyone knew the end was close. Finn could not be prouder of his team and radioed Dr. John Wright at the American Geographical Society of the "extremely rich harvest of results" that the Ronne Antarctic Research Expedition had obtained. Finally, it was time to leave.

The treacherous pack ice was moving in fast. Too fast for Finn's liking. He was well aware of the possible consequences if a shipbound expedition did not leave in time. In early February, Finn had been in contact with Gerald L. Ketchum, commodore of Task Force 39 and commander of the formidable U.S. Navy Wind-class icebreakers the USS *Burton Island* and the USS *Edisto.*[5] Ketchum was spearheading Operation Windmill, which was an exploration and training exercise designed to test equipment at Little America and conduct extensive surveying of the region. The *Burton Island* and *Edisto* were due to be in the vicinity of Marguerite Bay and were prepared to help the expedition if necessary. Jackie reported: "The possibility of having to remain another year here if the bay ice did not go out for the sake of a few more weeks of recordings, important as they were to our scientific program, was too great a risk to take."

It is not clear if Finn specifically requested assistance from Ketchum or if Ketchum himself determined that the Ronne Expedition needed rescuing — he may have come to this conclusion after he learned about the two women. Finn and Jackie's accounts of this episode suggest that the ships were already in the area. Yet, Boatswain's Mate Robert Pope Sr. assigned to the USS *Burton Island* later stated that the two ships incurred considerable risk in coming to the aid of *Port of Beaumont*. A detailed U.S. Navy map in Pope's possession that depicts the route taken by the ships prior to the rescue suggests that they deviated from their regular course and sailed at an increased pace to reach the Ronne party. In later years, Finn would downplay the rescue aspect of his interactions with these two ships.

As the water around *Port of Beaumont* continued to freeze, Finn's mind was made up. Suddenly, the evacuation plans from East Base kicked into high gear as the icebreakers would be arriving ahead of Finn's carefully planned schedule. All hands were on deck, making final observations for the scientific work and packing up all the equipment.

In these final days, the strained relations between the Ronnes and the Darlingtons boiled over with the disclosure of explosive news. As Finn and Jackie had suspected, Jennie was pregnant. This critical information about the health status of one of his team members had been withheld from Finn by Dr. McLean. It could have had potentially devastating consequences if the expedition had been snowed-in for the season, unable to leave Antarctica until the next year. Neither the American nor the British doctor had the specialist training or the appropriate equipment or supplies to deal with things should any complications arise. McLean had written in his final medical report that it was imperative that Jennie be evacuated at the earliest opportunity. There would be no possibility of a reconciliation between the Ronnes and the Darlingtons now.[6]

Jackie completed a few final stories and pitched in with the rest of them. Like the others, she was exhausted, admitting to herself if not to Finn that her heart was no longer in her work. Personal relations between team members remained fractious. Jackie reported: "[I]t got so bad that you'd become terribly irritated just by the way your neighbour tied his shoes."

Nicknamed "Hurtin' Burton," the flagship USS *Burton Island* led the way and arrived in Marguerite Bay on February 19, with socializing taking place on board and at East Base. It was a historic event since these were

A Ronne Antarctic Research Expedition flag.

the first icebreakers to travel to Antarctica. The meeting between *Port of Beaumont* and the two icebreakers marked the transition between the last major privately funded and organized expedition of the first half of the twentieth century and modern expeditions that operated on a grander scale and were characterized by the use of advanced technology.

On the USS *Burton Island*, Boatswain's Mate Robert Pope Sr. and his colleagues had great respect for the rugged conditions and hardships that the RARE team had faced and for all they had accomplished.

Finn, Jackie, and the rest of the American group bid farewell to the British team with mostly positive feelings on both sides. Finn remarked that "[e]ach of us had been able to help the other out of tight fixes; we had accomplished more together than either party would have separately and we had become good friends." Days later, Finn and Jackie walked the perimeter of the East Base camp for the last time. Their American flag was lowered, Finn checked that nothing of significance had been left behind and all doors were secured.[7]

That task completed, the Ronnes and RARE members left East Base and boarded the *Port of Beaumont*. For several hours, the USS *Burton Island* and USS *Edisto* broke up the ice in Marguerite Bay and forged a path out to sea. Then, attaching a cable to the *Beaumont*, the two icebreakers towed her out to the open water. Disconnecting the cable, Finn expressed his sincere appreciation for the rescue and wished them farewell. Everyone had their sights set on home.

After the icebreakers left, the weather turned against them. For the next five days, the *Port of Beaumont* was battered by the waves. Jackie suffered as much as the next person on the heaving ship. Food could not be served, so everyone lived on tomato juice and stale crackers. Likely, this is all that pregnant Jennie could keep down anyway. Water sloshed continually on the decks and the dogs that returned with the team howled mournfully. Travelling through the Drake Passage, Jackie's spirits began to lift despite the seasickness:

> Polar dress was rapidly discarded in favor of more conventional clothing used in more friendly climates. Fur parka and heavy boots were put aside and wrinkled civilian suits and washed but unpressed shirts and gay neckties were pulled from suitcase for inspection. Elaborate preparations were made with eager anticipation of leaving behind the isolation of a polar camp and returning to the civilized world.

The expedition team received a warm welcome during their stopovers in Punta Arenas and in Valparaíso, where they were feted at cocktail and dinner parties and granted a tour of the city. Jackie even fit in a lecture to the YWCA in Valparaíso. Jackie and Finn knew that this attention was in part due to the fact that the Chileans wanted the United States to support their Antarctic claims against the British.

Jackie enjoyed time by herself — a luxury she hadn't had for months. "Over the next few days I did a lot of shopping. It was pure ecstasy! Only a woman who has been deprived of shopping for a year could ever understand how I felt. I felt like a giggling schoolgirl again."

While in Punta Arenas, Harry and Jennie Darlington took advantage of the situation to slip away and leave the ship permanently. Ultimately, this furtive departure denied Jennie her triumphal return to the United States. Although she had not been an active expedition member with a formal role as Jackie had been, she was still one of the first women to overwinter in Antarctica. Her accomplishments should have been celebrated as well.

Feeling more rested but eager to leave, the Ronne Antarctic Research Expedition team made one further stop in Panama. Then *Port of Beaumont* set sail for the east coast of the United States and headed for home.

The newspaper coverage of the ship's return focused on the expedition's scientific accomplishments, but Jackie was mentioned as well. However, most articles about her, with headlines such as "Ever Try Domesticity at the Pole" and "Antarctic Housewife," focused on elements of Jackie's RARE experience that readers could identify with. One exception was an article entitled "Icewoman Cometh — From Pole," in which journalist Margaret Elliott wrote about the roles Jackie had played there:

> Dressed in gray slacks, a bright red sweater and a scarf over her freshly washed hair, Mrs Ronne sat in her bunk aboard the *Beaumont* and related what it was like to be the first of her sex to live in the Antarctic. She was the official historian of the expedition and also served as an assistant scientist.… During our chat, her husband, Commander Ronne began mentioning another Antarctic expedition. With a quick smile, Mrs. Ronne held up a protesting hand. "Not for me. It was fun, but the next time, I stay home."

Jackie later recalled intense feelings of joy welling up inside her as *Port of Beaumont* sailed toward the navy harbour in New York City: "As we passed the Statue of Liberty, no native or immigrant had ever gazed upon it with a heart more full of gratitude and relief than did I. HOME AT LAST! FREEDOM AT LAST! NEVER, NEVER AGAIN!!!"

ODE TO EDITH "JACKIE RABBIT" RONNE[8]
Talbert "Ted" Abrams

'Twas the Ronne Expedition, that started out brave,
To explore the Antarctic and start a new craze,
To prove the Antarctic was not all snow and fright
They took along "Jackie" to brighten the long winter night.

They explored the seas with the Beaumont Queen
And flew the interior with the Edward Swene
They mapped and tramped over penguins and seals
Jackie always came up with delicious meals.

The land was beautiful, also silent and white
A name was needed to record the site.
Edith Ronne Land seemed to tell the story fair
Our own "Jackie Rabbit" was the first to be there.

CHAPTER 7

AFTERWARD

What is it you plan to do / with your one wild and precious life?
— MARY OLIVER

AFTER MAKING HISTORY as one of the first women to overwinter in Antarctica and the first female Antarctic expedition member, Jackie returned to a rousing welcome home. She had braved the continual howling katabatic winds, the rough living conditions, and the desolation of the endless dark months during the austral winter when the sun never rose above the horizon. She had endured the relentless conflict between her husband and fractious team members and helped to defray the worst of the tension. On top of that, Jackie denied herself the much-needed female comradeship of the only other woman there. Both she and Jennie Darlington suffered from this separation that was caused in part by the clash of egos between their two volatile husbands. She had no choice but to put up with it all.

Few individuals, women or men, could have juggled the demands of a difficult, embattled, strong-willed spouse and helped maintain the peace within a group of (mostly) young, self-centred men jostling to protect their own turf, while at the same time performing their own job with such adroitness. If it had been bad for the others, it was worse for Jackie. Of all the RARE members returning home, Jackie was one of the happiest that the experience was coming to an end.

After being locked in the ice for nearly fifteen months and travelling nearly twenty-four thousand kilometres from Texas, along the west coast of South America, across the dreaded Drake Passage to Antarctica and back again, the valiant *Port of Beaumont* with the exuberant Ronne Antarctic Research Expedition team entered New York Harbor on April 15, 1948. On board, there was a melee of arms waving madly and weather-beaten faces

RARE crew on board *Port of Beaumont*. Back row (left to right): Ike Schlossbach, Don McLean, Jim Lassiter, Chuck Hassage, Larry Fiske, Finn Ronne, Jackie Ronne, Woody Wood, Bill Latady, Jimmy Robertson, Bob Nichols, Harcly Peterson, and Sig Gutenko. Front row (left to right): Chuck Adams, Bob Dodson, Smitty Smith, Mac McClary, Art Owen, and Andy Thompson. Missing: Larry Kelsey, Jennie Darlington, and Harry Darlington.

beaming, scanning the crowds for beloved faces. No one lingered below deck as the ship was greeted by tugboats madly honking their horns and spraying water hoses into the air. Jubilant friends and family and curious members of the public lined the navy pier, and Jackie and Finn were gratified to see esteemed polar explorer Sir Hubert Wilkins leading the cheers. They had been hopeful of a lusty welcome that would acknowledge their triumphant return. If they expected a tickertape parade or the illustrious accolades that were heaped upon Admiral Byrd when he came back from his Antarctica expeditions, they were sadly mistaken.

Prior to their arrival in New York, both Finn and Jackie sent a flood of telegrams to those who might arrange a whiz-bang celebration after the *Port*

Jackie and Finn return to New York, 1948.

of Beaumont docked. Finn wrote to Jackie's uncle Irvine: "As you know I … would rather have a simple dignified reception [than] a lot of ballyhoo.… Times certainly have changed." And yet it seems that ballyhoo was *exactly* what was wanted as he continued: "Dana might be able to assume some responsibility in New York with Dr Wright [of the American Geographical Society] in making arrangements for newsreels, reporters, Explorers Club representatives, Beaumont representatives, the Norseman Lodge representatives, which could easily be arranged. Assume upon my arrival NANA contract is over and I am free for spot news agencies."

He had been advised by a friend that the return date was not a propitious one: "You are arriving not exactly at the most favorable time. War with Russia is on everybody's lips. Yet, you can turn it all in your favor IF you stress the importance of Antarctica to the USA as a strategic necessity."

Finn and Jackie were pleased by the enthusiastic response of the American Geographical Society. A formal reception and dinner was held at the Hotel McAlpin and the Engineering Societies' Building Hall in New York with their friend and stalwart supporter Dr. Laurence Gould as toastmaster. Gould could not have been more generous in his praise. "You have proved what many of us have long believed, that a relatively small expedition can accomplish far more worth-while scientific results in proportion to its numbers than a larger, more cumbersome one could possibly do." Finn's explorer colleagues Lincoln Ellsworth, Sir Hubert Wilkins, Vilhjalmur Stefansson, and Anthony Fiala were in attendance; lavish toasts were offered and congratulatory telegrams were read from Sir Douglas Mawson, Paul Siple, and other polar luminaries. It was a night for Finn and Jackie to savour. But truth be told, Finn had secretly hoped for more. As always, he compared himself, and the reception he was given, to Byrd.

Jackie was thrilled to be home. There was so much to be grateful for and she felt a renewed appreciation for endless steaming hot water, electricity on demand, indoor heating, a flush toilet, an American-style bathtub, a comfortable bed with freshly laundered linen sheets and a fluffy pillow she could rest her head on, a closet full of clean clothes. Fresh milk, coffee, real eggs, hamburgers with all the fixings, crisp vegetables. And Jackie's favourite: potato chips and a chocolate soda with ice cream. Trusted friends and family with whom she could just relax. Shopping excursions to catch up on the latest fashions and trends. No more worrying about conflicts amongst the men, no more soothing Finn's bruised pride after a blow-up with Harry Darlington, no more anxiety about the men's safety when they left on reconnaissance missions by air or dog team. No more playing down her femininity, no disguising the love and intimacy between herself and Finn in public, no need to stifle her emotional self.

She was sick and tired of always being stern Mrs. Ronne, the boss's wife, who laid down the law and could never say what *she* really thought or do what *she* wanted. Now she could disagree with Finn as much as she liked, she could be frivolous and fun and free. Most of all, she treasured the newly found privacy and time to be herself. Just Jackie. She had earned it.

Although Jackie and Finn returned from Antarctica as conquering heroes and celebrities, when they arrived in the United States, there was literally nowhere for them to go. The lease on their former apartment had expired, and all their worldly goods were in storage. As usual, Jackie's aunt Merriel and uncle Irvine came to the rescue, allowing the couple to live with them until they found a place of their own. This must have been an uneasy, awkward situation since the couple was exhausted and culture-shocked and the modest home could hardly accommodate the whirlwind that was Finn Ronne. Merriel and Irvine Gardner were busy professionals with active social lives and likely would have preferred the Ronnes live elsewhere. In a letter to her aunt and uncle, Jackie expressed her thanks and outlined the couple's plans:

> Both Finn and I certainly appreciated your help and generosity in putting up with us for so long and we hope from now on we will be able to get organized so that we can plan what to do in the future. We should get our schedule from Colston Leigh and then decide on someplace to call our own

in Washington — even though small, it would at least house
our junk for a while, until we will want something better.

They may have felt some embarrassment in staying with Jackie's relatives. An article published in a Washington, D.C., paper, "Problem of Finding Home Here Now Occupying Finn Ronnes," broadcasting their "homeless" status to the world contributed to their discomfort.

After the initial flurry of excitement had worn off, Jackie felt bereft and at a loss. She had no home of her own and no money to speak of. The expedition to which she and Finn had committed their lives for so many years was over. Likely her unease about her unstable childhood stirred and resurfaced.

Still, Jackie's relationship with Finn was rock solid and he had her back as she had his. Their marriage had survived the test of Antarctica and sustained them both. A Christmas card from a girlfriend gushed that what she admired most about the couple was Jackie's great love for Finn. While this is beyond dispute, more telling was the implicit trust that she had in him. It was something she had sought all her life. She had found a worthy man in Finn, and he had found a perfect match in Jackie. What woman completely lacking in practical outdoor skills would have relinquished a fulfilling job, defied her loved ones, and indeed all conventional norms of the day to spend over a year in Antarctica with a newish, demanding husband? By the time they returned to civilization, Jackie knew without a shadow of a doubt that her future was tied to this man and everything she did going forward would support this.

Finn was nothing if not resilient. The expedition may have been over, but there was still lots of work for him to do. He never really took any time off but just pivoted to the next stage for any returning polar explorer. Heartily thank those generous sponsors who had supported him and ensure their good will for the future. Trumpet the significant achievements of the expedition. Gather the considerable data that had been collected, write it up, and publicize, publicize, publicize. If there was any opportunity to burnish

Finn Ronne in Decorated Parka. Painting by Thelma DeAtley.

his reputation and the Ronne family name, he and Jackie embraced it. Finn dutifully made the rounds to all the donors of the expedition and basked in their adulation.

While many of the RARE team members attended the celebratory dinner in New York, afterward, everyone went their separate ways. Happily, though, with only a few exceptions, the Ronnes maintained a long and friendly correspondence with the men, responding to their entreaties to join Finn on his next adventure, exchanging gossip about family members, and sharing news about the well-being of their Antarctic colleagues. The difficult times receded into the background and only the positive memories remained.

For most of them, the expedition was the highlight of their lives. Larry Fiske's daughter recalled her father saying, "As miserable as that bastard Finn was, I would go back in a heartbeat." Harries-Clichy Peterson confided years later: "Ronne could not achieve a close human relationship with any of his troops. But I thought he was right and American youth were wrong. I made up my mind I'd be with Finn." In the years following the expedition, Finn sent glowing reference letters to private companies and the military on behalf of RARE participants. The care he took in carefully crafting each letter far exceeded the requirements of a standard recommendation by an employer.[1]

Jackie was delighted to visit her best friend, Bettie; her old boss, John Steeves; and her former colleagues at the Department of State. What fun to be treated as a celebrity! With the end of the war, the department had suffered from cost-cutting measures levied across the federal government, which resulted in uncertainty and unrest amongst the staff. It was a happy reunion for Jackie although somewhat sobering as well.

Everyone agreed these were challenging and fast-moving times. By 1948, the Marshall Plan, also known as the European Recovery Program, had been introduced by President Truman; the World Health Organization had been formed; and Israel had declared its independence from Britain, which precipitated the First Arab-Israeli War. The Cold War was in full and dangerous swing. Momentous events were occurring on the world stage and America was involved in many of them.

Closer to home, Jackie heard whispered talk about the controversial activities of the House Un-American Activities Committee (HUAC). Formed in 1938 to investigate claims that Communists had infiltrated American organizations, including the U.S. government, HUAC was a profoundly divisive force from the outset. During that year, Secretary of State staffers, along with the rest of Americans, were riveted by the testimony of

Whittaker Chambers and their own Alger Hiss, who was a long-standing senior Department of State employee. Jackie had a front-row seat to the engrossing events and heard even more from her former co-workers. She also had a decision to make. Her State job was still available to her if she wanted it, even after the long absence. She knew, however, that if she went back, the deadlines and the pressure to perform would be the same. In the end, there was never any question in her mind about what she would do. She left the Department of State with a smile and a wave, and this would stand her in good stead in the future. The friendships she made there and the respect in which she had been held were intact.

Soon she was immersed in the life she had chosen, promoting the work of the Ronne Antarctic Research Expedition and Finn's career as an explorer. Her first U.S. lecture had been given at her alma mater, George Washington University. She had already started writing Finn's book about the expedition while they were at East Base. Finn was determined to have it published as quickly as possible. Written by Jackie, his personal account would capitalize on the expedition's accomplishments and firmly establish the Ronne legacy. In so doing, he would secure his much-desired place in the pantheon of legendary polar explorers. Counting on big sales in the gift-giving season, Jackie worked feverishly to get the book to a publisher in time for Christmas.

At the same time, she was busy writing articles for publications including the *Geographical Review, Photogrammetric Engineering*, the *Explorers Club Journal, Appalachia, Encyclopedia Americana Annual*, the *Standard Reference Encyclopedia*, and the *Encyclopedia Britannica*. This supported Finn's agenda and, as well, allowed them to make a living. At this time, writing represented the bread and butter of their income. But contrary to what many of their friends thought, writing and publishing was not always as glamorous as it sounded. Sometimes Jackie felt dismayed by the daily grind of it all. In a letter to her aunt and uncle, Jackie complained about the situation:

If our friend calls, can you tell him I expect to have a really good article for him upon my return. If the *Post* doesn't accept it, which I hope and think they probably will, I can always try and sell it to some other magazine. The *Post* circulation, of course, is the big thing. I have written the same things in so many different ways for a year now that I am getting a bit stale on new ways to tell the story — ah well.

Meanwhile, Finn had joined the profitable lecture tour circuit, crisscrossing the United States, and was engaged in planning his talks for the next two years. It was an ambitious program and provided a much-needed source of income for the couple.

The controversial participation of Jackie Ronne and Jennie Darlington had generated considerable buzz in the media due to the historic firsts that had been achieved. This publicity had benefitted the expedition overall. However, once the expedition was over, Finn worked hard to downplay the "woman aspect." Daughter Karen later reported:

> My father was frustrated that his RARE expedition was always being noted for the women being along and was not recognized more for the geographic exploration and scientific work that he and the other men accomplished. He would hardly mention the women in the lectures that he gave. I think he sometimes was a little ticked off when articles were published that were just about her. I'm not sure he ever really accepted that.

In this, Jackie was a willing partner, remarking blithely in an interview: "I just went along for the ride, and the ride lasted 15 months and 15,000 miles!" As far as Jackie was concerned, what she did to help Finn, helped her as well. In this, both she and Finn reverted to traditional gender roles of the 1940s. Jackie and Finn were still partners, but it was Finn who had made everything happen. Jackie's perspective on this would change later in life.

Throughout 1948, Finn kept in regular contact with Nichols, Peterson, Thompson, and Dodson as each were writing formal reports for the Office of Naval Research. The work accomplished by the expedition was impressive. Richard Light stated in a letter to Finn: "The excellent work done by your expedition stands as a landmark in modern scientific exploration. I have several times heard it used as a yardstick and you will never have to be ashamed of any part of the fine job you did there."

The expedition led by Finn Ronne and assisted by Jackie succeeded in exploring a significant section of Antarctica's coastline between the Palmer Peninsula and Coats Land. He achieved the primary objective of the expedition and proved once and for all that Antarctica was one continent only, not two continents bisected by a strait between the Weddell Sea and the Ross Sea. Over six hundred and fifty thousand square kilometres of unknown territory was explored by air and an area of 1.2 million square kilometres of land that had been known about but never mapped was photographed.

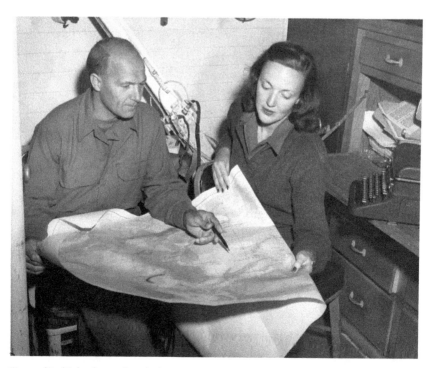

Finn and Jackie hard at work reviewing maps.

This resulted in the creation of fourteen thousand aerial photographs of an area as large as Mexico. These photographs were augmented by precise ground coordinates where available. (Some of this data had been generated and shared by the British FIDS team.) The ambitious scientific agenda that Finn had devised in consultation with his scientific staff had been achieved with new data being contributed in the fields of geology, geomorphology, human ecology, seismology, geophysics, meteorology, physics, astronomy, astrophysics, and glaciology[2] (see Appendix One).

As was his right as expedition leader, Finn officially named seventy-nine new geographic features — something done with the approval of the U.S. Board on Geographic Names. Numerous newspaper articles, with headlines including "Unexplored Tract in Antarctica Named for Woman Born Here" and "Polar Region Named for Mrs Edith Ronne," reported that Finn officially recognized Jackie's contributions to the expedition through naming a significant coastal area "Edith Ronne Land."

Interestingly, Finn imposed a hierarchical order in his naming process. A first-order feature was a region, sea, or extensive mountain range; peninsulas, significant mountains, or major glaciers were designated as second-order features; and third-order features included minor mountains, glaciers, and valleys. Those named by Finn fell into three categories:

Expedition members and members of their family: Gardner Bay (Dr. Irvine Gardner) and Dodson Island (Captain Harry L. Dodson);

Donors: Sweeney Mountains and Mount Edward (Edward Sweeney), Scaife Mountains (Alan Scaife), Hauberg Mountains (John Hauberg), Cape Wheeler (John N. Wheeler of NANA); and

Supporters: Wright Inlet (Dr. John K. Wright, director of the American Geographical Society), Mount Coman (Dr. Dana Coman), Mount Russell Owen — now Owen Peak (journalist Russell Owen), Gould Bay (Dr. Laurence Gould), Bowman

Peninsula (Dr. Isaiah Bowman), and LeMay Range (General Curtis LeMay).

Even Kasco Dog Food Company, which supplied dog food for the expedition, was recognized in Waverly Glacier, named after the town in which the company headquarters was located. No recommendation was made by Finn Ronne for a feature named after either Harry or Jennie Darlington. The rancour between the two men remained undiminished throughout their lives.[3]

Although they initially made their base at her aunt and uncle's home, Jackie and Finn spent part of 1948 renting homes elsewhere so they could focus on completing Finn's book. The work schedule they set for themselves was punishing. Jackie wrote about their work to her aunt Merriel:

> It is 9:30 pm and we are still working. Finn has just about completed his first rough editing of the film and we will probably preview it tomorrow night. I am on the second from last chapter in the book and hope to get it completed roughly in a

One of the American flags flown by RARE at East Base, Antarctica.

few days. I really have a great deal of work to do on it before it becomes anywhere near a creditable job and my mind is on nothing but getting the thing finished now.

Their work was spurred on by the publication of Finn's (and Jackie's) comprehensive scholarly article on the expedition that appeared in *Geographical Review*. They were also pleased with an article by Richard Light in the same issue lauding Finn as a true explorer:

> The days of discovery are not yet over, however; the "last secrets" have not been unveiled. And there are followers in the grand tradition. Finn Ronne is one of them. What impels him to see the far-off hills? The search that is bred in the bone, as it is in so many Norwegian explorers. It was his compatriot Nansen, immortal among geographers, who said: "Man wants to know and when he ceases to do so, he is no longer man." But exploration that makes a true contribution to geographical knowledge is no vague, impulsive wandering into the unknown.

Although Finn's star was shining bright in official circles, his trials with Admiral Byrd were not yet over. Finn suspected Byrd of interfering with an article on RARE that was supposed to be published in the *National Geographic*. Under unusual circumstances, Finn's deal with the prestigious magazine was abruptly cancelled, leading to a flurry of letters between Finn and his supporters. Near the end of the year, Finn and Jackie were further dismayed to learn that the film *The Secret Land* about Byrd and his last Antarctica adventure, nicknamed Operation Highjump, and starring Byrd as himself, had won the 1948 Academy Award for Best Documentary Feature. The competition between Ronne and Byrd remained fierce.[4]

In early 1949, Jackie and Finn finally moved to their own rented apartment in Silver Spring, Maryland, where they lived for the next two years. Even though the Ronnes and Merriel and Irvine Gardner were pleased to have their own private space, everyone remained on amicable terms. And since Jackie and Finn's new apartment was only a ten-minute drive away, they were able to visit each other often. Finn was still close to navy headquarters in Washington, and the seat of power for American explorers.

During that year, Finn was elected vice-president of the prestigious American Polar Society (APS), with his friend and RARE supporter Dana Coman as president. Polar luminary and member of the APS board of governors Marie Peary Stafford nominated him for this position. Stafford and Jackie were later to become good friends. Finn and Jackie lectured vigorously in the coming months, and Jackie often took the podium in Finn's absence. Travelling throughout the United States, they visited friends, including Ed and Kay Sweeney and RARE pilot James Lassiter in Idaho. In the fall, Jackie and Finn travelled to Norway at the invitation of the Royal Geographical Society and gave a series of lectures. Finn had been away from Norway for eighteen years, and this was the first time he was able to proudly show off his new American wife. As a result of an inspiring lecture at the University of Oslo, the couple were invited for an audience with King Haakon VII at the Royal Palace.

In late 1949, *Antarctic Conquest* by Finn Ronne was released by G.P. Putnam's Sons, which had published other spellbinding adventure works such as those by Admiral Byrd, Amelia Earhart, and Charles Lindbergh. The book was mainly written by Jackie, who had laboured mightily over it during the expedition and in the months following. She was well aware of how important the book was to Finn. When it was completed, the publisher was not entirely happy with the manuscript and suggested that a ghostwriter be called in to liven up the text.

Unusually, the fantasy and science fiction writer L. Sprague de Camp, author of *Lest Darkness Fall* and *The Incomplete Enchanter*, was hired for the job.[5] Hard up for cash at the time and eager to reinvigorate a flagging career, de Camp agreed to be paid more if Finn's name appeared as the sole author. Although the grandiose title, *Antarctic Conquest*, was derided by some in Antarctic circles (usually by Brits) as "typically brash American," it is possible this was de Camp's suggestion. He reported that Finn was a man of "austere standards" who preferred a more sedate narrative.

Jackie pointing to the Ronne Antarctic Research Expedition map.

Since she was one of the main writers of the book, the absence of Jackie's name is a conspicuous omission. The book's modest dedication — "To my wife Edith, who was an anchor to windward and saw the whole expedition through with me" — hardly acknowledges her contributions as a full expedition team member, her steadfast commitment to him personally, and the fact that she wrote most of the book. Finn was never shy about broadcasting his own accomplishments. He was a modern man in that he truly loved Jackie and considered her to be his partner in life and in work, but he was also a product of his culture and his time. What Jackie got out of it for herself was always secondary to him.

Portrait of *Port of Beaumont*.

In his 1996 autobiography, de Camp noted that *Antarctic Conquest* received generally positive reviews but had disappointing sales due to declining public interest in polar exploration. While the Ronnes would have welcomed the additional income, Finn was heartened by the praise for his (and, by extension, Jackie's) organizational abilities. M.C. Shelesnyak in *The Quarterly Review of Biology* reviewed the book:

> The document is a remarkable report on the "human ecology" in a remote and isolated scientific expedition. Moreover, the description of the infinitely detailed preparations and carefully meshed operations in the field gives the laboratory-trained reader a feeling of good research design.... A most commendatory note on the expedition is the plan regarding the workup and publication of the data. By the time *Antarctic Conquest* had been published, seven scientific papers on geophysics and

geology had been published, ten on other subjects and seven more in process.

The majority of the *Antarctic Conquest* reviews rarely mention the involvement of women in the expedition but, instead, reinforce the traditional masculinist narrative of the heroic polar explorer. In their review of the book in the *Boston Globe*, expeditionary team members Harries-Clichy Peterson and Bob Dodson commended Finn's initiative, stating: "It rekindles the old self-reliant spirit of America's pioneers of accepting all odds for the insistent drive toward new horizons. *Antarctic Conquest* is a fitting reply to skeptics of American virility." *Antarctic Conquest* remains the official public record of the Ronne Antarctic Research Expedition, but Jackie's deft hand within its pages remains invisible. She did not want to detract from Finn's own accomplishments and the expedition he had shed blood, sweat, and tears for, and so she wrote herself out of the story. In doing so, she contributed to and helped bolster the image of Antarctica as a cold continent inhabited by men alone.

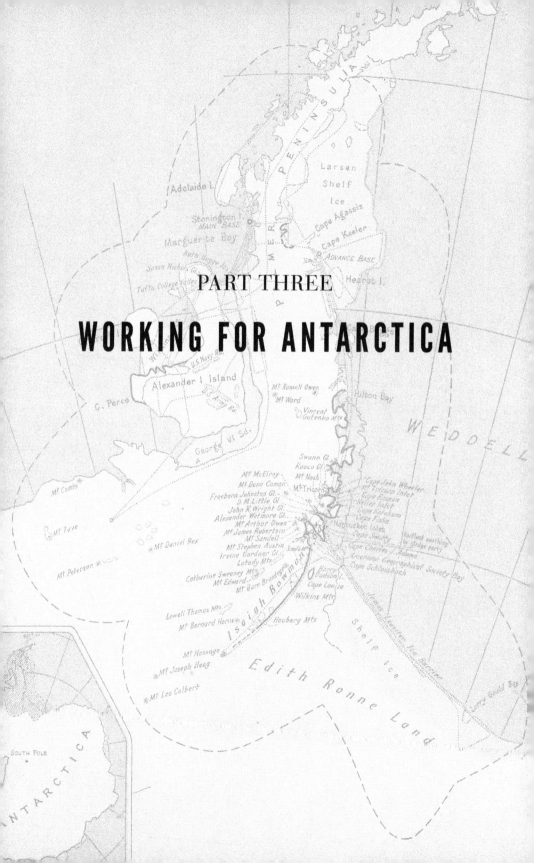

PART THREE

WORKING FOR ANTARCTICA

CHAPTER 8

AN EXPLORER'S PRIVATE LIFE

I wish you were out of it many times. But it is your field and I like to see you successful in it.
— JACKIE TO FINN, 1957

AS A NEW decade began, Jackie could be forgiven for hoping that after the expedition had ended and *Antarctic Conquest* was published, life for her and Finn would settle down. In the 1950s, the nuclear family was held up as the ideal family unit. Women and men had strictly delineated gender roles in society. In the United States, there was a huge surge in births and a significant move of young couples from the downtown to suburban areas where families could concentrate on child rearing, home decorating, and other domestic responsibilities. In *The Paradox of Change: American Women in the Twentieth Century*, William Chafe describes the situation that existed at

Jackie at home, early 1950s.

the time: "Perhaps most important, the suburban wife was expected to make the home an oasis of comfort and serenity for her harried husband and ... [represented] a model of efficiency, patience and charm." The pressure on Jackie to establish and maintain a well-ordered household, entertain friends and business associates, and support her husband in every way possible was significant.

Jackie did indeed "hold down the home front and provide a bedrock of security in a world of competition and chaos." Her husband was not the average male who worked a nine to five job, mowed the lawn regularly, and played golf on weekends. Most husbands faced fierce competition while clawing their way up the corporate ladder or negotiating the convoluted dynamics of the office workplace. Finn's "workplace" was entirely different. The world of the explorer is a singular and mysterious one. Jackie could not learn how to be the wife of an explorer from magazines or books or the radio. No family members could advise her. There were no ready role models for her, and so she was forced to learn as she went along. Hers was an unusual marriage to be sure, and she and Finn felt their way along together.

Whereas most 1950s American men wanted, first and foremost, to have a haven to return to, throughout their marriage, Finn's primary concern was that Jackie assist him in his work. He demanded much of her: an able workmate to help write his speeches, lectures, and books, and help him edit his films; a partner who could act as his legal proxy in all matters in his absence; an advisor who could help guide his career; and a "traditional" wife who would provide him with a happy home. Undoubtedly, he had his own mother in mind when considering the role of the perfect wife. In his 1979 autobiography, *Antarctica, My Destiny*, he writes admiringly of his mother, Maren Gurine Gulliksen:

> She practiced the highest standards in dignity, always looked at things in a positive way, and was equal to my father in strength and resourcefulness. These qualities served her well when my father was at sea. For example, she would paper and paint the rooms in our house, climb up on the roof to fix tiles, mix cement to patch the chimney or a garden wall, and do light carpenter work around the property. In addition, she hand-sewed clothing for all her seven children.

Jackie strove her whole life to live up to Finn's ideals.

Throughout 1950, the Ronnes were still living at the rented apartment in Silver Spring. With a surprising nod to domesticity, Finn bought several lots in Mohican Hills in nearby Bethesda with plans for development. He took pleasure in designing and constructing their first real home.

After returning from Antarctica, Finn had worked as an expert consultant for the Office of the Quartermaster General on matters pertaining to cold weather survival training. At the same time, he and Jackie undertook an ambitious twenty-thousand-kilometre lecture tour of the American West. Both Finn and Jackie were popular speakers. Jackie estimated that she had delivered two hundred lectures over the last five years.

Upon returning home, Jackie's schedule quickly filled up again. In a letter to Merriel and Irvine, she described her life:

> Went to a nice luncheon at the Washington Association of University Women. Katie and Bernie Horne came in town for a quick visit and I had lunch with her one day and saw *Tight Little Island* a British movie at the Little. The Sweeneys are building a swimming pool which will make Washington a much nicer place this summer! Kay is going to give a luncheon for 16 this Friday and Ruth Dudley and I are going. We may fly to Florida with them for three days starting Saturday. We have another lecture in Bridgeport, Conn. on the 19th, then the radio broadcast on the Bettie Crocker show on the morning of the 20th and a lecture in Poughkeepsie that evening. Saw George and Celia on Saturday — they are having their troubles. Saw Carl and Harriet yesterday. In between times of this activity have been working like a vertible [*sic*] dog.

Jackie could never complain that her life was boring. She had "regular" friends who she met through a mutual enjoyment of bridge, but increasingly, her life was dominated by weighty issues and important, often well-known people, who largely operated outside the norms of American society. She had had some preparation for that growing up since her aunt and uncle had never led conventional lives.

Jackie was always known for keeping a neat and elegant home, but it was a means to an end. Their home was a place to entertain important guests. While she did her best to cook for her family, the domestic sphere was not where she excelled. But her efforts at cooking Norwegian dishes were always appreciated by Finn.

JACKIE'S RECIPE FOR A FAVOURITE RONNE NORWEGIAN DISH, *KJØTTKAKER MED BRUN SAUS* (NORWEGIAN MEATBALLS IN BROWN GRAVY)

Ingredients

Meatballs
½ lb. ground beef
½ lb. ground pork
1 egg
½ cup bread crumbs
½ cup whole milk
To taste salt and pepper
Pinches of nutmeg, ginger, and/or allspice

Sauce
6 tbs. butter
¼ cup flour
½ onion, chopped or minced
3 cups beef broth
¼ cup sour cream
2 tbs. red wine

Directions: Mix all meatball ingredients and shape into small balls. Fry in skillet until browned. In saucepan, add meatballs, onion and broth and simmer about 20 min. Remove meatballs and place aside to add sauce later. For sauce, melt butter and stir in flour to make a roux and cook a bit. Whisk in the broth used with the meatballs; prevent from getting lumps. Simmer and just before serving, add in the sour cream and red wine.

She revealed her feelings about household chores to her aunt: "Today I have been working on the dog book and washing windows. The latter is not something I usually spend much time on, but I must say that now there is more light in the living room — a conservative estimate is about 60 percent more."

Her social life was filled with visits with women who lived extraordinary lives or who were married to high-ranking men with connections to the world of science and exploration. Men and women who could ultimately assist Finn in his chosen career of explorer.

During the early 1950s, Jackie and Finn's burgeoning friendship with famed Arctic explorer and millionaire Louise Arner Boyd developed further. Geographer, photographer, and botanist, Boyd was also a philanthropist

Arctic explorer Louise Arner Boyd prior to the 1928 Amundsen rescue expedition.

and socialite. She had participated in the 1928 international rescue mission to find Norwegian explorer Roald Amundsen and followed this with five daring expeditions by ship to Greenland, Jan Mayen Land, Franz Josef Land, and Spitsbergen.[1] Boyd was only a few years older than Finn and was delighted to extend hospitality to the Ronnes during their cross-country lecture tour. Jackie wrote to her aunt Merriel about their visit to Boyd's stately mansion in San Rafael, California. She was thrilled to chat with and learn from this Arctic pioneer and revelled in being "spoiled."

> Well, here we are back in California again — and this is just my dish. Swimming in Louise's private heated pool, having breakfast in bed, being driven around by a chauffeur in a big Packard is really very difficult to take. We really hit the right season of the year this time and at present it is very dubious whether you will ever see me back east again. What a set-up — Finn calls me Queen for a Day.

This was one group of individuals with whom Jackie shared a special bond. Only the exceptional female explorers like Louise Arner Boyd and the wives of other explorers could truly empathize with and understand Jackie's situation. Connecting with these women was important to her throughout her life.[2] Many opportunities arose to socialize with them at events hosted by geographic or scientific associations, particularly in Washington. She was on friendly terms with Mary Louise Ellsworth (wife of Lincoln Ellsworth), Marie Byrd (wife of Admiral Byrd), Evelyn Stefansson Nef (wife of Vilhjalmur Stefansson), Bess Balchen (wife of Bernt Balchen), and, particularly, Marie Peary Stafford (daughter of Robert Peary). Most of these women were of an earlier generation than Jackie and were from establishment American families. Breaking into this group of women must have represented a daunting prospect for Jackie, who was from a modest background. Still, she was nothing if not resourceful and would have taken her cues from them about what to say and how to behave. These powerful women were her friends, confidants, and allies, and helped to anchor her firmly within the upper echelons of Antarctic society.

Marie Peary Stafford, 1936.

During the early months of 1951, Finn was feverishly completing their new house as Jackie was awaiting the birth of their first child. Famous *New York Times* journalist and family friend Russell Owen wrote to the couple: "It's about time you intrepid explorers started off a new explorer. Besides it will keep Jackie out of the Antarctic. It's a wonder to me that you didn't start one down there!"

Daughter Karen was born on March 5 at Garfield Hospital. Jackie, aged thirty-two, and Finn, aged fifty-one, would have been considered older parents. Jackie was bearing her first child at a time when the majority of first-time American mothers were under twenty-five. Karen would be their only child. Congratulations poured in from friends far and near. Marie Peary Stafford wrote: "Well, Jackie, hooray for you and Finn and thanks very much for producing another Woman Geographer!"

Jackie, Finn, and Karen Ronne at home in Bethesda, Maryland.

When baby Karen was six weeks old, the young family moved to their new home at 6323 Wiscasset Road in Bethesda, Maryland, where Jackie and Finn lived for the remainder of their lives.

In 1949, while working for the Office of the Quartermaster General, Finn joined the recently formed Central Intelligence Agency (CIA) as a consultant. Throughout the 1950s, he worked as an intelligence officer in the Office of Policy Coordination, which was the covert operations wing of the CIA. This office later merged with the Office of Special Operations (OSO) to form the Directorate of Plans. The exact nature of the work that he conducted remains undefined. Even though he had been born in Norway, Finn was a patriotic American. Jackie was fully supportive of his CIA position. Of course, as a former Department of State employee, Jackie would have had her own security clearance and she would have understood the importance of keeping sensitive government information confidential. But she had now joined another unique, and secretive, group: the CIA wives. Bina Cady Kiyonaga described the lives of this group in her memoir, *My Spy: Memoir of a CIA Wife*: "We lied about our husband's jobs, stalled inquisitive policemen, befriended minister's wives, kept our ears open at parties, deflected the children's questions, and worried in silence alone. We were the CIA wives. You never knew us."

Finn's work for the CIA continued throughout the 1950s and 1960s. The couple, an intelligence officer with the organization and a wife who still maintained her connections with the Department of State, would have been privy to explosive information that would have been shocking to most Americans. This was a particularly volatile period, when the CIA was very active on the world's stage. As the Cold War raged, so too did fears about the spread of Communism throughout the world. It has only recently been confirmed that in the 1950s alone, the CIA was responsible for ousting the Iranian prime minister Mohammad Mossadegh in 1953 and the Guatemalan president Jacobo Árbenz in 1954.

Throughout their years together, the Ronnes' private and personal lives overlapped. Clearly, as the wife of a CIA intelligence officer, she knew how to keep secrets as well, but Jackie was a communications expert. She knew how to disseminate information in order to control and maintain a narrative.

Jackie and Finn had always enjoyed socializing. This was part of a good CIA wife's job, but for them, it served many purposes, both professional and personal. They loved to party, but they were also adroit at seeking out and nurturing networking opportunities with well-placed individuals who could further Finn's career.

One important friendship that crossed the professional-personal divide was their relationship with Ed and Kay Sweeney. Edward Cleaveland Sweeney was a former aide to Admiral Byrd and had accompanied him on a tour during the Second World War, surveying South Pacific islands. A former lieutenant commander, attorney, and a specialist in naval and aviation

Kay Sweeney and Finn and Jackie Ronne after Finn's return from Ellsworth Station.

intelligence, Ed became a close friend of Finn's. They met during the Second World War when they each served on an Arctic planning committee. Ed also had close connections with the CIA. He was married to wealthy heiress Catherine "Kay" Denkmann Hauberg. The two couples shared a passion for exploration, travel, and the outdoors, and Kay Sweeney became one of Jackie's most important female friends. Like Louise Arner Boyd and others, Kay was an unusual woman in her own right. She was down to earth and quiet but zealous about her own interests. A note from Finn to Jackie gives a sense of her: "Ed and Kay got off on Sunday. I was there when they left the house. From you I gave a beautiful orchid, $5 and she was very pleased to get it from you. It was the only going-away gift she had; but they do not care. Kay had an old coat on with the button missing. She was just as happy."

As a young woman, Kay had conducted graduate work in geology at the University of Arizona, loved hiking and riding, and had a lifelong interest in tropical botany. She was also a philanthropist, and both she, Ed, and her parents had been significant donors to the Ronne Antarctic Research Expedition.

The long-enduring relationship with the Sweeneys also helped the Ronnes to expand their circle of friends and to connect with supporters who might be useful to Finn. Throughout the fifties and sixties, Jackie and Finn circulated in high society when attending Kay's famous soirees. As time passed, Jackie and Finn's daughter, Karen, also socialized regularly with the Sweeney children. During the summer, Jackie and Karen spent every day at the Sweeney pool in Washington where the sculptress Julia Bretzman Shields and her husband, CIA officer (and soon to be CIA director) Richard "Dick" Helms, frequently did laps.

In the midst of their lecturing, writing, and socializing, Antarctica was never far from the minds of Finn and Jackie. Finn had begun scheming behind the scenes to kickstart another expedition, which he hoped to lead. He soon learned, however, that the world had moved on. The Ronne Antarctic Research Expedition had been historic in many ways, not just because of its substantial scientific achievements and its inclusion of women as team members. RARE truly was one of the last privately funded expeditions of its kind.[3] The times had changed, and the vast majority of Antarctic expeditions being planned at the time stressed international co-operation and engagement.

An interest in pursuing Antarctic science rather than exploration for its own sake prevailed in the early to mid 1950s. Led by John Giæver, the Norwegian-British-Swedish Antarctic Expedition (1949–1952), also known as NBSX or NBSAE, was the first Antarctic expedition involving an international team of scientists. The Commonwealth Trans-Antarctic Expedition (1955–1958), led by Sir Vivian Fuchs and Sir Edmund Hillary, was another international effort. Other missions such as the Sixth Norwegian Antarctic Expedition (1956–1960) ensured that Antarctic exploration remained in the public eye.

In the end, Finn's plans for his own post-RARE mission would be dashed, but his reputation as an experienced Antarctic explorer remained intact. Finn's plans to return to Antarctica with or without his own team continued with Jackie's support. They kept in contact with many RARE alumni, with the exception of the Darlingtons. Despite Harry's earlier threats that he planned to ruin Finn's reputation, no action was taken.

Unlike the Ronnes, the Darlingtons returned to an expansive property, Chilly Bleak Farm, located near Marshall, Virginia. They immediately disappeared from Antarctic circles. Harry Darlington retired from public life and became a respected cattle breeder. But in 1957, Jennie Darlington's book, *My Antarctic Honeymoon: A Year at the Bottom of the World*, in which she related her experiences as part of RARE, was published by Doubleday in the United States, dropping a bombshell on Jackie and Finn that reverberates throughout the Antarctic world even today.

Front cover of *My Antarctic Honeymoon* by Jennie Darlington.

Ghostwritten by her friend Jane McIlvaine (who later left her husband for Darlington crony and RARE alumnus Nelson McClary), Jennie's book was a no-holds-barred tell-all that differed sharply from Finn's official account, *Antarctic Conquest*. Until the publication of *My Antarctic Honeymoon*, polar expedition tales were mainly heroic sagas upholding the mythic image of the explorer as an untouchable, immortal conqueror. Jennie's book effectively destroyed this myth and portrayed Finn as a manipulative authoritarian leader.

Keith Holmes, who overwintered at the British base on Stonington Island a few years later and who met the Darlingtons, reported that it was never Jennie's idea to write the book in the first place, but that her writer friend Jane had eagerly promoted the project to her. He stated that both Jane and the editor were complicit in overdramatizing many of the more sensational aspects of the book, including the weaker aspects of Finn's character. Doubleday had recently had great success with the bestselling *The Caine Mutiny* by Herman Wouk and urged Jane to draw unflattering parallels between Finn and the despotic Captain Queeg.

Not surprisingly, the publication of *My Antarctic Honeymoon* turned the spotlight on the role of women in Antarctica. While it was entertaining and offered a glimpse into the daily lives of the team, it downplayed the very real accomplishments of Jackie and Jennie and shifted the focus away from the historic successes of the expedition. In her book, Jennie stated, "I do not think women belong in the Antarctic or on a similar expedition. The polar regions belong to those who know and respect them and can survive. Any weak link endangers the whole." She later recanted these comments, but they didn't help the cause of women eager to visit or work in Antarctica.

Jackie and Finn were incensed but could do nothing about it. In part because of the novelty of the subject matter, the book was widely and positively reviewed. Finn's supporters dismissed the book. Colleague Dr. Laurence Gould shared his views in a letter to Jackie: "Somebody gave me a copy of *My Antarctic Honeymoon*. I read it with much disgust and then heaved it overboard into the ocean so nobody else could see it. I hope this will be your reaction to it.... I hope very much that neither you nor Finn is unduly disturbed by it and I hope you will ignore it." Neither Jackie nor Finn were good at ignoring what they perceived as a betrayal. Loyalty meant every-thing to them. In future, they would take every opportunity to slight both Darlingtons, but ultimately, this approach would backfire.

In the late 1950s, Finn's efforts working behind the scenes, talking to the right people, and ensuring his name was uppermost in people's minds paid off. In this, Jackie was an astute and constant advisor. Karen later com-mented, "My father always believed that the work he did in the Antarctic, the land and features that he discovered and mapped, would stand alone as his legacy. What he didn't understand, and my mother did, was that you need to do more than that."

The Third International Geophysical Year (IGY) was an ambitious sci-entific project that was planned to run from July 1, 1957, to December 31, 1958. It involved sixty-seven countries working together in eleven scientific disciplines. It was designed to foster co-operation between the East and the West and involved an important polar component.

Finn's participation in the IGY was assured due to his prestige, experi-ence, and the hard work he and Jackie had put in to secure a role. He was deeply gratified to be offered the position of military leader of Ellsworth Station, one of the American Antarctic bases, located on the western coast of the Weddell Sea over the Filchner Ice Shelf. He accepted the position with alacrity and reported for duty. Four months later, he left for Antarctica.

This time, Jackie would not be accompanying him. Nor did she wish to. During the IGY, she joined the ranks of thousands of other military wives and wives of explorers who dealt with the prolonged absences of their hus-bands. But this time it was different, as she and young Karen were together. Even when Finn had been at home, Jackie had always been Karen's primary caregiver. Finn was a fond if, at times, preoccupied father, at least when his daughter was very young. Finn was first and foremost an explorer and his role as husband and father was secondary.

From the beginning of the IGY expedition, Jackie was worried about Finn, and her letters to him throughout the whole time he was at Ellsworth

Station are filled with concern. She was well aware that Finn's strict leadership style did not always stand him in good stead. Even Finn recognized this. He admitted in *Antarctica, My Destiny* that he had "rigorous standards of conduct — not always appreciated by those who served with me." Jackie's constant admonishments were not without cause.

> Please please try to work it out and be friends with as many as you can.... Try not to end up with enemies who will talk and write against you — it is the thing that does so much harm — even if you found a gold mine there — the public doesn't care — it is what the talk will be after they get back. Well you know how I feel and now I am going to drop the subject.

In Finn's absence, Jackie worked harder than ever on his behalf, despite the pain she experienced personally without her husband by her side. She was highly skilled at maintaining the network of supporters and colleagues who were sympathetic to Finn and was not afraid of sending in her proxies when necessary. When a *Time Magazine* article about Antarctic exploration

Jackie (far right) networking.

failed to mention the expedition, she persuaded RARE member Larry Fiske to write repeatedly to the *Time* editor and complain about this oversight. Social visits, parties, and geographic events were of great use even in Finn's absence and she nurtured relationships that would be beneficial.

Jackie was the consummate diplomat when it came to discussing polar politics. At events, it was not uncommon for politicians, military personnel, and institutional heads to approach Jackie informally and sound her out regarding Finn's opinions, and Jackie managed them all with aplomb. She was sharp, perceptive, and tactful, and she was fully capable of playing the game with the best of them.

Both Finn and Jackie recognized that Finn had a "low boiling point" and was not afraid of voicing his candid views. As with many explorer couples, they balanced each other perfectly — most of the time. Jackie stayed abreast of his current work and made sure he remained focused on what he was doing and, as much as she was able, buoyed his spirits. "Keep your chin up — don't argue — and don't worry about how things are going back here. Remember you have lots of high placed friends who will not forget you.... Just think of all those who think you are tops."

She made sure Finn knew which people he had to keep sweet. "I keep cautioning you to be careful what you say and do because I think this whole situation is in a complete flux and very messy diplomatically in good old polar politics. The less you get into it the better on every score. I am thinking of your future when I say this." She nurtured friendships with influential journalists, including Walter Sullivan of the *New York Times* and media personality Lowell Thomas, and reminded Finn to send regular personal updates, including a Christmas message from Ellsworth Station to two hundred American supporters. Jackie also kept in close contact with the U.S.-based wives of Finn's Ellsworth Station team. She was uniquely situated to understand the pain of having your man far from home.

Jackie was far better than Finn at juggling many balls in the air at any given time. Based near Washington, D.C., Jackie was painfully aware, as Finn was not, that the world was evolving and Finn's relevance as a "traditional" explorer was waning. She was contacted in late 1957 by Mary Louise Ellsworth, widow of the recently deceased Lincoln Ellsworth. Like Jackie,

Ellsworth was aware that political changes were underway in Washington regarding the American perspective toward Antarctica. Ellsworth bemoaned these changes, but Jackie was able to adapt and urged Finn to do the same.

> There is a new dynasty being formed and I don't think it will pay to cut ourselves off completely and I think every effort should be made to show that we harbor no ill feelings. I think eventually you will get the medal too if it is handled properly — I don't think they can do otherwise. But you must be diplomatic and not say anything to get them angry with you.... Oh boy there will be a lot of stuff going on when you get back. There will be decisions to be made and it won't all be easy.

Mary Louise Ellsworth preparing for a flight.

The year 1957 was a momentous one on the world stage, with ramifications for Finn and for Jackie. Admiral Byrd died in his sleep in March, marking the end of a contentious rivalry lasting several decades. He had always been gracious and civil to Finn's face, but the Ronnes believed that he constantly worked against Finn behind his back. Two years earlier, he had demeaned Jackie's historic RARE accomplishment by declaring that "no woman has ever set foot in the Antarctic. We found it to be the quietest and most peaceful place on earth."

Despite personal reservations, Jackie attended the funeral and described the event in a letter to Finn: "Well Admiral Byrd is dead. You would have thought a president at least had died. There was great hoopla in the papers all of which I saved for you. I had planned to go to the funeral of course as

EXPLORER RETURNS—Little Karen Ronne, who will be 7 in March, kisses her father, Navy Capt. Finn Ronne, today at National Airport. She had not seen him for the year he headed this country's Ellsworth Station in the Antarctic. Her mother, Mrs. Edith Ronne, flew here from Buenos Aires with her husband.—Star Staff Photo.

Finn's arrival home, 1958.

it was in my opinion the only thing to do. They were saving me a reserved seat in friends of the Admiral section in back of the family. And there I sat too."

When Finn returned from Antarctica, Jackie was shocked. He had survived the IGY expedition but had experienced none of the sense of accomplishment that he had felt following RARE. It took a heavy toll upon him, which he and Jackie did not try to disguise in their controversial book about his experience entitled *Antarctic Command.*[4] Finn had written to her about the continual personnel problems he was having at Ellsworth, so she had had some idea about what had transpired.

> I have had as a result, the most unpleasant year I have ever spent in my whole life. One thing I am proud of is that I have boosted the work of IGY as coming in the forefront of all my intentions and activities. Not once have I failed in that respect. I have gone against the grain of the station personnel to be certain that nothing ever would interfere with the obtaining of data valuable to the overall IGY program.

It was up to Jackie to put the pieces back together and support Finn despite the storm of negative attention that would come his way. It was a near-impossible task. According to David Stam, who sailed on the USS *Wyandot* and visited Ellsworth Station as a journalist in 1957:

> Ellsworth Station and its austral winter of 1957 is probably the best-documented of all the Operation Deepfreeze [*sic*] stations, not least because it was the most fraught and problematical. The leader, a well-known Norwegian explorer named Captain Finn Ronne, on his fourth or fifth expedition, was reputedly detested by most of the winter men for his authoritarian and dictatorial manner, his megalomania, his capricious direction, and his conflicts with both scientists and enlisted men. He tried to ban Jennie Darlington's *My Antarctic Honeymoon*, a book critical of Ronne and his wife, from the base library, not

knowing that other copies were in personal collections and much in demand.

Stam commented that Finn seemed "a very lonely man who'd been through some kind of hell." It would not be too far from the truth.

Finn was now nearly sixty years old, and this was his last major expedition. Despite the years of hard work that he and Jackie had put into the planning and organizing of his two last expeditions, his accomplishments and reputation were marred by the charges levelled against him by several members of his IGY team.[5] One of his harshest critics was astrophysicist and IGY team member J. McKim Malville, who later asserted that, while at Ellsworth Station, Finn's paranoia "threatened to bring the isolated base to the brink of insanity and mutiny."

As a loving wife and partner, Jackie had no choice in going forward. Finn had an intense nature and a no-nonsense leadership style developed during a lifetime of experience. His ways were based on traditional, old-fashioned European values, and he had learned from the best — his father, Martin Rønne, teaching him about how Amundsen guided his men. As a leader, Finn was often inflexible, intolerant, obstinate, petty, and intransigent. Accordingly, he was not loved and sometimes, not even respected by his men. But the facts remain: on both of the expeditions of which Finn Ronne was in charge, an impressive scientific agenda was accomplished, and no lives were lost.

The International Geophysical Year Expedition of 1957–1958 was difficult for Finn personally and professionally. Finn's work at Ellsworth Station, as well as all the work conducted during the IGY, was a precursor to an event that would change Antarctica forever. In the late 1950s, the Cold War was in full force and global disputes about Antarctica between Argentina, Chile, and the United Kingdom were escalating. In the United States, geographic work conducted by twentieth-century explorers, including Finn Ronne, increased international interest in Antarctica's economic, political, and strategic potential.[6]

The Eisenhower government initiated a dialogue with the twelve nations that had participated in the International Geophysical Year: Argentina,

Australia, Belgium, Chile, France, Japan, New Zealand, Norway, South Africa, the Soviet Union, the United Kingdom, and the United States. Jackie was already working on the important issues being discussed by those taking part. In 1954 she was hired as a freelance consultant by her former employer, the Department of State. She conducted research and wrote comprehensive technical reports on the accomplishments of recent American private expeditions and supplied briefs and background information to leading senators and congressmen involved in negotiations.

This dialogue, which produced what is formally known as the Antarctic Treaty, was directed by politicians, but the geographic contributions of U.S. explorers played a significant role. One of the main proponents of the treaty was James E. Mooney, the deputy United States Antarctic Projects officer from 1959 to 1965. He wrote powerfully about how his team had successfully used the discovery of the terrestrial features Edith Ronne Land, Marie Byrd Land, and the Ellsworth Highlands to justify U.S. interests in Antarctica and win over the U.S.S.R. during critical treaty negotiations.

> It was largely because of the explorations of Wilkes, Byrd, Ellsworth and Ronne, that the United States had such an important role in the establishment of the Antarctic Treaty and prestige with regard to Antarctic exploration.... The Ronnes have played an important part in Antarctic exploration. The father of Finn Ronne was not only a citizen of Norway but participated with Byrd in his explorations in Antarctica. It would be a pity to justify the elimination of Edith Ronne Land since Finn Ronne especially made major exploratory penetrations into the area now known as Edith Ronne Land on millions of maps and in our records. And Edith Ronne, his wife, was one of the first two and only women to winter over in Antarctica. Edith contributed tremendously to the success of the Ronne expedition.

Jackie promoted the objectives of the Antarctic Treaty and did what she could to secure its ratification. Even while Finn was still at Ellsworth

Station, Jackie argued for the internationalization of Antarctica, calling it a step toward world peace. In early 1958, she declared her emphatic support during a televised forum between herself and House Representative Thor Tollefson, in which she commended co-operative projects such as the IGY.[7] During this forum, Tollefson, a seasoned politician who endorsed the United States laying formal claim to part of Antarctica, scoffed at her comments, dismissing them as "utterly impractical."

Jackie's outspoken political stance was published in U.S. newspapers prior to the treaty's ratification with headlines including "International Antarctic Urged by Mrs. Ronne" and "Woman Asks Antarctic Be Open to All." She was vocal about this in public as well as within her circle of influential friends. These friends included Ambassador Paul C. Daniels, who served as the special advisor on Antarctica for the U.S. Department of State. Daniels was a critical member of the American team during Antarctic

Jackie conducting backroom diplomacy, late 1950s.

Treaty negotiations and Jackie hosted at least one dinner for him and his wife, Teddy, in 1959 while this process was underway. At this stage in her life, Jackie's skills as a political strategist were formidable.

The Antarctic Treaty was signed by the twelve signatories on December 1, 1959, and entered into force on June 23, 1961. Years later, the contributions of explorers such as Finn Ronne to the Antarctic Treaty were formally recognized by the secretary of the navy:

> Great Antarctic explorers like Amundsen, Scott, Shackleton, Byrd and Ronne have opened the way for the massive national and international assaults on the continent which are now underway. The fine work which was accomplished in Antarctica by many nations during the IGY and the progress which is now being made there under the terms of the 12-nation Antarctic Treaty, would have been impossible had it not been for the courage and indomitable spirit of men such as these.

Jackie had effectively played her role through the preparation of reports and briefing papers for individuals and the formal U.S. delegation. She had privately lobbied influential politicians at intimate social gatherings and boldly sparred with others on television in the public sphere. Jackie was, once again, uniquely situated at this stage in Antarctica's history. She continued to support the objectives of the Antarctic Treaty for the rest of her life, declaring in a March 18, 1981, *San Francisco Examiner* interview that she was happy that the treaty allowed for "a co-operative, peaceful and scientific sharing of Antarctica."

CHAPTER 9

A NEW ERA BEGINS

There's another horizon out there, one more
horizon that you have to make for yourself.
— GORDON PARKS

FINN'S RETURN IN January 1958 marked the last time he would ever come back from Antarctica as an expedition leader, the man in charge who made life and death decisions. There were other younger, stronger men and women with bright ideas about the future of polar exploration who were coming up behind him, eager to take his place. The 1957–1958 International Geophysical Year and the Antarctic Treaty irrevocably changed the future of Antarctica by regulating who could visit, when and how they could go, and what they could do there.

Jackie had been left on her own for a year and a half, and her reunion with Finn was a joyous one. Karen was still young when her father returned, and Jackie was keen to share parenting duties and spend time as a family. Her attempts to settle into a domestic bliss in which Finn's attention would

A formal portrait of Jackie and Finn.

be devoted to his wife and daughter were thwarted, however. He barely had time to unpack his suitcase before the couple were thrust into the limelight once again.

Throughout the late 1950s and into the early 1960s, Finn and Jackie were sought-after celebrities on the Washington social circuit, attending diplomatic and high-level soirees two or sometimes three times a week. The Ronnes were part of the "Embassy Set," which intersected occasionally with the famed "Georgetown Set," with links to the Office of Strategic Services (OSS) and, later, the CIA. The parties were attended by Washington social-ites, American politicians, international diplomats, and Hollywood starlets, as well as a smattering of well-known figures, including Finn and Jackie Ronne. Karen remarked on Jackie's vivacious nature: "My mother came from humble beginnings and ended up being world-famous in her day. She

Joan Kennedy, Finn Ronne, and Martha Mitchell at a Washington party.

was chatty and lively and could as easily talk to a beggar in the street as to the king of a country. She got on well with everybody." Finn may have lost some of his star appeal, but he and Jackie still represented Antarctica both privately and publicly. Throughout their lives, they continued to exchange social visits and maintain a lively correspondence with respected twentieth-century polar icons including Henryk Arctowski, Paul-Émile Victor, Baron Gaston de Gerlache de Gomery, and Bernt Balchen.

A new chapter began for Finn and Jackie when they received a tantalizing invitation from the Argentine navy. Two of four nations claiming rights to the Antarctic Peninsula, Argentina and Chile, were pioneers in Antarctic tourism.[1] From January to February 1958, Argentina launched the first two cruises to Antarctica for a select group of tourists on the Argentine navy transport ship *Les Eclaireurs*. Despite the cruise's historic significance, it had been a low-key affair conducted with little fanfare. The next year, the Ronnes were invited as honoured guests on the vessel M/V *Yapeyú* on what was billed as the first commercial tourist cruise to Antarctica. Organized by the state-owned cargo shipping company Flota Argentina de Navigación de Ultramar (F.A.N.U.), this adventure was a landmark in the history of Antarctic tourism.

The Ronnes eagerly embraced this new opportunity to share Antarctica with the world. Neither of them had seriously considered polar tourism as a way of promoting Antarctica, but it was a natural fit. Both of them were passionate and knowledgeable about the continent and were veteran travellers. Jackie had no idea how important this first cruise would be or what a

F.A.N.U. advertisement for Antarctic cruise, 1959.

significant role Antarctic tourism would play in her later life. She wrote to her aunt and uncle:

> I have been invited to go on the Antarctic tourist cruise as a Guest of the Argentines and it looks as though one of the travel agencies here will give me a free air ticket to and from Argentina, since there will be six tickets purchased through them by the Sweeneys. I have thought a lot about it and feel that there are some good aspects in it that would never present themselves again and since I am really so identified with this field ...

Jackie and Karen Ronne relaxing by the pool in the 1960s.

Travel for Jackie and Finn as a couple was not as easy as it was before. She was divided between her responsibilities as a mother and her work as an advocate for Antarctica. Jackie never forgot being abandoned by her own parents who had focused more on the bitter strife between them than on raising their child. In contrast, Jackie was a devoted, hands-on mother, attending all school events and encouraging her daughter in every way possible. Despite Finn's absences during Karen's formative years, Jackie ensured that she passed on the Ronne family legacy. Fostered by her caring mother and awestruck by her famous if sometimes distant father, Karen grew up proud to be a Ronne. Finn never experienced conflict between his role as an Antarctic explorer and his role as a father. The domestic side of life was always Jackie's responsibility.

The unique concept of Antarctic tourism had been envisioned decades earlier when the tour company Thomas Cook advertised a trip to Antarctica in *The Press* in 1910.[2] These plans did not come to fruition. In 1930 Lieutenant Commander Joseph Stenhouse proposed taking the Norwegian-owned *Stella Polaris* on an exclusive four-month cruise to various exotic locations, including Antarctica. The Antarctica portion of the itinerary was of particular interest to those fascinated by polar history. Stenhouse had commanded the SY *Aurora* during Ernest Shackleton's 1914–1917 Imperial Trans-Antarctic (*Endurance*) Expedition, and his chosen ice pilot for the 1931 journey would be his *Endurance* colleague, Frank Worsley. Opportunities for cruise passengers to do some exploring of their own would also be provided with a not-inconsiderable hike over the treacherous ice to Hut Point, Cape Evans, and Cape Royds, previously occupied by Scott and Shackleton. An October 24, 1930, *Daily Mail* article about the proposed December 1931 expedition stated that this trip would be of particular interest to women, and indeed, other newspapers carrying this story touted headlines including *The Press*'s "Women's Antarctic Tour." Although this exciting cruise never materialized, it was not due to lack of interest on the part of potential Antarctic visitors. Most of those who signed up early were women, and included Emily, Lady Shackleton, widow of Sir Ernest Shackleton.

Over the next few decades, other ideas for Antarctic journeys for non-explorers were developed but did not make it past infancy. In fact, these plans were not realized by any company until the late 1950s. The first tourist flight to Antarctica was in December 1956, when a Chilean DC-6B from Linea Aerea Nacional flew with sixty-six passengers over the South Shetland Islands and Trinity Peninsula. The first tourist airplane landed in Antarctica in October 1957, when the Pan Am Boeing Stratocruiser *Clipper America* left Christchurch, New Zealand, and travelled to McMurdo Sound.

The 1959 Argentine F.A.N.U. cruise promised to be something special. Built in 1951, the M/V *Yapeyú* was 158 metres in length with a full passenger complement of 753 and 165 crew. The 1959 cruise in which the Ronnes took part was offered to only two hundred and sixty passengers, so the passenger to crew ratio was appealing. There were only thirteen luxury staterooms, one of which was offered to the Ronnes. Jackie wrote: "Having breakfast served to you in bed in your stateroom was a new wrinkle in polar exploration and not all that hard to take. A good dress, nylon stockings and high-heeled shoes were suddenly not so out of place in Antarctica after all."

Jackie was excited about participating in this cruise, stating in her autobiography that she began packing her bags as soon as she was asked to go. She couldn't wait to share her good news with her friend Lady Suzanne Wilkins, widow of Sir Hubert Wilkins. On this first commercial Antarctic cruise, Jackie and Finn invited a small group of friends along, including Talbert "Ted" Abrams, known as the "father" of aerial photography and an early aviator whose pilot's licence was signed by Orville Wright.

On board, the Ronnes also made new friends, including members of the wealthy, influential Argentinian Dodero family. The *Yapeyú* had belonged to the Doderos until it had been "liberated" by the Perón regime's nationalization program a few years earlier. The Doderos had been good friends with President Juan Perón and his stunning wife, Evita. Mrs. Dodero confided that if Evita ever admired any of her jewellery, it was an invitation to send it to the presidential palace the next day.

The Antarctic cruise lasted from January 23 to February 8, 1959, and had an intriguing itinerary: Ushuaia; the Melchior Islands; Schollaert Channel; Paradise Harbour; Lemaire Channel; Lighthouse Bay; Neumayer Channel; Wilhelmina Bay; Maxwell Bay; Jubany Base (now known as Carlini Base); Half Moon Island, where the Argentine Cámara Base was located; and Deception Island. The Ronnes were especially delighted to visit Deception Island, the starting point for the 1928–1929 Wilkins-Hearst Antarctic Expedition — it accomplished the first flight over Antarctica.

Despite the historical importance of the 1959 F.A.N.U. cruise, neither Finn nor Jackie wrote much about the trip itself. Perhaps they did not fully realize its significance at the time. After these pioneering cruises and flights, tourism to Antarctica was halted until the late 1960s, as international policies and regulations relating to this burgeoning industry were formulated and implemented. Participation in this early cruise made converts out of Finn and Jackie, and they would continue to advocate the benefits of Antarctic tourism. Once again, Jackie was swept along in the tide of history as she participated in one of the earliest cruises to Antarctica.

Embracing a passion for Antarctic tourism would not be the only change she faced. By the mid to late 1960s, the United States was buffeted by unrest and societal transformations wrought by the civil rights and anti–Vietnam War movements. The feminist movement during the same period had an equally dramatic effect. Jackie was no "women's libber," but even she could not fail to be aware of and affected by the evolving role of women. It was a time of upheaval in society and in the Ronne household, too, as Jackie struggled to define her role outside of her life as a wife and mother. The 1960s was an era during which the traditional gender roles of women and men were questioned. In 1960 the first commercially produced birth control pills were available for sale, thus providing a woman with the choice about whether or not she wanted to bear children. In 1962 the Equal Pay Act was designed to prevent gender-based discrimination in the workplace. In 1963 *The Feminine Mystique* by Betty Friedan shattered the stereotype that all women felt fulfilled solely by their roles as housewives and mothers.

These changes were mirrored in Antarctica also. Although little publicized, a few years earlier, Russian marine geologist Maria Klenova became the first woman scientist to take part in an Antarctic expedition while working on board the icebreakers *Ob* and *Lena*. In 1957 flight attendants Patricia Hepinstall and Ruth Kelly became the first women to visit McMurdo Station, the American research base on Ross Island. These were small but important steps, even though a seemingly progressive *Christian Science Monitor* article entitled "Antarctic Role Pioneered by Women" downplayed these achievements by remarking that Hepinstall and Kelly "judged a beard-growing contest, modelled the latest in male fur-trimmed parkas and generally proved themselves as a great attraction to the 'natives.'"

Despite her own role as an Antarctic pioneer, Jackie did not get involved in, nor was she particularly sympathetic to, the feminist movement. Still, Jackie seemed to demonstrate a need to put herself forward. No matter how much she loved Finn and was committed to Antarctica, she wondered when her own time to shine would come. Jackie certainly had expectations that Finn would slow down or retire so they could spend more time together. She remarked to her aunt: "Hope we get over there one of these days, but probably not before Finn retires because he never has any leave as he uses it in the winter for lecturing." There were, after all, no more expeditions for him to plan and seemingly, no pressing need for him to be elsewhere. At an American Polar Society meeting, Finn even referred to himself as one of the "few old-time explorers still kicking around." Surely now would be the time for Finn to commit fully to being with his wife and daughter, but this never happened. Cracks were beginning to appear in their relationship as Finn showed few signs that he recognized or cared about Jackie's needs.

Finn's career as an explorer was always the focal point in the Ronne household. The program of the twenty-fifth anniversary of the American Polar Society held at the Cosmos Club in Washington was dedicated to Finn's accomplishments. With Jackie by his side, Finn was made an honorary member of the society, joining the ranks of a select group of only seven individuals, including Louise Arner Boyd, Lincoln Ellsworth, Vilhjalmur Stefansson, and Admiral Byrd. At the same time, Jackie's contributions were also, finally, publicly recognized. John Roscoe, a friend and Antarctic

Glamorous couple Jackie and Finn Ronne.

colleague of Finn, wrote: "In honoring Finn, we must not forget to recognize the able assistance rendered him by his understanding wife and explorer-colleague, Jackie Ronne."

Finn requested retirement with pay from the navy in 1961, but, to Jackie's displeasure, there is little evidence that his workload diminished. That year, he applied to work as a consultant with the Department of State and his lecture schedule was busier than ever. Following an exhaustive solo summer lecture tour in Europe, he visited Norway, where he was delighted to meet up with Rønne relatives, as well as with Ingrid and Lars Christensen.

Finn and Jackie were already well known to the wealthy ship-owning couple. Of course, Ingrid Christensen had travelled extensively in the Antarctic region and had been the first woman to set foot on the Antarctic mainland. In a letter to Jackie, Finn remarked: "Ingrid Christensen gave a splendid dinner for me last night with 14 persons only in a style that surpasses Louise Boyd — a beautiful dining-room and the meal was out of this world. We spoke about you many times with her as well as the other 2 ladies who went to Antarctica with her in 1933–1935. This house is a huge one — most luxurious."

He had scarcely returned home to his family when, as the son of Martin Rønne, he was invited by the U.S. Navy to visit the South Pole as part of the celebrations of the fiftieth anniversary of the discovery of the South Pole. Also present was Baron Gaston de Gerlache de Gomery, whose father, Adrien de Gerlache, led the *Belgica* Expedition of 1897–1899, during which Amundsen served as first mate. Gaston had followed in his father's footsteps by leading the second Belgian expedition to Antarctica in 1957–1958, sixty years after his father. Director of the Scott Polar Research Institute Gordon de Q. Robin remarked:

> Amundsen and his party, as a result of years of experience in the Arctic and Antarctic, were superb masters of technique. Captain Robert Falcon Scott and his men, of whom his chief scientist, Edward Adrian Wilson, should be especially mentioned, led the world with their attainments in the scientific study of Antarctica. The United States South Pole Station, named after Amundsen and Scott, provides an outstanding example of what can be accomplished by close cooperation between the present-day masters of polar technique and the scientists studying natural phenomena at the ends of the earth.

Although there is no question that Jackie wanted desperately to accompany him on both exciting trips, Finn's letters home to her express no remorse over the fact that Jackie was unable to join him because of her responsibilities as a mother.

By 1962, the friction between Jackie and Finn had developed further. The couple tried to make more time for the family and took a European road trip ending in Norway, where Finn and Jackie met up with another polar power couple — Lars and Ingrid Christensen.

Finn was a local celebrity and the couple appeared on the cover of *Vi Menn*, the equivalent of *Life Magazine* in Norway, both in 1962 and in 1964. Finn had another surprise for his family once they had arrived in Norway. This was a cruise to Spitsbergen, which, at that time, was a remote destination, seldom visited by outsiders. Finn, Jackie, and eleven-year-old Karen were joined by their friends Kay and Ed Sweeney, their daughter Harriet, and another couple. Although Jackie and Karen found it vastly enjoyable, the trip was not primarily taken to please Jackie or to allow Finn to spend time with his family.

Finn had an ulterior agenda. Although Finn had officially retired from the CIA a few months earlier, his trip to Spitsbergen was undertaken with American interests in mind. He was keen to visit Barentsburg, a Russian mining town rarely seen by Westerners. As he noted in a report to the CIA:

Jackie and Finn on the cover of *Vi Menn* in Norway.

"Undoubtedly, Spitsbergen is assuming increasing strategic importance and might well form a major focal point in any future world-wide conflict between Communism and the free world."[3]

The Cold War was in full swing and tensions between the United States and the U.S.S.R. were running high. The Ronne party was granted permission to visit but was treated with kid gloves. And no wonder, as the group contained a wealthy and well-connected Washington lawyer with close ties to the president, a member of the virulently anti-Communist Subversive Activities Control Board, and a famous American explorer who commanded newspaper headlines around the world. While the group was treated with respect by the governor and his wife in Spitsbergen, in Barentsburg, they were treated like royalty. Finn collected as much information as possible and later submitted a report on this Spitsbergen trip to

Finn Ronne, Lars Christensen, Ingrid Christensen, and Jackie Ronne, 1964.

his former CIA masters. Years later, a CIA historian would contact Karen about this trip.

In 1964 the couple visited Norway again and Jackie was delighted to spend time with Ingrid Christensen, another Antarctic pioneer. Returning to the United States, she was thrilled to be presented with the Antarctica Service Medal. This was a military award established by Congress in 1960 to replace several earlier commemorative awards given for participation in Antarctic expeditions. Finn was pleased for her, but, as time went on, he continued to spend too much time away from home.

Finn and Jackie's interest in Antarctic tourism as an innovative way of introducing more people to the icy continent was reawakened in 1965 with a chance meeting between Finn and Lars-Eric Lindblad. Lindblad was a native Swede who, like Finn, had become a naturalized American citizen. By the time they met, Lindblad had a reputation as a successful promoter of high-end adventure tours. Between them, they discussed Lindblad's plans to launch a luxury Antarctic tourist cruise.[4] Finn was delighted and eager to build on his early cruise experience in 1959. The cruise would be taking place between January 11 and February 11, 1966, on the Argentine ship *Lapataia*, offering accommodation for fifty-eight passengers. All but four of them were Americans. Similar to his earlier 1959 trip on the *Yapeyú*, the trip would leave from Ushuaia and travel across the Drake Passage to many small and larger islands, including Smith, Melchior, and Deception Islands; Half Moon Bay; and Hope Bay. There were important differences, however. Unlike the 1959 journey, Finn held the official position of "expedition leader" and was responsible for lecturing and working with the guests on a full-time basis.

The Lindblad expedition also had a strong, well-defined scientific component. This was no mere sightseeing junket but catered to a well-educated and intellectually curious clientele. An on-board scientific laboratory was set up, and passengers were promised that the comprehensive program included lectures and workshops in marine biology, meteorology, ornithology, wildlife conservation, geology, glaciology, and the history of Antarctic exploration. A reading list was provided to passengers beforehand, and they were encouraged to fully immerse themselves in the experience.

Lindblad's ambitious agenda immediately got a lot of attention, and he had no problem meeting his passenger quota. Finn was delighted to be working in an official capacity on the upcoming cruise. He had no idea that the plan for the *Lapataia* to visit the official bases of various countries was generating concern in unexpected quarters.

The *Lapataia*'s schedule included visits to the Argentine Admiral Brown Station near Paradise Harbour and Groussac Hut on Petermann Island, as well as the American Palmer Station on Anvers Island, and areas claimed both by Argentina and Britain. This captured the attention of the British government, as the cruise "raised all sorts of jurisdictional problems that had not been contemplated when the Antarctic Treaty had been signed only a few years before." Throughout 1965 and until Lindblad's Antarctic cruise was completed, the British Foreign Office kept a close eye on all aspects of the cruise.[5]

The fact that Finn Ronne was promoting it only served to increase their suspicion. Brian Roberts, who had represented Britain during the Antarctic Treaty process, believed that Finn had not always worked in support of British interests. While the Antarctic cruise was conducted without international incident, it helped to highlight gaps in the nascent Antarctic Treaty, which would need monitoring in the future.

Several of the Ronnes' friends participated in this cruise, including socialite and philanthropist Rose Saul Zalles and eighty-six-year-old Bessie Sweeney, mother of Ronne friend and RARE supporter Ed Sweeney. Sweeney called it "the most thrilling travel experience of a travel-packed life" and that the highlight "was holding a penguin in my arms, stroking his chest and observing him relax and even enjoy being petted."[6]

Jackie did not accompany Finn on this trip. At this stage, fifteen-year-old Karen was a high school student at Sidwell Friends School in Washington and ensuring her consistent education and care was always Jackie's priority. Jackie's hopes that she and Finn would spend more time together had long since been replaced by feelings of bitterness and resentment. Throughout 1965 and 1966, harsh words between them turned into acrimonious arguments. Despite her opposition, Finn continued to travel on his own. In a heartfelt letter, Jackie revealed her true feelings to Finn.

> My whole life was devoted to promoting you in your Antarctic career — you retired and looked for other interests. These interests not only left me out but offered me no future interests to supplant that which you had retired from. Oh yes, I had the house and Karen, both of which are major concerns. But it ended there and I needed more.... There has been very little give and take in our marriage — just mostly take — you have never been a companion to me — my worries have never been taken to heart by you — you have always been too preoccupied with your own affairs.

Despite the problems in their personal lives and the conflict they experienced, Finn and Jackie's marriage survived. Over the next few years, Finn and Jackie presented a united front as they were recognized for their work advancing the cause of Antarctica. Finn was declared a Knight, First Class of the Royal Norwegian Order of St. Olav and, in 1966, he was awarded the Elisha Kent Kane Medal by the Geographical Society of Philadelphia.

That same year, his expertise was requested by a Japanese team planning the first ascent of Mount Vinson as part of the Japanese West Antarctica Expedition 1966–1967. Over a two-year period, Finn maintained an ongoing correspondence with the team and flew with Jackie to Tokyo in the summer of 1966. Although he was successful in assisting their cause and earned their goodwill, Finn was mortified when an American team summited Mount Vinson on December 17, 1966, thereby usurping the Japanese plans.

Three years later, Finn and Jackie were delighted to attend a special ceremony at the National Archives in Washington. Finn's colleague Talbert Abrams had donated a large, illuminated, rotating Terr-A-Qua Globe to the National Archives in honour of the geographic contributions of both Finn and Jackie.[7]

In the fall of 1971, both Jackie and Finn were invited by the U.S. secretary of defense to visit the South Pole as part of the sixtieth anniversary of its momentous discovery by Roald Amundsen. This would be Finn's ninth trip to Antarctica and Jackie's third. In early December, the Ronnes flew from Washington, travelling almost sixteen thousand kilometres. With stopovers in Honolulu, Hawaii, and Christchurch, New Zealand, the flight took nearly two days. Everyone on board was exhausted and jetlagged upon arrival. Another record had been achieved as Jackie and Finn Ronne were the first married couple to visit the pole itself. She recalled her excitement as she and Finn broadcast to famous journalist (and Ronne family friend) Lowell Thomas from the American base. This time around, Jackie could not be prouder of her own role in Antarctic history.

> Although the round trip from McMurdo Sound on Antarctica's icy coast to the geographical South Pole can be achieved by air in one good flying day, women who had made the trip were scarcer than penguin chicks at a zoo. Many women have crossed the Antarctic Circle via tourist ships in

Jackie at the South Pole, displaying the Society of Woman Geographers flag.

recent years, but you could count in an ice tray those who have contributed to on-the-spot history of the Continent.

Left unspoken was that she herself was one of those select women. The only other female member of the American party was journalist Louise Hutchinson who worked as the Washington correspondent for the *Chicago Tribune*. She reported the Amundsen-Scott South Pole Station as "a scene of desolation — an ice runway, six buildings breaking the bleak landscape, a small forest of radio antennae, a bright torrent of flags of nations that have signed the Antarctic Treaty, a barber pole that marks the 'tourist pole.'"

As she and Finn toured the facility, Jackie marvelled at the scientific work being conducted: "geological, biological and upper atmospheric information [was] being systematically inventoried at all of our Antarctic bases ... Some immediate applications of the results already obtained provide us with more accurate predictions in long-range radio transmission and weather forecasting. And in a somewhat lighter vein, there was a fascinating three-year study of the sleep and dream patterns of personnel to help understand human adaptation to isolation." She enjoyed learning about all of it.

While the trip was supposed to be mainly ceremonial in nature, it was not without thrills and excitement. With sixteen other men in their party, the Ronnes climbed aboard a UH-1N helicopter for a survey of the nearby historic huts officially designated as historic sites. Unexpectedly, while visiting Sir Ernest Shackleton's base at Cape Royds, a blizzard blew in, marooning the party. Overnighting and even spending a few days there was a very distinct if disconcerting possibility. Constructed by Shackleton's men during the *Nimrod* Expedition, the hut offered no heat and scant protection from the elements. Jackie and the others were tired, cold, and hungry. She commented ruefully:

> As time wore on, the dingy hut took on new dimensions. In spite of a New Zealand Government notice cautioning all visitors from removing any item whatsoever from the historic shrine, we began to eye the corroded cans of Bird's Eye Powder, Cabbage, Ox Tongue, weathered boxes of hard tack biscuits and bottles of brandy with more than casual indifference ...

Subconsciously, each of us picked out a corner or niche on a hard bench, which might possibly afford some relative comfort during the forthcoming night.

Luckily, no consumption of the historic comestibles took place as the helicopters were able to lift off following a long six hours on the ground. Crisis averted, the Ronnes returned home to the United States with more Antarctic tales to share. The Hercules that was due to pick up journalist Louise Hutchinson was delayed, and she inadvertently became the first woman to spend the night at the South Pole.

In 1973 Jackie lost both her aunt and uncle as they passed away within eight months of each other. Although they met and married later in life, Merriel and Irvine Gardner's marriage had been a long and fulfilling one. Likely, children had not been in their plans, but they lovingly raised Jackie as their own. It was due to their tender care and attention that she received an excellent education and unique opportunities in life. When her father had died a few years previously, Jackie opened her heart to the Gardners:

> I could think of nothing except how little of the past I had really understood growing up and that to my dying day I will be eternally grateful for you and uncle having the understanding, compassion and interest to have made it possible for me to lead a different life.... In the past you may not think at times I have shown the proper appreciation, but you must know now how in my own heart I feel. I am particularly grateful that Karen need never know of all of this and how different her childhood has been.

Their deaths also ensured Jackie's financial well-being, as Jackie and her daughter, Karen, were the primary beneficiaries of the Gardners' wills. This final loving gift from her aunt and uncle provided Jackie with the complete freedom to follow her own pursuits with no reliance on Finn.

Jackie's work writing about Antarctica for publications including the *International Geophysical Year Monograph*, *Américas Magazine*, the *Encyclopedia Britannica*, and Funk & Wagnalls *Standard Reference Encyclopedia* continued as she sought new avenues to communicate her passion for Antarctica. Karen recalled: "She wrote annual articles for the encyclopedias — she did that for years and spent a long-time researching material for the chapters on Antarctica. She always stayed current on everything going on there by reading about it and through the experienced people she knew in the field."

Throughout the period between the 1950s and 1970s, encyclopedias represented a vital information source for the general public although they are considered obsolete today. The articles she wrote on science and politics provided cutting-edge research on Antarctica to eager Americans — most of whom would never visit this continent.

In the 1940s, Jackie controlled the media coverage about the Ronne Antarctic Research Expedition through writing and editing the vast majority of RARE newspaper articles. Similarly, her later encyclopedic entries helped establish the public narrative on Antarctica. Written under the byline "Edith M. Ronne, Antarctic specialist," most articles focused on scientific work and events at research bases, but she still managed to slip in references to her own accomplishments. Her article in the 1967 edition of the *Encyclopedia Britannica* states: "For the first time, women scientists worked in Antarctica as part of the U.S. Antarctic Research summer program, including Lois Jones of OSU Institute for Polar Studies. The only women to have spent a year in Antarctica are Edith Ronne and Jennie Darlington of the Ronne Antarctic Research Expedition." Similarly, the 1973 edition mentions that she and Finn visited the South Pole on the sixtieth anniversary of Amundsen's discovery of the South Pole and that they were the first husband and wife team to visit the pole.

She visited her dear friend Kay Sweeney in Florida and returned to Norway with Finn. He still enjoyed travelling and meeting people, with or without Jackie. In the late 1970s, Finn had a heart attack, but this did not stop him working with Jackie on his final book entitled *Antarctica, My Destiny*. As with all his previous books, Jackie and Finn worked on it together as partners. That same year, the couple celebrated the marriage of their beloved daughter, Karen.

On January 12, 1980, at the age of eighty, Finn died peacefully in his sleep. As with many outstanding polar explorers, Finn Ronne was a charismatic individual, flawed, uncompromising, and self-absorbed. Jackie was never under any illusions about her husband and did not pretend to herself or others that he was other than an imperfect man. But whereas others saw only these faults, she recognized and loved the principled, hard-working, courageous, innovative, determined man he was and celebrated the visionary within.

Finn Ronne at the South Pole.

CHAPTER 10

LIFE AFTER FINN

No woman should say, "I am but a woman!" But
a woman! What more can you ask to be?
— MARIA MITCHELL

FINN'S DEATH WAS unexpected and sudden. He had always been fit and vigorous throughout his life, but with a twenty-year age gap between them, Jackie knew it could happen at any time. Condolences and tributes poured in from all quarters, but Jackie had work to do. She was determined that Finn should have an honourable resting place suitable for a military figure of his stature. There was only one option: Arlington National Cemetery. It is the burial place for U.S. presidents, including John F. Kennedy and his family, and the son and grandson of Abraham Lincoln, and the pre-eminent cemetery for military men and women. Impressively located within 639 acres, Arlington officially became a national cemetery in 1864. It holds a hallowed significance for American polar explorers. Richard Byrd, Robert Peary, Adolphus Greely, Charles Wilkes, Matthew Henson, and Bernt

Balchen all found their resting place in Arlington, as did revered astronauts John Glenn, Gus Grissom, Roger Chaffee, Pete Conrad, and all members of space shuttle *Challenger* and space shuttle *Columbia*.[1]

Jackie knew that this was exactly where he would want to be. Even though Finn was a military man with a distinguished career as a polar explorer, there was no guarantee that his burial there was assured. According to their official policy, "eligibility for in-ground burial at Arlington National Cemetery is the most stringent of all U.S. national cemeteries." Jackie did not see this as an impediment; she was determined and worked her extensive list of influential contacts, including ex-ambassador, prominent lawyer, and Ronne ally Ralph Becker, to ensure that this would be Finn's final resting place and her own. Her perseverance paid off, and Finn was laid to rest with full military honours in a prestigious plot located a few rows away from Byrd, Peary, Balchen, and Henson. After Finn's funeral, Jackie was at loose ends. It was time for her to take stock of her life and move forward.

If the 1960s and 1970s were revolutionary decades for women, the 1980s was a time in which the consequences of this social, cultural, and political upheaval became evident.[2] During this period, the systemic changes prompted by the women's movement began to reverberate throughout society. In 1981 Sandra Day O'Connor became the first woman sworn in to serve on the U.S. Supreme Court. In 1983 Sally Ride became the first American woman in space. In 1984 Geraldine Ferraro became the first woman nominated as vice-president for a major political party in the United States. That same year, discrimination on the basis of sex was banned for members of all-male organizations such as the Rotary Club, the Kiwanis Club, and the Jaycees.[3]

Changing attitudes toward women were also apparent in Antarctica. In 1969 American geochemist Lois Jones led the first all-female expedition to the McMurdo Dry Valleys, and Australian women were finally permitted to travel to the Australian Antarctic Territory in an official capacity.[4] In the 1970s Mary Alice McWhinnie became the chief scientist at McMurdo Station — the first woman to serve in this capacity. She and Mary Odile

Dr. Lois Jones and her scientific team in the late 1960s: (left to right) Kay Lindsay, Terry Tickhill Terrell, Lois Jones, and Eileen McSaveney.

Dr. Mary Alice McWhinnie in the laboratory.

Cahoon become the first women to overwinter in Antarctica at McMurdo Station, and in 1979 the U.S. Navy advertised for "qualified female volunteers to over-winter in Antarctica" for the first time. While these are important milestones, change in Antarctica was still slow to arrive, as Cornelia Dean described in her 1998 *New York Times* article "After a Struggle, Women Win a Place on the Ice; in Labs and in the Field, a New Outlook."

Glaciologist Colin Bull was an early supporter of women scientists working in Antarctica. "One of the surprising results of my efforts to liberate a whole continent for women was the reaction of some of my male friends. One chap, who had been at South Pole Station for the first winter, so much resented that he had lost the exclusivity of the 'Antarctic Club' that he wrote to me a very short letter: 'Dear Colin, Traitor!'" The degree to which different countries supported this change varied greatly. Women's presence in polar research communities did not fully normalize until the late 1980s and 1990s.

The 1980s was a period in which Jackie mourned the death of her husband and then got back on her feet, brushed herself off, and went on with life. She immersed herself in renovations at her Maryland home, tailoring everything to her own taste. Indulging her love for penguins, she and Karen had started their own prolific collection of all-things penguin — figurines, tea towels, china, books, and, of course, real stuffed penguins that Finn had brought back. It became a shared passion between them, and they delighted in gifting penguin items to each other on special occasions. Now Jackie let this obsession run wild, so penguins overtook every room in her house. She spent more time visiting with friends, socializing, and playing bridge, and she found renewed joy in her grandchildren, Michael and Jaclyn. As always, she travelled extensively with Karen and her family, and spent time socially with Karen's friends as well as her own. Often the line between the two was blurred. Joani Graves was a long-time friend of both mother and daughter and recalled, "Whenever us girls went places, Jackie was one of us and came too. She was so much fun and so interesting!" But Jackie's work with Antarctica was not over yet.

She had always found comfort and pleasure in the company of other women. From her girlfriends at Girl Scout camp to her sorority sisters in Phi

Mu and her colleagues at the State Department, female friendship filled a deep need inside her. It was no coincidence that many of her closest friends were strong women such as Bettie Earle (later Heckmann) and Kay Sweeney. After Finn's death, Jackie continued to be active in, and inspired by, an all-women's organization that remained important to her throughout her life.

The Society of Woman Geographers (SWG) was founded in 1924 by a group of four adventurous, risk-taking friends to promote women's participation in exploration, geography, anthropology, and related fields. At that time, women explorers, no matter how renowned, were refused admittance to the prestigious, males-only Explorers Club. SWG members included famous names such as Amelia Earhart, Margaret Mead, Eleanor Roosevelt, Mary Leakey, Margaret Bourke-White, and Jane Goodall, as well as a host of lesser-known but equally charismatic personages, including diplomat/socialite Courtney Letts Adams, East Asia expert Eleanor Holgate Lattimore, and Spanish journalist Isabel de Palencia.

Proposed by fellow polar colleague Evelyn Stefansson Nef, Jackie had joined SWG in the 1940s shortly after her return from the Ronne Antarctic Research Expedition. She had been a keen supporter ever since. In the late 1970s, she headed up the SWG Washington group and served as SWG vice-president and president, continuing in this capacity until 1981. She had proudly carried the SWG flag to the South Pole when she visited there with Finn in 1971. She also served seven years as SWG treasurer. Karen shared her commitment to this organization, and they often attended meetings together. As SWG president, Jackie was invited to present a memorial lecture to the Explorers Club entitled "The Ronne Antarctic Research Expedition 1946–1948." She was the first woman ever to carry a full program before that group. In 2002, Jackie was thrilled to receive the Society of Woman Geographers Outstanding Achievement Award "for a lifetime of living on, studying about, lecturing on and writing about the continent of Antarctica."

At long last, Jackie felt free to revel in her achievements. There was no one to watch over her shoulder jealously and no concern that, in accepting her own share of the glory, she was trying to eclipse Finn. Karen remarked: "Previously Jackie downplayed her own role in the expedition because she thought that's what he wanted ... and she was right." She was regularly sought out by journalists eager to learn about her experiences, and she was more willing to embrace her accomplishments. In her later interviews, Jackie Ronne is less self-deprecating and more likely to state proudly that she had been "busy documenting history" during the Ronne Antarctic Research Expedition. Regrettably, she did not actively promote the cause of women in Antarctica. Like many women pioneers, she was, in many ways, very traditional. In contrast to her male Antarctic colleagues, Jackie never sought the attention but, later in life, accepted it graciously when it found her.

In her autobiography, she wrote that during Finn's lifetime, she "felt uncomfortable in the spotlight as I also was conscious about taking some of the spotlight away from Finn's accomplishments." In her heart of hearts, her primary role was caring for Finn and the Ronne legacy and promoting Antarctica. These factors were always intertwined. Jackie was relentless in protecting Finn's life work and did so with tenacity and utter fearlessness. She even took on august publications such as *National Geographic* and the *New York Times*.

> Why is it that Finn seems to be your chosen whipping boy continually — he doesn't deserve your incessant poor treatment. If you are seriously interested in what actually happened on "that" expedition as you profess, I shall be very happy to enlighten you anytime — and you can be very sure I have back-up documentation. Surely you know well enough that men who do not get what they want from an expedition are the most vocal in placing the blame on the leader after returning. R.A.R.E. was no different. I am well aware of all the axes there were to grind. To me your bias is distasteful, untruthful, offensive and hurtful. In addition, your male chauvinism is unbecoming…. Just lay off your constant snide remarks about Finn or you will continue to get static a plenty from me.

This active defence of her husband was directed toward individuals who had written about Antarctican history and whose work portrayed Finn in an unfavourable light or ignored or slighted the Ronne legacy. In this, Jackie more than fulfilled Finn's expectations that his wife would always protect and promote his reputation. Until her own death, it was always more important to Jackie to protect Finn's reputation than uphold her own. This stalwart protection of the Ronne legacy was no mere loyalty on the part of a grieving widow for her husband. Jackie understood that what was written about Finn would stand for all time. It would determine if Finn Ronne was remembered as an accomplished American Antarctican explorer or a tyrannical wannabe. Despite Jackie's best efforts during her lifetime, Jennie Darlington's 1957 memoir, *My Antarctic Honeymoon*, written by a ghost-writer and sensationalized by a sales-hungry editor, continues to adversely affect Finn's reputation. Further damage has been inflicted by derogatory comments made by members of Finn's 1957–1958 IGY team at Ellsworth Station.[5]

In the early 1980s, Jackie inaugurated the Finn Ronne Memorial Award with the Explorers Club, which was given every four years to an "individual noted for accomplishments in polar field research or exploration."[6] Finn and Jackie's friend Sir Wally Herbert was the first recipient in 1985. Described by Sir Ranulph Fiennes as "the greatest polar explorer of our time," Herbert had a long and illustrious career as a polar explorer, including serving as the leader of the 1968–1969 British Trans-Arctic Expedition. This nearly six-thousand-kilometre journey with dogs was the first surface crossing of the Arctic Ocean. British prime minister Harold Wilson called it a "feat of endurance and courage which ranks with any in polar history." Herbert; his wife, Marie; and Jackie maintained a cordial relationship even after Finn's death.

Jackie was always keen to speak with other explorers about the polar regions whether in the north or the south. This had largely been missing from her life since Finn died. In the late 1980s, Jackie got to know Wally Herbert well. The National Geographic Society had invited him to conduct research on Robert Peary's original February–April 1909 diary, requesting that he closely study the astronomical observations, soundings, and other historic data written and collected during Peary's epic quest to conquer the North Pole. Peary's claim to have reached the North Pole first had been bitterly contested and Wally Herbert's thorough investigation was designed to settle the question once and for all. Despite being a Peary admirer, Herbert was the right man for the job and was delighted with the opportunity of being one of the first people to read Peary's diary apart from Peary family members.

Prior to beginning research at the National Geographic office in Washington, Herbert rented accommodations within walking distance of Jackie's home. Karen and her husband, Al Tupek, lived nearby and usually drove Herbert into the office each morning. Afterward, Herbert spent dinners with Jackie and the Tupeks and reviewed his findings with them. Jackie was never afraid of offering her own opinion and enjoyed discussing this significant Arctic mystery with him. Herbert later wrote *The Noose of Laurels: Robert E. Peary and the Race to the North Pole* based on the research he had conducted. While his book acknowledges his colleagues, friends, and family, he neglects to mention the assistance offered by Jackie and her family during his research stay in Washington. But Jackie did not hold this against him and only a few years later, she and Herbert would meet up again. In 1999, she was happy to send a commendation for knighthood to Sir Ranulph Fiennes who was spearheading the initiative.

In between a busy lecture and writing schedule, volunteer commitments (apart from the Society of Woman Geographers, the Antarctican Society, and the Explorers Club, she also served as the vice-president for the National Society of Arts and Letters), and time with her family, Jackie carried on socializing with girlfriends. Daringly, she had purchased a condominium in Boca Raton, Florida, something that Finn had always wanted to do. Florida was a haven of sorts and Jackie remarked, "After the pressures of the lecture circuit and the urban life of my home near Washington, D.C., I come here to unwind. I do my writing and prepare my slide shows here. And I go swimming every day."

She was highly respected in Antarctic circles for her accomplishments and, most importantly for Antarctic veterans, for her time on the ice. She remained active in Antarctican Society meetings and events where she was considered a "rock star" by many of the society members. She was friends with other female elders of the society, including Ruth Siple, widow of Antarctic geographer/explorer Paul Siple. Like Jackie, Ruth Siple had also

Karen Ronne Tupek, Monica Kristensen (later Kristensen Solås), and Jackie Ronne.

worked for the National Geographic Society and later became president and one of the guiding lights of the Antarctican Society. Another colleague was Mildred Crary, a journalist, gifted photographer, and avid traveller who had journeyed over the Khyber Pass on a camel at the age of eighty-five. She was the widow of Albert "Bert" Crary, a noted polar geophysicist and glaciologist, who was the first person to stand at both the North and South Poles.

Jackie remained active in the Society of Woman Geographers and the Explorers Club, where she mentored up-and-coming female explorers such as Kathryn Sullivan. Sullivan was the first American woman to walk in space and a crew member on three *Challenger* missions. A geologist, she also became the first woman to dive to the Challenger Deep in the Mariana Trench and became known as "the most vertical woman in the world." Jackie sponsored Sullivan for membership in the SWG and Sullivan always viewed her as a respected colleague.

Not surprisingly, Jackie had a special interest in supporting women polar explorers. She was friendly with thirty-six-year-old Swedish-Norwegian glaciologist and explorer Monica Kristensen (later Kristensen Solås) and met her several times at her Bethesda, Maryland, home. Amongst other accomplishments, Kristensen was the leader of the 1986–1987 Norwegian-British 90 Degrees South Expedition which sought to retrace Roald Amundsen's historic route to the South Pole. She was the honoured recipient of the Founder's Medal bestowed by the Royal Geographical Society and the first president of the Norwegian chapter of the Explorers Club. Jackie admired Kristensen and cheered her on as another strong woman leader in the Antarctic. They met again in New York City and in Oslo at important Explorers Club events. Although they later lost touch, Kristensen considered Ronne a friend.

Jackie's interest in Antarctic tourism had continued unabated. She retained a lively curiosity about all things Antarctic. Antarctic cruising held a special fascination for her due to the Ronne family involvement in its early years. Since the late 1950s, cruises to Antarctica had captured public attention and were now offered by many countries as a premiere tourist destination. Increased popularity and consumer demand precipitated the need to manage visitor use and ensure the long-term conservation of natural and cultural resources. In 1991 the Protocol on Environmental Protection to the Antarctic Treaty was signed, which protected Antarctic wildlife and vegetation, established special area and heritage protection, protected against marine pollution, and established rules for waste disposal and management. The same year, the International Association of Antarctica Tour Operators (IAATO) was established to "practise and promote safe and environmentally responsible travel to this remote and delicate region of the world." Strict guidelines regarding how cruise operators and the ever-present stream of enthusiastic visitors behaved in Antarctica offered an elevated level of protection to the vulnerable Antarctic environment and its living resources.

In 1995 Jackie received a tantalizing invitation that would allow her to combine her love of Antarctic cruising with her past experience as a member of the 1946–1948 Ronne Antarctic Research Expedition. As Finn had done before her, Jackie was invited to sail on board the M/V *Explorer* as guest lecturer. Organized by Abercrombie & Kent, this would be no ordinary cruise for Jackie. She would be returning to Antarctica and, most importantly, to that godforsaken lonely place she loved with all her heart. The place that had shaped her life and, quite literally, put her name on the map. But going back there meant invoking painful memories, including the bitter feud between Finn and Harry Darlington, the near-death experiences of several of the men, and the estrangement with Jennie Darlington caused by their loyalty to their husbands. Never an introspective woman, this dredging up of memories was one aspect of the upcoming cruise that she dreaded. She had always remarked, "I had never expected to gaze upon Stonington Island's magnificent scenery again."

The objective of the cruise was reaching Stonington Island, which allowed Jackie to visit East Base for the first time since the departure of the Ronne Antarctic Research Expedition in 1948. Members of both the Society of Woman Geographers and the Washington branch of the Explorers Club signed on. Jackie brought with her a group of friends, including several children of Ronne family friends Kay and Ed Sweeney, and her daughter, Karen, to share this unique experience. There was no guarantee, however, that the *Explorer* would be able to reach its destination given the vagaries of the unpredictable weather and the frozen pack ice that crowded the region. Then as now, Stonington Island in Marguerite Bay is notoriously difficult to reach and is rarely included on cruise itineraries. In fact, in 1995 (the year of Jackie's cruise), there were only two ice-free weeks in this area. Against all odds, the ship made it through. It was an emotional time for Jackie, and she was flooded with memories of Finn and the momentous experiences they had shared. As Stonington Island drew nearer, everyone on board the M/V *Explorer* marvelled at the splendour surrounding them.

> To the east the luminous blue ice of the glacial cliffs faced us, and above them, long white slopes of the glaciers rose to peaks of black stone crowned with ice ... the sea was a sheet of shine scattered with decaying icebergs, and along the shoreline thousands of broken bits of brash ice, moving in an imperceptible swell, gurgled and sang.

Jackie hadn't been there for nearly fifty years, but it could have been yesterday.

Jackie revisiting East Base, Stonington Island, Antarctica, 1995.

Words can hardly describe how I felt as I stood once again in this place and re-lived all of the memories that lay hidden within its walls. All of the joys and sorrows, the happy times and the petty rows that had been something of a trauma for me then, flooded through my mind. It was an unforgettable lesson in raw basic human nature without any of the veneer of civilization. It is not something that I would want to repeat. It was only by re-visiting these memories in this place that I was able once and for all to face them down and finally feel able to share them with the world. Free at last!

The East Base that Jackie remembered from fifty years earlier was long gone. The machine shop had fallen to pieces, the exterior canvas covering had disappeared from the bunkhouse, and the science building and the ground surrounding the buildings was littered with rusting twisted metal, broken jars, and rotted seal carcasses. Peering through the shattered

Modern-day East Base, Stonington Island, Antarctica.

windows, she was dismayed to see that the buildings had been completely stripped. Recently designated a National Historic Site, there was evidence that National Science Foundation staff had visited and conducted conservation work. "Metal plaques had been placed on all the buildings attesting to the action, including one marking the 'Ronne Hut.' Suddenly my old little shack where I had hibernated for a year, while I unwittingly made history, had become an internationally recognized historic building worthy of being preserved, partly because I had lived there."[7]

Now a government historic preservation architect, Karen had brought three panels to erect on the site commemorating Jackie and Finn's accomplishments and the Ronne Antarctic Research Expedition. For Jackie, it was wrenching to see the condition of her previous home, but for the rest of her life, she was thankful she had made the difficult journey. To her friends and family who had accompanied her, she stated with a smile, "I wouldn't have given up that experience for a million dollars. Nor would I ever have done it again." Jackie and Karen were later shocked to learn that the M/V *Explorer*, on which they had sailed in 1995, would be the first cruise ship to sink in the Antarctic after striking an iceberg only twelve years later.

While she never returned to Stonington Island again, this 1995 cruise whetted her appetite for more. She remarked in her autobiography, "Almost despite myself, I had become a true Antarctican.... When a person has once overwintered in the Antarctic, a great desire to return will invariably occur and I was no different. The wild grandeur of nature at its most primitive and man's untiring battle to survive and cope with the worst that it has to offer, are the strong ties of the continent which continue to draw Antarcticans back, even on a tourist ship."

It didn't take much for her friend Erland Fogelberg, vice-president of Orient Lines, to convince Jackie to sign on as a guest lecturer on the former icebreaker MS *Marco Polo*. For the next several years, Jackie revelled in her role as an Antarctica expert while sailing the frigid waters around the southern continent. Antarctic cruises were considerably more upscale and sophisticated than those of the 1950s. Savvy cruise entrepreneurs promoted these trips as "voyages" and "expeditions," using language "imbued with exploration rhetoric and informed by the narratives of Antarctic heroic age explorers. Antarctic tourism offer[ed] insights into boundaries between tourism and exploration."

Jackie won the hearts of hundreds of cruise passengers due to her natural charm and she was a popular draw. There were few people like Jackie — a woman who spoke from first-hand experience, conversing informally and lecturing knowledgeably about the world of the Antarctic explorer, the historical origins of polar exploration, and the early years of Antarctic tourism. An Antarctic pioneer in every sense of the word. In 1997, Jackie celebrated her fiftieth anniversary in Antarctica while lecturing on the *Explorer*. Another cruise the following year on the *Marco Polo* was significant as Karen; son-in-law, Al; and Jackie's grandchildren, Michael and Jaclyn, accompanied her. They were the first family to have a historic four generations visit Antarctica.

The last decade of Jackie's life started with a celebration. On October 13, 1999, Karen honoured her mother's eightieth birthday with a surprise "Cruise to Antarctica" party. Guests feasted on a sumptuous and imaginatively named menu, including Wooster College Shrimp Mold, Phi Mu Cheeses, Stonington Island Beef Tenderloin, McMurdo Broccoli Casserole, Palmer Peninsula Potatoes, and Antarctic Ice Cream Cake featuring Ronne Ice Shelf Icing while Jackie was feted by family and friends. In the coming years, Jackie received awards honouring her long service to Antarctica. In 2004 she was asked to join astronaut Neil Armstrong in signing the American Geographical Society's Fliers' and Explorers' Globe in Atlanta. Jackie's friend and mentor Louise Arner Boyd had signed it years earlier.

Later that year, at the age of eighty-five, Jackie had finally decided that the time had come for her to commit her memories to paper. Surprisingly, for someone who had spent a significant portion of her life promoting her family legacy, she displayed a marked aversion for sifting through her own archives. Karen had encouraged her mother for years but with little success. Despite a lifetime of writing for others, Jackie did not find self-reflection or the writing process to be pleasurable experiences.

She eventually plunged in and completed the book with Karen's aid and with the assistance of her good friend, Antarctic historian and fellow cruise lecturer David Wilson. It was challenging for her to write about herself and reveal her personal history. Comprised primarily of diary extracts, her autobiography, entitled *Antarctica's First Lady: Memoirs of the First American Woman to Set Foot on the Antarctic Continent and Winter-Over*, focused less on her own life and more on the Ronne Antarctic Research Expedition. Despite her extraordinary achievements in Antarctica, Jackie struggled to find a publisher. Finally, wealthy Beaumont, Texas, philanthropist and owner of the Clifton Steamboat Museum David W. Hearn Jr. agreed to publish it.

The modest book launch took place in Beaumont, Texas, the site of *Port of Beaumont*'s departure for Antarctica in January 1947. At the same time, other activities were planned by the Three Rivers Council of the Boy Scouts. The Scouts had maintained an interest in RARE ever since sending local Beaumont resident and Eagle Scout Arthur Owen on the expedition. A special Art Owen–Ronne Antarctic Medal was struck by the Scouts commemorating Owen's participation and themed Scouting programs focusing

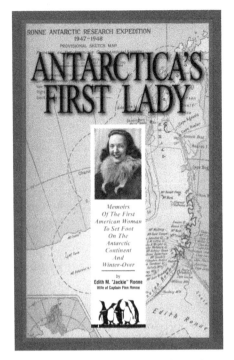

Front cover of Jackie's published autobiography.

on the "adventuresome spirit of the expedition" were developed. In coordination with the publication of Jackie's book, the Clifton Steamboat Museum
opened an impressive Ronne Expedition exhibit attended by Jackie, family
members, and local VIPs and which garnered considerable local interest.
Senior Scout executive Jack Crawford commented to Jackie that the Ronne
Expedition had been beneficial for Beaumont and was the catalyst that
brought many different organizations together in service for a good cause.

The Three Rivers Council also hosted a RARE reunion at the same time.
There had been earlier reunions, but these had not always gone well. A 1983
reunion hosted by Nelson McClary and his wife Jane had been attended by
Admiral Richard Blackburn Black, a former Byrd colleague much disliked
by the Ronnes. Black's comment that Finn had been no leader of men and
that it had been a wasted year for many RARE members was reported in the

local newspaper and drew Jackie's ire. She lost no time in replying: "Leaders certainly cannot please everyone (as anyone knowledgeable with Antarctic history is well aware) and in this instance, I believe your reporter was misled into presenting a highly negative viewpoint. Most Ronne Expedition members continue to be proud of their part in the expedition and consider it to be the high point of their lives." The 2004 reunion would be the last one held for RARE members.

Over the next few years, Jackie's health declined. She became increasingly frail and scaled back her social engagements. More dependent on her daughter and son-in-law, she suffered increasingly from dementia and passed away on June 14, 2009, in Bethesda, Maryland. In death, her role as an Antarctic legend was recognized and her obituary was featured on ABC News and in the *New York Times*, *Time Magazine*, and other leading newspapers, and flashed around the world. Stephen Miller of the *Wall Street Journal* referred to her as a "rare female in a formerly all-male bastion" and Patricia Sullivan of the *Washington Post* applauded her expeditionary contributions and geographic work. In *Polar Record*, her close friend, polar historian David Wilson wrote glowingly of her accomplishments as well as her personal attributes: "Jackie was a lady of considerable charm, loyalty and affection with a wonderful sense of humour. She liked nothing better than a game of bridge or a long chat over a scotch and soda with a bowl of potato chips, preferably a penguin bowl, for penguins appeared in every aspect of her home in Bethesda, Maryland." But none of the obituaries acknowledged the full breadth of Jackie's contributions to Antarctic history.

As Jackie had done for Finn, Karen ensured that her mother was laid to rest in Arlington National Cemetery alongside her beloved husband, Finn. Her funeral was well-attended with family, friends, and admirers from around the world and Karen's eulogy was heartfelt.

> My mother was a great woman, not only because she was a most devoted and loving mother but also because she was the First Lady of the Antarctic. She was first and foremost a lady, with many social graces and a vivid personality. Secondly, she was a pioneer. As the first American woman to set foot on the

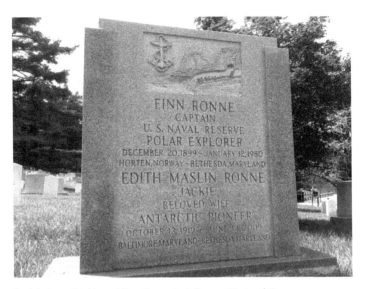

Burial place of Jackie and Finn Ronne in Arlington National Cemetery.

Jackie Ronne later in life.

Antarctic continent, she was also the first woman in the world to be a working member of an Antarctican expedition and to winter-over on the frozen continent. The experience made her life and opened doors she never imagined. She felt privileged to have been exposed to such a rich and stimulating life that came from her year in the Antarctic. She never envisioned that she would be celebrated upon her death, but so she has been. I'm grateful that so many people recognize her lasting legacy.

Jackie had commemorated the Ronne family legacy following Finn's death with the creation of the Finn Ronne Memorial Award given through the Explorers Club and did so once again with another award following her own death. In so doing, she ensured that the Ronne family would continue to support vital work in Antarctica in perpetuity and that the Ronne name would forever be associated with Antarctic exploration. Established under the terms of Jackie's will, the Ronne Award for Antarctic Research or Exploration was established in 2010 through the Society of Woman Geographers. This award is granted to an early or mid-career member or non-member who has made a significant contribution to the Antarctic region. Recipients of these two Ronne awards include Antarctic scientists and explorers such as Monica Kristensen Solås, Will Steger, David Hempleman-Adams, James McClintock, Polly Penhale, and Jill Mikucki. Although the awards honoured both Ronnes, it was Jackie who had made the awards possible.

Karen believes that, by the time she died, Jackie accepted her honoured place in the pantheon of Antarctic exploration. Her name had even entered popular culture as the answer to a question on the revered American game show *Jeopardy*. "Over time, she began realizing more and more that she had accomplished something. As she matured and looked back, she thought, *Yeah! I was the first woman to do that. It's pretty cool*."

EPILOGUE

And the desire was as pure as the polar snows:
to go, to see — no more, no less.
— Ursula K. Le Guin

JACKIE RONNE HAS been marginalized in the annals of polar exploration, which is defined in masculinist terms, with women largely invisible and irrelevant. Even gender-based histories of Antarctica have ignored her. Despite her own Antarctic accomplishments, she has been overlooked and relegated to the role of a passive appendage to her flamboyant husband. In this, she was complicit. In many ways, although Finn did the exploring, it was Jackie who created "Finn Ronne, Antarctic hero." In the process, she did herself no favours. Due to her own conventional views about women and out of an unwavering sense of loyalty, Jackie promoted her husband, but she failed to promote herself. Jackie was not an explorer in the traditional sense as Finn was. Her story offers an "alternative history of Antarctic exploration that is not premised on conquest, nationalism, fame or a race to the finish line."

She did not achieve a new record through participating in a major sledging operation or pilot the Beechcraft along a virgin stretch of rugged coastline. She did not identify a species new to science or discover a new geographical terrestrial or marine feature. In fact, she never wrote about or voiced a desire to reach any of these objectives. The reality is, in the late 1940s in the United States, it was hardly an option for well-behaved, middle-class women such as Jackie.

Regardless, Jackie Ronne's contributions to Antarctic history are impressive. As the first female Antarctic expedition member who overwintered on the continent, she proved that women could survive and thrive. Her role in charge of communications and media relations for the Ronne Antarctic Research Expedition during and following this adventure helped shape the expedition narrative and create its legacy. She proved herself as a RARE team member, demonstrating that a woman's place was in Antarctica or any place she damn well wanted it to be. Later, as a respected and well-known Antarctic figure, she advocated on behalf of the Antarctic Treaty and promoted early Antarctic tourism. Her passion for Antarctica and love for her Antarctic-mad husband guided her adult life yet the breadth of her accomplishments remained unknown during her lifetime. Jackie would be thrilled to learn that today, RARE's historic and valuable trimetrogon photographs are still in use by scientists within the U.S. Geological Survey and the British Antarctic Survey.

A newspaper advertisement supposedly placed by Sir Ernest Shackleton in the (London) *Times*.

More so than any other place on Earth, Antarctica has been controlled by men. Ernest Shackleton's apocryphal advertisement conveys a potent message. It wasn't just challenging for women to go there — until quite recently, it was virtually impossible. There have been generations of powerful men in official organizations, including the U.S. Navy, the British Antarctic Survey, and the Australian Antarctic Division who vigorously opposed it. Acting as gatekeepers, they reinforced the deeply entrenched myth that polar regions were best preserved for men. Until the mid-twentieth century (and even later in some countries), sexist attitudes prevailed in national Antarctic programs. Regardless of their qualifications, gutsy women were obliged to (meekly) obtain the permission of unyielding admirals, captains, and, perhaps most galling of all, husbands.

It is an undisputed fact that Jackie Ronne was the first American woman to step onto the Antarctic continent and the first female participant in an Antarctic expedition; this occurred because Finn Ronne wanted her there. Like Ingrid Christensen and Caroline Mikkelsen before her, it was Jackie's husband who offered the key to her remarkable life and they both knew it. It is because of him that Jackie became an Antarctic pioneer and was presented with unique opportunities to contribute to Antarctic polar history throughout her life. But Finn supported Jackie's work only insofar as it helped him. She was devoted to her husband and to maintaining the Ronne family legacy and raised her only child to do the same. Jackie pushed the envelope for women who, later, wanted to go to Antarctica based on their own merits. She was one of the first to go there, and every woman who takes for granted that she can be a research station leader, manage a scientific project, launch a trek to the South Pole, or work as a chief mechanic there, should remember that they owe her a debt of gratitude.

During Jackie's waning years and after her death, the access of women to Antarctica improved slowly but gradually, as one barrier after another was overcome. Jan Strugnell commented: "When we think about Antarctic science and the history of that, it's all tied up in exploration…. If you think of Mawson and Scott and Shackleton — you still think of these beardy guys."

A number of notable accomplishments by "non-beardy types" occurred in 1993, when American Ann Bancroft led the American Women's

Expedition to the South Pole and became the first woman to reach both the North and South Poles across the ice; Norwegian Liv Arnesen became the first woman to ski solo and unsupported to the South Pole in 1994; Ann Bancroft and Liv Arnesen became the first women to cross the Antarctic continent from Queen Maud Land to the Ross Ice Shelf in 2000–2001; and Briton Felicity Aston became the first woman to complete a solo crossing of Antarctica in 2012.

Access to senior decision-making and management positions improved also. This process began in the 1980s and 1990s and included milestones such as Liz Morris becoming head of the Ice and Climate Division in 1986, Carol Roberts becoming the deputy director of the National Science Foundation's Office of Polar Programs in 1988, and Gillian Wratt being named director of the New Zealand Antarctic Programme in 1992. Following that, Karin Lochte became head of the Alfred Wegener Institute in 2007, Kelly Falkner became head of the National Science Foundation's Office of Polar Programs in 2012, Jane Francis became director of the British Antarctic Survey in 2013, and Jenny Baeseman became head of the Scientific Committee on Antarctic Research in 2015 (followed by Chandrika Nath in 2018).

Today, there are few boundaries for women in Antarctica — mostly, they are able to work wherever they want and do whatever they want to do. However, sexist attitudes are still prevalent in this remote land and women's struggles to overcome them continue.[1] The significant role played by Jackie Ronne and other historic female Antarctic pioneers, and the challenges they bravely faced and overcame, should always be remembered.

Jackie Ronne (1919–2009).

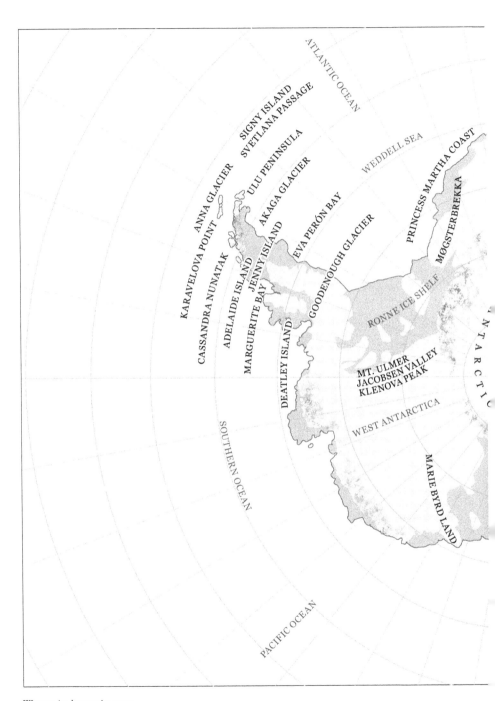

ATLANTIC OCEAN

SIGNY ISLAND
SVETLANA PASSAGE

ULU PENINSULA

ANNA GLACIER

AKAGA GLACIER

KARAVELOVA POINT

WEDDELL SEA

PRINCESS MARTHA COAST

MØGSTERBREKKA

EVA PERÓN BAY

CASSANDRA NUNATAK

JENNY ISLAND

GOODENOUGH GLACIER

ADELAIDE ISLAND

MARGUERITE BAY

RONNE ICE SHELF

ANTARCTIC

DEATLEY ISLAND

MT. ULMER
JACOBSEN VALLEY
KLENOVA PEAK

WEST ANTARCTICA

SOUTHERN OCEAN

MARIE BYRD LAND

PACIFIC OCEAN

Women in Antarctica map.

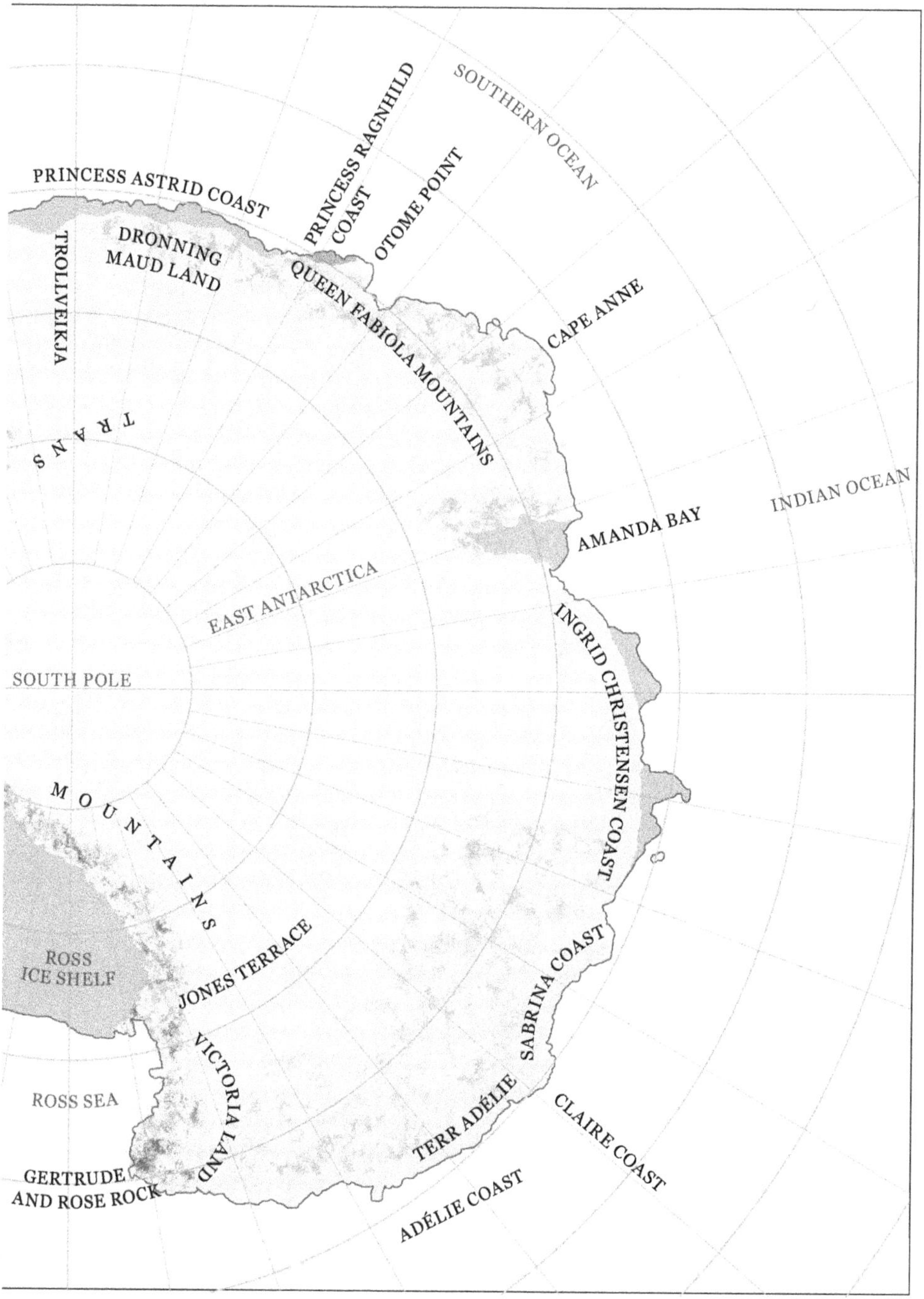

SOUTHERN OCEAN
PRINCESS RAGNHILD COAST
OTOME POINT
PRINCESS ASTRID COAST
DRONNING MAUD LAND
TROLLVEIKJA
QUEEN FABIOLA MOUNTAINS
CAPE ANNE
TRANS
AMANDA BAY
INDIAN OCEAN
EAST ANTARCTICA
INGRID CHRISTENSEN COAST
SOUTH POLE
MOUNTAINS
SABRINA COAST
JONES TERRACE
ROSS ICE SHELF
VICTORIA LAND
TERR ADÉLIE
ROSS SEA
CLAIRE COAST
GERTRUDE AND ROSE ROCK
ADÉLIE COAST

AUTHOR'S NOTE

AS A BIOGRAPHY of Jackie Ronne, this book, in part, examines her role in the Ronne Antarctic Research Expedition and does not attempt to provide a comprehensive history of this scientific mission. Likewise, Finn Ronne appears in these pages primarily as his life and career impacted on his wife. The time is long past due for a full and balanced account of this important Antarctic expedition as well as a biography of the complex explorer Finn Ronne.

ACKNOWLEDGEMENTS

A SERENDIPITOUS MEETING with Karen Ronne Tupek during the book tour promoting my biography of Arctic explorer Louise Arner Boyd led to enthusiastic discussions about her mother, Jackie Ronne. I already knew about Jackie, as she was a friend of Miss Boyd, a fellow member of the Society of Woman Geographers, and an Antarctic icon in her own right. Like Boyd and so many other extraordinary women whose lives and accomplishments remain obscured and unsung, Jackie Ronne's biography had not yet been written. I took my meeting with Karen to be a good luck sign from Boyd.

Over the three-and-a-half-year period of this book's gestation, Karen generously placed the voluminous family archives fully at my disposal, participated in extensive interview sessions, shared Ronne family contacts, and answered hundreds of my probing questions with endless patience, grace, and good humour. And she never once emailed this slow and methodical writer to ask about the book: "So, is it done yet?!"

I was mindful of the fact that Jackie and Finn Ronne are renowned public figures, but, at the same time, they were Karen's own mom and dad. The trust she placed in me to write a fair-minded, balanced, well-documented, and accurate life of her mother was deeply felt and appreciated. From a professional perspective, I would like to recognize and celebrate Karen's lifelong commitment to nurturing the Antarctic legacy of the Rønne/Ronne family. It is due to her diligence that the significant Ronne family archives and artifacts have been conserved in institutions around the world and she has done future historians (and her parents) a tremendous service in doing so.

One of the great joys of being a biographer is being let into the private world of one's subject if only for a short time. I have considered it a privilege to speak with the friends and family members of Jackie and Finn Ronne, as well as those connected with members of the Ronne Antarctic Research Expedition. In particular, I was privileged to interview at length the two surviving members of the expedition: Robert R.H. Dodson and Jorge di Giorgio, and I am grateful for their insight and memories. Jahn Rønne in Norway provided important assistance to me at various stages in my journey and his kindness was appreciated. A special thanks to Kevin Latady for providing access to his voluminous family archives and for his hospitality and ongoing support.

I thank the following individuals for sharing their precious research, photographs, maps, and stories with me and for encouraging me on this journey: Roberta Akin, John C. Behrendt, Joan Boothe, Noel D. Broadbent, Caroline F. Butson, Rick Butson, Eleanor "Lee" Byrd, Dean Chance, Rosalie Thompson Dale, the late Paul C. Dalrymple, Carol Devine, *Ernest* Journal, Jane Fanshawe, Kathryn Fiske, Susan Fiske Gagne, Joani Graves, Guy Guthridge, Jimmy Hassage, Ann Park Hawthorne, Laura Jeffery, Robb Kendrick, Jane-Alexandra Krehbiel, Kristin Larson, Jere H. Lipps, Clyde McCauley, Christopher McClary, Ian McLean, J. McKim Malville, Sarah Marlow, Aidan Meighan, William G. Meserve, Michael Parfit, Polly Penhale, Robert Pope Jr., James B. Robertson, Arthur Schlossbach, Marilyn Schlossbach, Paul Schlossbach, Laurie Gwen Shapiro, Monica Kristensen Sølas, Catherine Holder Spude, Robert Spude, Jane Storey, William Sumrall Barton A. Thompson, Daniel G. Thompson, Alan Tupek, Jonathan Walton, Robert M. Weaver, David Wilson, and several other individuals who wished to remain anonymous.

In addition, I would like to thank the following for their professionalism and willingness to assist me in clarifying abstruse matters relating to my project: Adrian Almond; the American Alpine Club; the American Heritage Center, the University of Wyoming; the Antarctican Society; Beverley Ayer, the British Antarctic Survey; Daniel Barbieri, the National Academy of Sciences; the BAS Club, Marian Bauman, the Neptune Public Library; Fran Becque; Dian Belanger; Cynthia Darlington Beyer; Robert Blanchette, Naoma Boneham, Scott Polar Research Institute; the Brooks School; Tiffany H. Cabrera, U.S. Department of State; Peter Clarkson, Scott Polar Research Institute; Geoff Cooper, British Antarctic Survey; Alan Delozier, University Archivist, Seton Hall University; Noel Downham; the Fay School; Nathan Fenney, British Antarctic Survey; Lacey Flint, the Explorers Club Archives; Adrian Fox, British Antarctic Survey; Melissa Francis, Stewart Library, Special Collections, Weber State University; Brett Freiburger, Institution Archivist, Woods Hole Oceanographic Institution; Becky Fullerton; Thad Garrett, Cosmos Club; Janice Goldblum, National Academy of Sciences; William Grace, Tyrrell Historical Library, Beaumont, Texas; Robert Headland, Scott Polar Research Institute; Keith Holmes; Ieuan Hopkins, British Antarctic Survey; Laura Hovenac, formerly of the Curator Branch, Naval History and Heritage Command; Mary Jane Johnson, Phi Mu Headquarters; Brigette Kamsler, Special Collections Research Center, Gelman Library, George Washington University; Susanne Kayyali; Laura Kissel, Byrd Polar and Climate Research Center; the Library of Congress; Philip Lund, Scott Polar Research Institute; Paulette Lutz, Howard County Historical Society; Allison Maier, Tufts University; the Maryland Historical Society; the Maryland State Archives; Lizzie Meek, Antarctic Heritage Trust of New Zealand; Denise D. Monbarren, Special Collections, the College of Wooster; the National Archives, London; the National Archives for Records Administration, Washington, D.C.; Pamela J. Overmann, Navy Art Collection, Naval History and Heritage Command; Philip Pelkey; Kevin Roberts, British Antarctic Survey; Jahn Rønne; Karin Schaefer; Rob Schoeberlein, City Archivist, Baltimore City Archives; Richard Scoffom; the Scott Polar Research Institute; Laura Snow; Andre B. Sobocicnski, Historian, Communications Directorate, U.S. Bureau of Medicine and Surgery; Ramona Stoltz, the Columbian Women of George Washington University; the UK Antarctic Heritage Trust; Mary van Balgooy, Society of Woman Geographers; Myra Walton; Allan Wearden; and Robin Fanning White, Phi Mu. I am also grateful to my editor, Dominic Farrell, for his careful wordsmithing, as well as to Elena Radic and Kathryn Lane and all the team at Dundurn Press for their stewardship of this book.

Finally, I express my thanks to my family and friends for their ongoing love, support, and interest in my work. And to Duncan, I owe my gratitude for technical assistance, maps, and a listening ear, but mostly, for his love, respect, and unyielding belief in me as a writer.

APPENDIX ONE

MAJOR SCIENTIFIC FINDINGS OF THE RONNE ANTARCTIC RESEARCH EXPEDITION: SUMMARY

1. GEOLOGY AND GEOMORPHOLOGY

Studies conducted by Robert L. Nichols, Tufts University.

Studies conducted at over twenty sites with 150 days committed to field study.

Data collected on deglaciation, the average thickness of the Antarctic continental ice cap, ice, features including talus, marine cliffs, block terraces, elevated beaches, and mudflows. A significant collection of geological specimens was gathered.

Organizations that benefitted were the Geological Society of America and Tufts College.

2. SEISMOLOGY AND GEOPHYSICS

Studies conducted by Andrew Thompson, Columbia University, with Jackie Ronne as (unacknowledged) assistant.

Maintained continuous seismological, tidal, and magnetic observations at Stonington Island. Recorded 170 earthquakes and forty local disturbances.

This data was critical in locating southern earthquakes near South America and New Zealand.

Provided information to, and worked co-operatively with, the Jesuit Seismological Association, Columbia University, and the U.S. Coast and Geodetic Survey.

3. METEOROLOGY AND ASTROPHYSICS

Studies conducted by Harries-Clichy Peterson, Cornell University.

Collected weather data from shipboard observations to and from Antarctica, East Base, on Stonington Island, several outposts, and locations identified during long-distance trail parties. Additional data was gathered on specific meteorological problems in Antarctica.

Data shared with the U.S. Weather Bureau.

4. SHIP ENGINEERING

Studies conducted by Charles Hassage.

Provided information about the performance of the ship's engines to the U.S. Navy.

Results for geology, geomorphology, seismology, geophysics, meteorology, astrophysics, and ship engineering provided in "Scientific Results of Ronne Antarctic Research Expedition 1946–1948. Compiled by Ronne Antarctic Research Expedition September 1, 1948."

Submitted to the Office of Naval Research, U.S. Navy, Washington, D.C.

5. AVIATION AND AERIAL PHOTOGRAPHY

Studies conducted by William Latady, photographer; James Lassiter, pilot; Charles Adams, pilot; and James Robertson, mechanic; with Jennie Darlington as (unacknowledged) assistant.

A detailed analysis was conducted about: (a) the performance and procedures of the use of three airplanes and aircraft equipment; (b) cameras, film, development, and airplanes used during aerial photography; (c) radio communications; and (d) operations of the army cargo carrier Weasel.

Results provided in "Reports Covering Tests conducted on the Ronne Antarctic Research Expedition of the American Antarctic Association, Inc. for U.S. Air Force under Contract No. W33-038 ac-16047 (17112) July 15, 1948."

6. HUMAN ECOLOGY

Studies conducted by Robert Dodson, Harvard University.

Presented a detailed analysis from data collected on the use of cold-weather equipment and supplies used by RARE members, including food, clothing, tents, stoves, lanterns, eating utensils, and dog-team equipment.

Results provided in "Report of Quartermaster Equipment on the Ronne Antarctic Research Expedition" (1948) submitted to the Office of the Quartermaster General, Military Planning Division, Research and Development Branch.

7. GEOGRAPHY AND EXPLORATION

Studies conducted by Finn Ronne, expedition leader.

From Marguerite Bay, travelled along the west coast of the Palmer Peninsula, over Alexander I Island, Charcot Island, Ruth Bugge Islands, through the George VI Sound, and along the Robert English Coast. Also, up to Adelaide Island and Mikkelson Island.

From Marguerite Bay, travelled along the east coast of the Palmer Peninsula, over the Larsen Ice Shelf, Hearst Island, Cape Boggs, Hilton Bay, Wright Inlet, along the Lassiter Ice Shelf into what became known as "Edith Ronne Land." Also, as far as Coats Land.

With the British team, surveyed the Richard Black Coast on the east side of Palmer Land from Cape Knowles to Gardner Bay.

Data used in the generation of maps for the U.S. Geological Survey.

APPENDIX TWO

WOMEN IN ANTARCTICA TIMELINE

1935

Caroline Mikkelsen becomes the first woman to set foot on an Antarctican island.

1937

Ingrid Christensen, along with daughter Augusta Sofie Christensen, Lillemor Rachlew, and Solveig Widerøe become the first women to set foot on the Antarctican mainland.

1947–1948

Jackie Ronne is the first American woman to step onto the Antarctic continent and the first woman to actively participate in an Antarctic expedition.

Jackie Ronne and Jennie Darlington are the first women to overwinter in Antarctica.

1956

Marine geologist Maria Klenova is the first female scientist to participate in an Antarctic expedition as part of a team from the U.S.S.R.

1957

Pan-Am flight attendants Patricia Hepinstall and Ruth Kelly are the first American women to visit McMurdo Station as part of a commercial flight.

Publication of *My Antarctic Honeymoon: A Year at the Bottom of the World* by Jennie Darlington. This is the first book about Antarctica from a woman's perspective.

1960

Artist and poet Nel Law becomes the first Australian woman to visit Antarctica when she travelled to Mawson Station with her husband, explorer Phillip Law.

1969

First all-female expedition to Antarctica. Led by geochemist Dr. Lois Jones, the team includes geologist Eileen McSaveney, biologist Kay Lindsay, and chemistry student Terry Tickhill Terrell. Also accompanying them are science writer Jean Pearson and biologist Pamela Young.

Biologist Christine Müller-Schwarze is the first American woman to work on the mainland of Antarctica, doing so with her husband, a fellow biologist.

1970

Engineer Irene Peden becomes the first American woman to work in the interior of Antarctica as the principal investigator on a project.

1971

Jackie and Finn Ronne are the first married couple to visit the South Pole.

1974

Mary Alice McWhinnie is the first woman to serve as a chief scientist at an Antarctic research base (McMurdo Station).

McWhinnie and Sister Mary Odile Cahoon are the first women to over-winter at McMurdo Station.

Australian women travel to Antarctica in an official capacity for the first time.

Elena Marty and Jan Boyd are the first female civilian contractors to work in Antarctica.

1975

Eleanor Honnywill is the first female recipient of the Fuchs Medal from the British Antarctic Survey.

1975–1976

Mary Alice McWhinnie is the first female scientist to work at Palmer Station.

1978–1979

Dr. Michele Raney is the first female physician to overwinter at the South Pole and the first woman to overwinter at an Antarctic inland station (Amundsen-Scott South Pole Station).

U.S. Navy advertises for "qualified female volunteers to overwinter in Antarctica" for the first time.

1983

Janet Thomson becomes the first British woman scientist to work inside the Antarctic Circle.

1985

Scientist Ann Waylette and cook Rebecca Heimark are the first women to overwinter at Palmer Station.

1986

Virginia Fiennes is the first female recipient of the Polar Medal from the British Antarctic Survey.

1988

Lis Densmore is the first woman to summit Mount Vinson, the highest peak in Antarctica, located in the Ellsworth Mountains.

1989

Americans Shirley Metz and Victoria "Tori" Murden are the first women to reach the South Pole overland by ski. They are part of a privately funded group led by Adventure Network International.

Diana Patterson becomes head of Australia's Mawson Station and is the first female Antarctic station leader.

1990

German polar medicine specialist Monika Puskeppeleit is the doctor and station leader of the first all-female team to overwinter in Antarctica (at the Georg von Neumayer Station).

1992

Botanist Gillian Wratt becomes the first woman director of the New Zealand Antarctic Programme.

Judy Chesser Coffman of the U.S. Navy becomes the first female helicopter pilot to fly in Antarctica.

1993

American Ann Bancroft leads the American Women's Expedition to the South Pole.

Ann Bancroft becomes the first woman to reach both the South and the North Poles.

1994

Norwegian Liv Arnesen becomes the first woman to ski solo and unsupported to the South Pole.

1995–1996

Carol Devine leads the first civilian cleanup of Antarctica, working with the Russian Antarctic Expedition.

2000–2001

Liv Arnesen and Ann Bancroft become the first women to cross the Antarctic continent from Queen Maud Land to the Ross Ice Shelf.

2004

Publication of Jackie Ronne's autobiography, *Antarctica's First Lady: Memoirs of the First American Woman to Set Foot on the Antarctic Continent and Winter-Over*. This is the first autobiography of an active female Antarctic expeditioner.

2011

Barbara Hillary becomes the first Black American woman to reach the South Pole.

2012

Felicity Aston becomes the first woman to cross Antarctica solo.

2013

Paleoclimatologist Jane Francis becomes the first female director of the British Antarctic Survey.

2016

The organization Homeward Bound launches the first all-female expedition to train STEMM (science, technology, engineering, medicine, and mathematics) leaders.

2020

Anja Blacha from Germany conducts the longest solo, unsupported, unassisted polar expedition by a woman.

2022

Preet Chandi becomes the first woman of colour to complete a solo expedition in Antarctica.

NOTES

Prologue

1   Only books by American expedition members Finn Ronne (1949, 1971), Jennie Darlington (1957), and Jackie Ronne (2004) have been published about the Ronne Antarctic Research Expedition. Books by Falkland Islands Dependencies Survey (FIDS) members Kevin Walton (1982) and Dr. Richard "Dick" Butson (2010), who were stationed at the British base on Stonington Island during the same period, relate their own personal experiences.

2   In 1968 the U.S. Geological Survey formally determined that the Ronne Ice Shelf was "[n]amed for Edith Ronne, wife of Captain Ronne, who made important contributions to the planning, organization, and operation of Ronne Antarctic Research Expedition (RARE) and who served as observer at the Stonington Island base while Ronne Antarctic Research Expedition (RARE) members were in the field."

Jackie Ronne would have been surprised when the Ronne Ice Shelf made the headlines over a decade after her death. In May 2021, Iceberg A-76 calved from the western side of the Ronne Ice Shelf into the Weddell Sea. Heralded as the world's largest iceberg, it measured 170 kilometres in length and just under twenty-six kilometres in width. A-76 was created as a result of the natural cycle of calving in the region.

3   However, Admiral Byrd's supporters objected to the truncating of the name "Marie Byrd Land" to "Byrd Land." Although she never visited Antarctica, Admiral Byrd's wife is still commemorated by the terrestrial geographic feature Marie Byrd Land, as well as the marine feature Marie Byrd Seamount.

     In "Women and Civilisation on Ice," Lisbeth Lewander writes: "Although female explorers and travellers have been present in both polar areas ... men's biographies, travel accounts, reports and so on have simply failed to present the few women who have visited ... the Antarctic. Moreover, on the few occasions when women are mentioned, they are marginalised or even made fun of."

4   Naturalist-explorer Jeanne Baret is sometimes mentioned as travelling to the Falkland Islands (see Elizabeth Chipman, *Women on the Ice: A History of Women in the Far South*), but Baret's biographer, Danielle Clode, disputes this claim. For more information on Baret, see *In Search of the Woman Who Sailed the World* by Danielle Clode.

5   In *Women on the Ice*, Elizabeth Chipman records that in 1839 an unknown woman on board either the British ship *Eliza Scott* or the *Sabrina* may have been the first woman to sight Antarctica. She states: "Perhaps it is appropriate that this first woman known to cross the Antarctic Circle and to see the land of the Antarctic continent is anonymous. Without name, nationality, race, nor social status, she may have been any one of us."

6   See *Such is the Antarctic* by Lars Christensen for further details about Ingrid Christensen's adventures in Antarctica. Lars dedicated this book: "To my wife who accompanied me on my voyages in the Antarctic."

7   Columnist J.B. Martin wrote in his column Shipwise in the *Anderson Sunday Herald* on August 7, 1960, "I can frankly say that we do not know who or when the first woman visited the Antarctic. No doubt the lady would not want us to know or publish her name." Martin

implies that a true "lady" would not be interested in claiming a momentous geographic first in the same way that a man would. Rather (he believes), it would be an accomplishment of which she would likely be ashamed.

PART ONE: BEFORE ANTARCTICA

Chapter 1: Overcoming the Odds

1 Jackie Ronne was an intensely private person and rarely revealed her true feelings about her parents and childhood. However, in a letter written on the occasion of her father's death, she refers to him as "nearly a saint" and implies that he had had a difficult life with her mother.

2 Founded in 1852, Phi Mu is the second oldest sorority in the United States. Other well-known Phi Mu sisters are aviator Jerrie Mock, who was the first woman to fly solo around the world, and astronaut Mary Ellen Weber. For more information, see phimu.historyit.com.

3 The Columbian Women was known for its support of women's equality. For example, it sent a contingency to the suffrage memorial ceremonies in 1921 for the unveiling of a statue of Susan B. Anthony, Elizabeth Cady Stanton, and Lucretia Mott, and contributed to the work of Nobel laureate Marie Curie, who visited the United States in 1921. The Columbian Women also marched with three thousand other women on August 26, 1977, in support of the ratification of the Equal Rights Amendment. For more information, see Eden Orelove's GW Today article, "Looking Back: The Columbian Women."

4 In 1948, after Jackie had left the department, Alger Hiss was charged with being a Communist spy by the infamous House Un-American Activities Committee. He was found guilty and served almost four years in prison. His conviction remains contentious to this day.

Chapter 2: Meeting Finn

1   Dr. Irvine Gardner became chief of the Division of Optics and Meteorology for the National Bureau of Standards in 1950 and president of the Optical Society of America in 1958.

2   According to the U.S. Department of Labor, the number of female employees working at the Department of State increased steadily from 2,074 (1939) to 2,277 (1944) to 3,860 (1947). The number of men employed there fluctuated from 3,685 (1939) to 1,327 (1944) to 3,935 (1947). A similar rate is evident in some but not all U.S. government departments during this period.

3   Rønne is the correct spelling of the Norwegian family name. Finn anglicized his surname when he moved to the United States in 1923. Today, Norwegian family members are known by Rønne and American family members are known by Ronne.

4   Before he had even met Jackie, Finn had filed for divorce in 1939 on the grounds of desertion, but a divorce was not formally granted until June 1943.

PART TWO: THE RONNE ANTARCTIC RESEARCH EXPEDITION (1946–1948)

Chapter 3: The Beginning

1   Known in the United States as the Palmer Peninsula at the time, it is now called the Antarctic Peninsula. It is known as Graham Land in the United Kingdom, Tierra de O'Higgins in Chile, and Tierra de San Martin in Argentina. It is the northernmost point of the Antarctic mainland.

2   The association between Byrd and Finn was always difficult; ideas about the reasons behind that difficulty divided the polar community in their time and still does today. The lengthy correspondence between

the men reflects the ebb and flow of a tempestuous relationship. Many of the letters are filled with angry recriminations and defensive posturing. Both Jackie and Finn Ronne reveal their animosity toward Byrd in their books.

Although his stellar reputation as an American polar explorer has been tarnished in recent years, Byrd still inspires intense loyalty in Antarctic circles. But Byrd's critics exist as well and attest to his active opposition to Finn's planned expedition. Roger Revelle worked in the Office of Naval Research at that time. He was a neutral party since he knew both men on a professional rather than a personal basis.

> The Antarctic man on the staff of the CNO [Chief of Naval Operations] was Rear Admiral Richard Evelyn Byrd, the famous polar explorer. He was dead set against the Navy giving any support at all to Ronne. The reason was that Ronne had "betrayed" him.
>
> "How [has] Ronne betrayed you, Admiral?" [I asked]. I have a vivid picture of this in my mind still, because he literally was somewhat insane, Admiral Byrd, I think.
>
> His eyes flashed and his face got flushed and he said, "He arrived in New York a day before I did and he gave a press conference!" Literally the word he used was "betrayal."
>
> So the result was that we got nothing out of CNO. (R. Revelle, 1984, Oral History interview)

3 Erling Strom is considered the father of alpine skiing in the Pacific Northwest and became well known for making the first successful assault on Mount McKinley by ski.

4 The poem "Vanity — Thou Art A Woman" was written by the Ronnes' good friend Harold Merriman Dudley upon the occasion of Jackie Ronne participating in the expedition. Although tongue-in-cheek, it is

typical of most written work about women explorers from this period, as it focuses exclusively on Jackie's appearance. No mention is made of her intelligence and talents (beyond the ability to attract men) or what she contributed to the team.

Chapter 4: Getting There

1   In a September 22, 1977, letter to Jere H. Lipps, Finn placed the blame squarely on Harry's shoulders, stating that Harry had instructed that the tanks of the plane be filled prior to being loaded on the ship. This additional weight had caused the lug to break as the plane was loaded on board the *Port of Beaumont*. Subsequent testing of the lug later revealed a hairline fracture.

2   At the time the American team arrived on Stonington Island, a contingent of the British team were away conducting fieldwork. Although Dr. Dick Butson neglects to mention the incident in his own memoir, Jennie Darlington reported that he responded with utter shock, dismay, and embarrassment when meeting her unexpectedly for the first time on a hill outside the British base.

3   The British did a rigorous job of documenting the condition and contents of East Base over an extended period of time, from early 1946, when they first arrived on Stonington Island, to late 1948 after RARE left. They also monitored the activities of the Argentine and Chilean naval forces during their unexpected visits to Stonington in 1947.

4   For a further discussion of the U.K.-U.S. relationship in Antarctica, see *Claiming the Ice: Britain and the Antarctic 1900–1950* by John Dudeney and John Sheail.

5   Interestingly, the two countries have a further point of difference regarding the island. Americans pronounce it "Stōnington," with a long "o," whereas the British pronounce it "Stŏnington," with a short "o."

6 Upon their arrival at the base, newlywed Jennie Darlington was quickly disabused of any romantic notions she might have harboured: "I had a last, lingering, bridelike thought. I wondered if it would occur to Harry to carry me over the threshold. It was a silly, feminine thought, as out of place in this man's world as I felt."

Chapter 5: The Adventure Gets Underway

1 As Klaus Dodds et al. note in *Handbook on the Politics of Antarctica*, "There have been strong links between the news media and Antarctic exploration since the Heroic Era began. Fame was a product not only of [an] explorer's abilities, but of the way their feats were marketed to the public." Beau Riffenburgh investigates this in *The Myth of the Explorer: The Press, Sensationalism and Geographical Discovery*.

2 Harry's lack of emotional control had already been in evidence at the Fay School and Brooks School he had attended as a young man. His school reports record his "poor judgement," "temperamental upsets," and the fact that "Harry resents discipline of any kind."

3 Like Finn, Harry had also been a team member of the 1939–1941 U.S. Antarctic Service Expedition, in which he had held a junior position.

Chapter 6: Striving for Glory

1 In 1948 Dr. Richard Butson received the Albert Medal in Gold for Saving Life on Land (supplanted, in 1972, by the George Cross) in recognition of this selfless act.

2 The American Meteorological Society defines a "water sky" as "the dark appearance of the underside of a cloud layer when it is over a surface of open water." This term is frequently mentioned in polar accounts, including Francis McClintock's *The Voyage of the 'Fox' in Arctic Seas: In Search of Franklin and His Companions* and in Fridtjof Nansen's *Farthest North* when discussing George De Long's U.S. Arctic Expedition.

3   Unbeknownst to Harry or the rest of the team, Harry's mother, the formidable Ethel Darlington Garrett, had donated a number of books to the RARE library. This donation was not formally recognized.

4   Unfortunately, Jorge's imagination ran away with him, as he later publicly declared that he and Jennie had been in love during the expedition and would ask to wash dishes together so they could surreptitiously hold hands. This would have been an impossibility in such close quarters. There has never been a hint that Jennie focused on any other man than her husband while at East Base. However, it was later stated that after the expedition was over, she received three proposals from team members.

5   Between 1948 and 1956, the USS *Burton Island* took part in nineteen Arctic and Alaskan cruises. In 1966 it was transferred from the U.S. Navy to the U.S. Coast Guard and went on eight Operation Deep Freeze operations to Antarctica.

6   It was lucky that the expedition returned to the United States when it did, as Cynthia Darlington, daughter of Jennie and Harry Darlington, was born only five months later.

7   Finn thought that he had carefully removed everything of value; he would have been shocked to learn that one of the American flags that he had taken to Antarctica and used at East Base ended up in British hands. Unbeknownst to the American team, one of these flags was purloined by a FIDS member and kept in his attic for many decades with an explanatory note attached. It is currently in the possession of the Byrd Polar and Climate Research Center at the Ohio State University. Additionally, an incriminating paper containing notes in Finn's handwriting about possible retaliatory action Finn contemplated taking against Harry Darlington should Harry attempt to discredit him or the expedition was found in the snow near East Base after the departure of RARE. This note was found by a FIDS member and is currently in the British Antarctic Survey archives.

8 Talbert Abrams. Undated. "Ode to Edith 'Jackie Rabbit' Ronne." Unpublished. Finn Ronne and Edith M. Ronne Papers, 1900–2012 MSS 86269 Manuscript Division, Library of Congress, Washington, D.C.

Chapter 7: Afterward

1 The letter of reference sent on September 10, 1948, by Finn Ronne to General Clifton B. Cates, Commandant of the U.S. Marine Corps, on behalf of Harries-Clichy Peterson is characteristic of many such letters in the Ronne Archives located in the Library of Congress.

> Dear Sir,
>
> It gives me pleasure to advise you of the excellent service performed by Lt. Harries-Clichy Peterson, expedition physicist with the Ronne Antarctic Research Expedition, 1946–48. The example set by his extremely loyal and energetic support of exped-ition aims made him a most valuable man to have on my staff. In addition to the excellent work he and his assistants achieved in physical sciences research, Lt Peterson proved outstandingly helpful in the organ-ization of the expedition, during the sea voyages, and in numerous ways at the Antarctic base. During the nearly two years in which he served the expedition, Lt Peterson displayed the highest degree of initiative, responsibility and wholehearted cooperation in even the most difficult of circumstances. It is hoped that if future events recall him to active duty, the Corps will give due recognition to the abilities he has acquired and demonstrated.
>
> Respectfully yours, (Finn Ronne and Edith M. Ronne Papers, 1900–2012 MSS 86269 Manuscript Division, Library of Congress, Washington, D.C.)

The majority of the RARE members also kept in contact with each other and with FIDS members for many years. For example, Dr. Don McLean, the Darlingtons, and the McClarys remained close to Andy Thompson and his family, and Kevin Walton of the FIDS team maintained regular contact with Bob Dodson and Bill Latady.

2   Despite widespread acknowledgement amongst Antarctic historians of the scientific accomplishments of the Ronne Antarctic Research Expedition (see Kenneth Bertrand's *Americans in Antarctica, 1775– 1948*; Joan Boothe's *The Storied Ice*; and David Day's *Antarctica: A Biography*), the image of the expedition is still negatively affected by the personal conflicts that developed between team members. Some writers focus more on Finn's success as an explorer and downplay the scientific achievements of the expedition. See G.E. Fogg's *A History of Antarctic Science*, where the author writes: "Some highly successful explorers of the Antarctic ... have left no appreciable legacy of science, amongst these are Amundsen and Ronne."

3   On January 1, 1953, the U.S. Board on Geographic Names designated a headland at the entrance to Hilton Inlet on the east coast of Palmer Land as Cape Darlington. This had been discovered during the U.S. Antarctic Service Expedition (1939–1941), during which Harry Darlington (also a participant in the later Ronne Antarctic Research Expedition) had participated. This feature was originally thought to be an island, but RARE flights later determined it to be a headland. Finn Ronne did not make this recommendation on behalf of Darlington.

4   Byrd's granddaughter Eleanor "Lee" Byrd cannot recall Byrd privately expressing any rancour toward Finn Ronne. According to her, Byrd's animosity was reserved exclusively for Bernt Balchen, who publicly disputed Byrd's claim to have been the first to have flown to the North Pole in 1926. For further information, see *Explorer: The Life of Richard E. Byrd* by Lisle A. Rose.

5　L. Sprague de Camp later "immortalized" the Ronne–de Camp part-
nership in his short story "The Hand of Zei," published in 1951. Set in
Antarctica, the protagonists are a stalwart explorer and his ghostwriting
assistant.

PART THREE: WORKING FOR ANTARCTICA

Chapter 8: An Explorer's Private Life

1　For a more complete examination of the life and remarkable accom-
plishments of intrepid explorer Louise Arner Boyd, see *The Polar
Adventures of a Rich American Dame: A Life of Louise Arner Boyd* by
Joanna Kafarowski.

2　Research into the lives of polar wives and their impact on their ex-
plorer husbands is fairly modest. Most notable are *Widows of the Ice:
The Women that Scott's Antarctic Expedition Left Behind* by Anne
Fletcher; *Snow Widows: The Scott Expedition and the Women They
Left Behind* and *Woman with the Iceberg Eyes: Oriana F. Wilson* by
Katherine MacInnes; *Polar Wives: The Remarkable Women Behind the
World's Most Daring Explorers* by Kari Herbert (herself the daughter
of Sir Wally Herbert); *Lady Franklin's Revenge* by Ken McGoogan; *My
Arctic Journal: A Year Among Ice-Fields and Eskimos* and *The Snow
Baby* by Josephine Diebitsch Peary; *Green Seas and White Ice* and *I
Married an Explorer* by Miriam McMillan; *The Snow People* and *The
Reindeer People* by Marie Herbert; *This Everlasting Silence: The Love
Letters Between Paquita Delpratt and Douglas Mawson, 1911–1914*,
edited by Nancy Robinson Flannery; *An Antarctic Affair* by Emma
McEwin; and *A Great Task of Happiness: The Life of Kathleen Scott* by
Louisa Young.

3　Other less significant, privately funded Antarctic expeditions that followed RARE included one led by David Lewis sailing on the *Ice Bird*
in 1972, and another sailing on the *Solo* in 1977–1978. On this latter

expedition, Lewis collected data on sea temperature and salinity measurements near icebergs, as well as biological and geological specimens.

4   Published in 1961, *Antarctic Command* held nothing back. His 1949 book about the Ronne Antarctic Research Expedition conformed to the unspoken code adhered to by polar explorers in which successes were valorized and failures disguised. However, in *Antarctic Command* Finn and Jackie enumerated everything that went wrong on that expedition. In a review of the book, Finn's Antarctic colleague and friend John Roscoe wrote:

> [It] may make him few friends and many enemies. He could be considered either brave or a professional fool to describe the details of an expedition on which young civilian scientists and Navy personnel found themselves pitted against one another for status symbols, living comforts, peculiar privileges and opportunities to work effectively. It was old explorer vs. neophyte, enlisted man vs officer, Navy vs civilian, airman vs groundling, ship's crew vs shore party, wintering party vs visiting summer VIPs and within these groups, individual against individual. ("Finn Ronne Blasts Antarctic Expedition," *Washington Post*, Oct. 29, 1961, p. E6)

As an experienced Antarctic colleague, Roscoe knew what he was talking about and recognized that, as the leader, Finn was ultimately held accountable. With prescience, Roscoe wrote, "[S]ome explorers may come to call [this book] 'Ronne's Revenge' or 'Ronne's Frustrations.'" Writing the book might have eased some of the angst experienced by Finn during the expedition in the short-term. However, in the long-term, *Antarctic Command* has damaged Finn, as several living expedition members continued to malign him long after Finn's death.

5   Today, over fifty years later, former members of Ronne's IGY team remain critical of his leadership abilities. It is important to keep in mind, though, the results of a little-known psychological study conducted of all members of the Ellsworth Station (including Finn) immediately following the conclusion of the IGY mission in 1958. In an article, "Psychological Study at an Antarctic IGY Station," published following their study, psychologists Charles Mullin and H.J.M. Connery concluded that although a "generally critical attitude toward the policies and practices of the leader" existed, this attitude had a positive impact on the group dynamic by providing a focus for the "hostilities that are inevitably generated in a group of men whose interests and backgrounds are disparate and who are thrown together under conditions of enforced close personal associations for a long period of time."

The psychologists noted that the men at Ellsworth Station endured greater isolation from outside contacts than the other six American IGY stations in Antarctica. Mullin and Connery identified unrealistic expectations on the part of most of the expedition members as a problem, as the enlisted men had anticipated "a democratic Utopia relatively free of discipline and with an equal sharing of both chores and amenities," while the civilian scientists had expected "an academic cloister free of 'military interference' and the distraction of extracurricular duties." A hard group for any leader to deal with!

The psychologists' conclusions were significant. "There was general agreement that the 'basic objectives of the mission of the station were realized and, in some ways, exceeded,' despite their feelings about the leader." These results concur with a newspaper article in the *Washington Evening Star* ("Friction in Expedition at Antarctica Reported") on February 10, 1958, in which both the scientists and military team members acknowledge the scientific work was competently and thoroughly done.

Nevertheless, scathing comments by Malville (as quoted in Behrendt, 1990) and Behrendt (1998), combined with remarks made by Finn's Second Byrd Expedition colleagues Charles Passel in *Ice: The Antarctic Diaries of Charles F. Passel* and Stuart Paine in *Footsteps on the*

Ice: The Antarctic Diaries of Stuart D. Paine, Second Byrd Expedition and discussed in Lisle A. Rose's *The Life of Richard E. Byrd* and Dian Olson Belanger's *Deep Freeze: The United States, the International Geophysical Year, and the Origin's of Antarctica's Age of Science*, are revealing.

6   See *China as a Polar Great Power* by Anne-Marie Brady. According to Brady, "Antarctica is widely believed to be rich in mineral resources, however, the scientific evidence of this so far is scant."

7   As always, Jackie and Finn stood together on Antarctic matters. Finn declared to the American Polar Society on February 6, 1960: "The impact which the IGY made in opening up the Antarctic should not be underestimated. It provided the necessary wedge to renewed interest on an international scale undreamed of by the pioneers.… These worthy objectives have also been materially aided by the new international treaty on the Antarctic recently signed here in Washington."

This was a curious point of dissent between Thor Tollefson and the Ronnes. Tollefson was otherwise a strong supporter of Finn and commended him at length on June 12, 1963, in the House of Representatives when Finn was awarded the Citation of Merit from the Explorers Club.

Chapter 9: A New Era Begins

1   These four nations were Argentina, Chile, the United Kingdom, and the United States. Finn had a reason not to love the Argentine navy as it had actively cannibalized the American supplies at East Base on Stonington Island in the 1940s prior to the Ronne Antarctic Research Expedition. Although this had jeopardized the early success of his mission, Finn later chose to forget this.

2   Reich (1980, 203) wrote: "Information on the subject [of the development of commercial tourism in the Antarctic] has proved to be elusive, scattered and, in some cases, difficult to confirm."

Published in the November 4, 1910, issue of *The Press*:

> There is a possibility of the Antarctic regions be-
> ing visited by a party of tourists next year, Messrs
> Thomas Cook and Sons having put forward propos-
> als for the despatch of a vessel to McMurdo Sound.
> The trip, it is estimated, will take fifty days, and it
> is intended that the vessel should leave some New
> Zealand port about the end of the year, so as to arrive
> at the Antarctic in mid-summer. Already some mem-
> bers of the New Zealand Parliament, a number of
> ladies and several gentlemen interested in scientific
> matters, have made enquiries about the trip, which
> it is likely, will include a visit to the Sub-Antarctic
> islands of the Dominion.

3   From an unpublished report by Finn Ronne dated September 20, 1962, sent to the Central Intelligence Agency, titled, "Spitsbergen and Soviet Activities There." Finn Ronne and Edith M. Ronne Papers, 1900–2012 MSS 86269 Manuscript Division, Library of Congress, Washington, D.C.

4   The two men remembered the genesis for the idea of the first Antarctic cruise quite differently. In *Antarctica, My Destiny*, Finn states that since 1930 he himself had "harbored the dream of starting regular tourist cruises to Antarctic" (257); that he had lobbied various tour operators about this idea and had finally managed to convince Lindblad of the efficacy of this idea. In *Passport to Anywhere*, Lindblad claimed this idea was wholly his own.

5   See "Capt Finn Ronne's tourist expedition to Antarctica 1965." National Archives, London, England. FO371/179736. This is the file kept on Ronne's participation in this trip. It was primarily compiled by British polar scientist Brian Roberts, who had been one of the main proponents

of the Antarctic Treaty process from the United Kingdom. He was highly suspicious of Ronne's motives, in particular, and of the United States in general.

6   Mrs. Bessie Sweeney, "Women Find Antarctic Trip Is Filled with Thrills," *Baltimore Sun*, February 7, 1966. Guidelines and regulations regarding the behaviour of tourists around wildlife, environmental and heritage sites would not be identified and implemented for several decades.

7   The Terr-A-Qua Globe was on display for many years in the now-defunct Center for Polar Archives in the National Archives building in Washington, D.C. It is currently on display in the basement of the Library of Congress building in the Geography and Map Division. Sadly, the electric motor that enabled the globe to rotate and the illuminated element of the globe no longer function. See Jessie Kratz, "The 'Terr-A-Qua Globe,'" *Pieces of History* (blog), National Archives, January 17, 2018, prologue.blogs.archives.gov/2018/01/17/the-terr-a-qua-globe/.

Chapter 10: Life After Finn

1   In life as in death, most polar wives are recognized only as mere appendages of their renowned husbands. Wife of Robert Peary and explorer and author in her own right, Josephine Diebitsch Peary is buried in Arlington National Cemetery with her husband and is memorialized as "Beloved Wife." Also buried in Arlington are Marie Ames Byrd, wife of Admiral Byrd, who is remembered as "His Wife;" Henrietta Nesmith Greely, wife of Adolphus Greely, is remembered by her birth and death dates; and the second wife of Matthew Henson, Lucy Ross Henson is remembered as "beloved wife." Neither of Charles Wilkes's two wives or Bernt Balchen's ex-wife are buried there.

2   The period between roughly 1960 and 1980 is known as the "second wave of feminism" following the "first wave," which was characterized by the fight for women's suffrage in the early decades of the twentieth

century. The term was coined by journalist Martha Lear in the *New York Times* in 1968.

The effects of this second wave were not all positive, as there is evidence that there was a backlash against the women's movement during this era. The Reagan era was a long period of conservatism in which reproductive rights and affirmative action were under threat.

3 The Explorers Club opened its membership to women in 1981. Among the first female members were marine biologist Sylvia Earle, astronaut Kathryn Sullivan, mountaineer Vera Komarkova, and aviator Ingrid Pedersen.

4 Artist and wife of Phillip Law, Nel Law travelled to the Australian Antarctic Territory in an unofficial capacity in 1960, landing at Mawson Station.

5 For example, former IGY team member J. McKim Malville commented in his review of *Crevasse Roulette: The First Trans-Antarctic Crossing* by Jon Stephenson in *Arctic, Antarctic, and Alpine Research Journal* 42, no. 2 (May 2010): 238:

> Finn Ronne, our leader at Ellsworth, had little interest in the scientific program of the IGY. As far as we could tell, he was primarily interested in geographical discoveries for which he could get credit. Jon Stephenson, in fact, notes the problems we had at Ellsworth during the winter of 1957 and judges that "the greatest difficulties [at Ellsworth] probably resulted from his [Ronne's] inflated opinion of his own experience and knowledge."

6 There have been seven recipients of this award, including two women: Monica Kristensen Solås (1991) and Polly Penhale (2011).

7   Since the departure of the Ronne Antarctic Research Expedition on February 23, 1948, significant damage has occurred at East Base due to extreme weather and the salt-laden onshore drift storms. Conservation work was conducted there from the late 1970s until the early 1990s after it was declared a National Historic Site. See Lipps (1976, 1977, 1978), Broadbent (1992), Parfit and Kendrick (1993), and Spude and Spude (1993). Surprisingly, no conservation work was conducted again until an extensive project was carried out in 2017 by the United Kingdom Antarctic Heritage Trust. Antarctica's harsh environment continues to have an adverse effect there. More recently, scientists have identified an alarmingly increased rate of deterioration of the buildings and the historic artifacts caused by fungal growth. Due to climate change, this fungal growth has grave consequences for the future of East Base and other Antarctic historic sites and artifacts. See Blanchette and Held (2002), and Arenz and Blanchette (2008, 2009).

Epilogue

1   One example is the so-called "Sistine Ceiling" of the Weddell Hut at Australia's Mawson Station. The "Sistine Ceiling" was actually an eye-boggling collage of ninety-two 1970s and 1980s pornographic pin-ups described as a "shrine to the red-blooded male" and labelled as part of the national heritage. It was mysteriously destroyed in 2005.

BIBLIOGRAPHY

MANUSCRIPT COLLECTIONS

Andersen, Peter J. Papers. Polar Archives, Byrd Polar and Climate Research Center, Ohio State University, Columbus, Ohio.

Byrd, Robert E. Papers. Polar Archives, Byrd Polar and Climate Research Center, Ohio State University, Columbus, Ohio.

Darlington, Harry. File. Brooks School Archives, North Andover, Massachusetts.

———. File. Fay School Archives, Houston, Texas.

Falkland Islands Dependencies Survey Papers. British Antarctic Survey Archives, Cambridge, U.K.

Fiske, Clarence O. "Larry" Collection. Accession no. 9458. American Heritage Center, University of Wyoming, Laramie, Wyoming.

Latady, William R. File. Explorers Club Archives, New York, New York.

———. Latady family papers. Bedford, Massachusetts.

Lipps, Jere H. Papers. Polar Archives, Byrd Polar and Climate Research Center, Ohio State University, Columbus, Ohio.

McClary, Jane McIlvaine. Papers, 1947–1956. ARC 20737576. National Archives, Washington, D.C.

McLean, Donald. Expedition Diary. Michael Parfit papers. Sidney, British Columbia.

———. File. Explorers Club Archives, New York, New York.

Nichols, Robert L. Collection. Tufts University Archives and Special Collections, Tufts University, Medford, Massachusetts.

Ronne, Edith "Jackie." File. College of Wooster Archives Collection, College of Wooster, Wooster, Ohio.

———. File. George Washington University Special Collections, George Washington University, Washington, D.C.

———. File. Phi Mu Archives, National Headquarters, Peachtree City, Georgia.

———. Papers. Library of Congress, Washington, D.C.

———. Papers. Ronne family archive. Bethesda, Maryland.

———. Papers. Society of Woman Geographers Archives, Library of Congress, Washington, D.C.

Ronne, Finn. Archive. Naval History and Heritage Command, Washington, D.C.

———. Papers. Explorers Club, New York, New York.

———. Papers. FO 371/179736; OD 6/894; CO 78/267/1. National Archives, London, England.

———. Papers. Library of Congress, Washington, D.C.

———. Papers. 1942–1978. ARC 21986108. National Archives, Washington, D.C.

———. Papers. Ronne family archive. Bethesda, Maryland.

———. Papers. Stefansson Collection, Rauner Special Collections Library, Dartmouth College, New Hampshire.

Ronne Antarctic Research Expedition. Papers. American Geographical Society, University of Wisconsin, Milwaukee, Wisconsin.

Schlossbach, Isaac. File. Neptune Public Library, Neptune, New Jersey.

———. File. Tyrrell Historical Library, Beaumont, Texas.

———. Papers. 1928–1973. ARC 20014734. National Archives, Washington, D.C.

Smith, William. Papers. Polar Archives, Byrd Polar and Climate Research Center, Ohio State University, Columbus, Ohio.

Sweeney, Edward. File. Explorers Club Archives, New York, New York.

Wilkins, Hubert. Papers. Polar Archives, Byrd Polar and Climate Research Center, Ohio State University, Columbus, Ohio.

AUDIOVISUAL MATERIALS

Antarctic Heritage. "Stonington Island: Conserving the Historic Bases of the Antarctic Peninsula." YouTube video. 2:10. July 8, 2018. youtube.com /watch?v=EEe0as0kv-E.

"Antarctica, 1939–1941." Public.Resource.org. YouTube video. 1:10:16. youtube .com/watch?v= rjUJqTWeQwg.

Cravos, Claudia. "Antarctic 2014: Stonington Station." YouTube video. 10:45. July 8, 2016. youtube.com/watch?v=-B7BAN_1Eao.

"The Ends of the Earth: Finn Ronne's Antarctica." Video. n.d. Ronne family archives. gwillow.com. (2015, March 29).

Gould, Laurence M. "My 50 Years in Antarctica." Antarctican Society Memorial Lecture, Washington, D.C., April 19, 1979. Part 1: Introduction, Background of First Byrd Expedition, 31:00; Part 2: Selecting BAE I members, Crash in Rockefeller Mtns., Sledge Journey, 30:00; Part 3: ICY, SCAR, Antarctic Treaty, Women, Conclusion, 31:00. antarctican.org/my-50-years.

Krinke, Tyler. "Georges de Giorgio." YouTube video. 3:30. February 25, 2017. youtube.com/watch?v=f_4a5N1EKXg.

"Longines Chronoscope with Richard E. Byrd." YouTube video. 14:33. 1947. youtube.com/watch?v=PrdSal9uH28.

Mom & Pop Productions. "First Woman on the Ice." Vimeo video. 14:47. 2002. vimeo.com/195047920.

Naval History and Heritage. "Operation Deep Freeze I." YouTube video. 22:02. 1957. youtube.com/watch?v=uA-1F5NSjsU.

Tahiwi, Kingi Te Aho Aho Gillings. "Admiral Byrd's Third United States Antarctic Service Expedition." Ngā Taonga Sound and Vision video. 29:17. December 1939. ngataonga.org.nz/collections/catalogue /catalogue-item?record_id=194362.

ARTICLES, REPORTS, AND THESES

Anonymous. "The Cordell Hull Conference Room — Room 208." Eisenhower Executive Office Building. Life in the White House. Accessed on July 7, 2019. georgewbush-whitehouse.archives.gov/history/eeobtour/room208-flash.html.

Anonymous. "Finn Ronne." In *Exploring Polar Frontiers: A Historical Encyclopedia*, edited by W. Mills, 554–557. Santa Barbara, CA: ABC CLIO, 2003.

Anonymous. "Stonington Island." In *Antarctica: An Encyclopedia*, edited by John Stewart, 1510–1511. Jefferson, NC: McFarland & Company, 2011.

Anonymous. "Women Explorers." In *Exploring Polar Frontiers: A Historical Encyclopedia*, edited by W. Mills, 716–717. Santa Barbara, CA: ABC CLIO, 2003.

Anonymous. "Women in Antarctica." In *Antarctica: An Encyclopedia*, edited by John Stewart, 1722. Jefferson, NC: McFarland & Company, 2011.

Arenz, Brett E., and Robert A. Blanchette. "East Base, SOS: Assessment of Deterioration and Recommendations for Conserving This Important Antarctic Historic Site." In *Cultural Heritage in the Arctic and Antarctic Regions*, edited by S. Barr and P. Chaplin, 79–84. Volume 17 in the ICOMOS Monuments and Sites Series. Charenton-le-pont, FR: Council on Monuments and Sites, 2008.

———. "Investigations of Fungal Diversity in Wooden Structures and Soils at Historic Sites on the Antarctic Peninsula." *Polar and Alpine Microbiology* 55 (2009): 46–56.

Asbury Park Press (Asbury Park, NJ). "Week to Honor Commander." July 4, 1971.

Aston, Felicity. "Women of the White Continent." *Geographical Magazine* (September 2005): 27–30.

Balch, Edwin Swift. "Antarctic Names." *Bulletin of the American Geographical Society* 44, no. 8 (1912): 561–581.

Bathie, Carol, and Janet Pett. "The Four Ladies of Prydz Bay: Notes on the Naming of a Submarine Formation in Australian Antarctic Territory." *Victorian Naturalist* 136, no. 1 (2019): 44–46.

Beaumont-Enterprise (Beaumont, TX). "Ceremonies to Mark Ronne Sailing." January 25, 1947.

Bergmann, Linda S. "Woman Against a Background of White: The Representation of Self and Nature in Women's Arctic Narratives." *American Studies* 34, no. 2 (1993): 53–68.

Berkowitz, E.A. "Frozen in Place: American Policy and Practice in Antarctica." Ph.D. diss., Scott Polar Research Institute, University of Cambridge, 1986.

Bingham, E.W. *An Account of the Proceedings of the Falkland Islands Dependencies Survey, 1946.* Unpublished report. 1946. AD6/2E/1946/B1. Falkland Islands Dependencies Survey, British Antarctic Survey Archives, Cambridge, U.K.

———. *The Establishment of Base E. Falkland Islands Dependency Survey.* 1953. AD6/2E1966/A. British Antarctic Survey Archives. Cambridge, U.K.

Black, R.B. Foreword for *Environmental Impact along the Antarctic Peninsula*, edited by B.C. Parker and M.C. Holliman, vii–ix. Blacksburg: Virginia Polytechnic Institute, 1978.

———. "Geographical Operations from East Base, United States Antarctic Service Expedition, 1939–41." *Proceedings of the American Philosophical Society* 89, no. 1 (1945): 4–12.

Blackadder, Jesse. "Frozen Voices: Women, Silence and Antarctic." In *Antarctica: Music, Sounds and Cultural Connections*, edited by Bernadette Hince, Rupert Summerson, and Arnan Wiesel, 169–177. Canberra, AU: ANU Press, 2015.

———. "Heroines of the Ice." *Australian Geographic* 113 (March/April 2013): 88–98.

———. "Illuminations: Casting Light Upon the Earliest Female Travellers to Antarctica." Ph.D. diss., University of Western Sydney, 2012.

Blanchette, Robert, and Benjamin W. Held. "Defibration of Wood in the Expedition Huts of Antarctica: An Unusual Deterioration Process Occurring in the Polar Environment." *Polar Record* 38, no. 207 (2002): 313–322.

Booker, Maia. "Breaking the Ice Ceiling: The Women Working in Antarctica Today." *Time*, March 8, 2019. Accessed on June 9, 2019. time.com/longform/women-antarctica-iwd-scientists-explorers/.

"Brigadier General Charles J. Adams." U.S. Air Force. September 1, 1971. Accessed on June 13, 2019. af.mil/About-Us/Biographies/Display/Article/107880/brigadier-general-charles-j-adams/.

Broadbent, Noel D. "From Ballooning in the Arctic to 10,000-Foot Runways in Antarctica: Lessons from Historic Archaeology." In *Smithsonian at the Poles: Contributions to International Polar Year in Science*, edited by Igor Krupnik, Michael A. Lang, and Scott E. Miller, 49–60. Washington, D.C.: Smithsonian Institution Scholarly Press, 2009.

———. "Project East Base: Preserving Research History in Antarctica." National Science Foundation. *Directions* 5 (1992): 1–2.

Broadbent, Noel D., Catherine Holder Blee, and Robert L. Spude. "Reclaiming U.S. Antarctic History: The Restoration of East Base, Stonington Island." *Antarctic Journal of the United States* 17, no. 2 (1992): 14–17.

Broadbent, Noel D., and Lisle Rose. "Historical Archaeology and the Byrd Legacy. The United States Antarctic Service Expedition, 1939–41." *Virginia Magazine of History and Biography* 110, no. 2 (2002): 237–258.

Bulkeley, Rip. "The Curious Incident of the Missing Cleaner." *Polar Record* 46, no. 236 (2010): 84–86.

Bull, Colin. "Behind the Scenes: Colin Bull Recalls His 10-Year Quest to Send Women Researchers to Antarctica." United States Antarctic Program *Antarctic Sun*. Accessed Nov 13, 2009. antarcticsun.usap.gov/features/1955/.

Bureau of Labor Statistics. *Retail Prices: 1913–December 1919*: Bulletin of the United States Bureau of Labor Statistics, 270. Washington, D.C.: Bureau of Labor Statistics, 1921.

Burns, Robin. "Investigating Women's Antarctic Experiences: Some Methodological Reflections on a Qualitative, Feminist Project." *Resources for Feminist Research* 28, nos. 1/2 (2000): 133–139.

———. "Women in Antarctic Science: Forging New Practices and Meanings." *Women Studies Quarterly* 28, nos. 1/2 (2000): 165–180.

———. "Women in Antarctica: Sharing This Life-changing Experience." Fourth Annual Phillip Law Lecture, June 18, 2005. Hobart, Australia.

Burton, Bob. "The Changing Face of Antarctica." *BAS Club Magazine* 53 (2005): 15–17.

———. "Remembering Kevin Walton." *BAS Club Magazine* 63 (May 2010): 10–11.

Butson, A.R.C. "Mountaineering in the Antarctic." *American Alpine Journal* 57, no. 279 (1949): 198–204.

Carrere, Sybil. "Physiological and Psychological Patterns of Acute and Chronic Stress During Winter Isolation in Antarctica." Ph.D. diss., University of California, Irvine, 1990.

Chaplow, Lester. "The First-Women's Club of Antarctica: Remembering Dorothy Braxton." *Antarctica* 32, no. 4 (2014): 51.

Cimons, M. "Forty Years of Women Researchers in Antarctica." U.S. News and World Report, December 2, 2009. usnews.com/science/articles/2009/12/02/forty-years-of-women-researchers-in-antarctica.

Codling, Rosamunde. "Wilderness and Aesthetic Values in the Antarctic." Ph.D. diss., Open University, 1999.

Cole, William. "Explorer and Wife in the Antarctic." *Smithsonian,* June 1972.

———. "The Ronnes: The First and Last Husband and Wife Exploring Team." Draft article for the *New York Times*. 1971. Finn Ronne and Edith M. Ronne

Papers, 1900–2012 MSS 86269. Manuscript Division, Library of Congress, Washington, D.C.

Collis, Christy. "The Australian Antarctic Territory: A Man's World?" *Signs* 34, no. 3 (2009): 514–519.

Cook, A., A. Fox, D. Vaughan, and J. Ferrigno. "Retreating Glacier Fronts on the Antarctic Peninsula over the Past Half-Century." *Science* 308, no. 5721 (2005): 541–544.

Crary, M. "It's About Time." *Antarctican Society Newsletter* 2 (December 1978): 3–7.

Cruwys, Liz, and Beau Riffenburgh. "Bernard Stonehouse." Obituary. *Polar Record* 38, no. 205 (2002): 157–169.

Daily Mail (London). "Women's Antarctic Tour." October 24, 1930.

Daily Telegraph (London). "Anglo-U.S. Co-operation in Antarctic Surveys." June 23, 1947.

Dalrymple, P. "The End of a Great Era." *Antarctican Society Newsletter* 2 (December 1978): 7–10.

Dean, K., S. Naylor, S. Turchetti, and M. Siegert. "Data in Antarctic Science and Politics." *Social Studies of Science* 38 (2008): 571–604.

Debenham, Frank. "Lady Kennet: An Appreciation." *Polar Record* 5, nos. 35/36 (1948): 147.

Department of State. *Register of the Department of State 1942*. Washington, D.C.: United States Government Printing Office, 1943.

———. *Register of the Department of State 1945*. Washington, D.C.: United States Government Printing Office, 1946.

———. *Register of the Department of State 1946*. Washington, D.C.: United States Government Printing Office, 1947.

Devine, Carol. "The Year of Antarctic Women." *Medium*. January 17, 2017. doi.org/medium.com/@caroldevine/the-year-of-the-antarctic-woman-and -humanity-ff1f3b73eafe.

Dieter, R.A., E.R. Dieter, and D. McWhinnie-Rousseau. "Mary Alice McWhinnie: First Woman to Over Winter in Antarctica." *Arctic Medical Research* 53, Suppl. 2 (1994): 339–340.

Dodds, Klaus. "The 1959 Antarctic Treaty: Reflecting on the Fiftieth Anniversary of a Landmark Agreement." Guest Editorial. *Polar Research* 29, no. 2 (2010): 145–149.

———. "Putting Maps in Their Place: The Demise of the Falkland Islands Dependency Survey and the Mapping of Antarctica, 1945–1962." *Ecumene* 7, no. 20 (2000): 176–210.

———. "Settling and Unsettling Antarctica." *Signs* 34, no. 3 (2009): 505–508.

Dodson, Robert H.T. "Antarctic Rescue." *American Alpine Journal* 3 (September 1949): 361–362.

———. "Crevasse." *Polar Times* 3, no. 26 (2015): 16–26.

———. "Lassiter of the Ronne Antarctic Research Expedition (1920–1992)." *Antarctican Society Bulletin* 92/93, no. 5 (1993): 5–6.

Downham, N.Y., and E.B. Armstrong. *Report on the State and Contents of Refuges and Stations Visited in the Antarctic Peninsula by BAS Personnel.* 1964. AD6/2E/1964/21. British Antarctic Survey Archives, Cambridge, U.K.

DSP. *British Antarctic Survey, Stonington Island Journal, 1965.* 1965. AD6/2E/1965/B1. British Antarctic Survey Archives, Cambridge, U.K.

Duffin, Erin. "Percentage of the U.S. Population Who Have Completed Four Years of College or More from 1940 to 2018, By Gender." Statistica.com. Accessed December 1, 2019. statista.com/statistics/184272/educational-attainment -of-college-diploma-or-higher-by-gender/.

Dumenil, Lynn. "The New Woman and the Politics of the 1920s." *Organization of American Historians* 21, no. 3 (July 2007): 22–26.

Eklund, Carl R. "Farthest South." USAS1939.org. n.d. Accessed May 16, 2019. usas1939.org/carl.eklund/Carl_Eklund_Farthest_South.pdf.

Enterprise. "Naval Officer-Arctic Explorer with Seven Lives." September 1, 1955.

Erceg, Diana. "Explorers of a Different Kind: A History of Antarctic Tourism 1966–2016." Ph.D. diss., Australian National University, 2017.

Erikson, Patricia Pierce. "Homemaking, Snowbabies, and the Search for the North Pole: Josephine Diebitsch Peary and the Making of National History." In *North by Degree: New Perspectives on Arctic Exploration,* edited by Susan A. Kaplan and Robert McCracken Peck, 225–285. Philadelphia: American Philosophical Society, 2013.

———. "Josephine Diebitsch Peary." *Arctic* 62, no. 1 (2009): 102–104.

Evening Sun (Baltimore, MD). "Edith Ronne One of Just 8 Women at South Pole." August 1, 1972.

Explorers Journal. "Captain Charles J. Adams." New Member. *Explorers Journal.* 28, no. 1 (1950): 48.

Explorers Journal. "James Walter Lassiter." New Member. *Explorers Journal.* 28, no. 3 (1950): 33–34.

Explorers Journal. "Lawrence De Wolfe Kelsey." New Member. *Explorers Journal.* 26, nos. 3/4 (1948): 35–36.

Explorers Journal. "Robert H.T. Dodson." New Member. *Explorers Journal.* 28, no. 1 (1950): 48.

Fairchild, Wilma B. "Explorers: Men and Motives." *Geographical Review* 38, no. 3 (1948): 414–425.

Fitzgerald, P. Review of *Innocents on the Ice: A Memoir of Antarctic Exploration, 1957,* by John C. Behrendt. *Eos* 80, no. 27 (1999): 304.

Fogg, G.E. "The Royal Society and the Antarctic." *Notes and Records of the Royal Society of London* 54, no. 1 (2000): 85–98.

Fox, Adrian J. "Unlocking the Time-capsule of Historic Aerial Photography to Measure Changes in Antarctic Peninsula Glaciers." *Photogrammetric Record* 23, no. 121 (2008): 51–68.

———. "Using Multiple Data Sources to Enhance Photogrammetry for Mapping Antarctic Terrain." *Polar Research* 14, no. 3 (1995): 317–327.

Frederick, Guy, and Jenny Rock. "The Influence of 'Place': A Case Study of Antarctic Scientists." *Polar Journal* 8, no. 1 (2018): 126–140.

Freeman, R.L. *F.I.D.S. Report on Local Survey, 1947–48.* 1947. AD6/2E/1947/ L2. Falkland Islands Dependencies Survey, British Antarctic Survey Archives Cambridge, U.K.

Frey, Joseph. "Ice Scream." *Medical Post,* January 8, 2002, 42.

Friedman, Paul D. Review of *East Base: Historic Monument, Stonington Island/ Antarctic Peninsula,* by Catherine Holder Spude. *Public Historian* 17, no. 1 (1995): 103–106.

Fuchs, Sir Vivian. "The Falkland Islands Dependencies Survey, 1947–50." *Polar Record* 6, no. 41 (1951): 7–27.

———. "The Human Element in Exploration." *British Antarctic Survey Bulletin* 1 (June 1963): 1 8.

———. Statement Concerning the Condition of the American Base on

Stonington Island as Found on 23 February 1948. 1948. AD1/D1/6.06. Falkland Islands Dependencies Survey Archives, British Antarctic Survey Archives, Cambridge, U.K.

Gephart, Louise. "The Honeymoon's on Ice." *Courier-Journal* (Louisville, KY), October 23, 1956.

Giegerich, Steve. "'Ike' Schlossbach: Truly 'a Legend.'" *Asbury Park Press* (Asbury Park, NJ), August 26, 1971.

Glasberg, E. "'Living Ice': Rediscovery of the Poles in an Era of Climate Change." *Women's Studies Quarterly* 39, nos. 3/4 (Fall/Winter 2011): 221–246.

Goodrich, Peggy, and Bernard Stonehouse. "Isaac Schlossbach." Profile. *Polar Record* 24, no. 149 (1988): 119–124.

Gurling, Paul. "Some Notes on a Sledge Journey from Stonington Island, 1940–41." *Polar Record* 19, no. 123 (1979): 613–624.

Haddelsey, Stephen. "The 'Heroic' and 'Post-Heroic' Ages of British Antarctic Exploration: A Consideration of Differences and Continuity." Ph.D. diss., University of East Anglia, 2014.

Hansson, Heidi. "Feminine Poles Josephine Diebitsch-Peary's and Jennie Darlington's Polar Narratives." In *Cold Matters: Cultural Perceptions of Snow, Ice and Cold*, edited by Heidi Hansson and Cathrine Norberg, 105–123. Umea, Sweden: Umea University and the Royal Skyttean Society, 2009.

Harrowfield, D.L. "Conserving Antarctica's Earliest Buildings." *New Zealand Antarctic Record* 10, no. 3 (1990): 3–11.

Hart, Ian. "Pierce-Butler, Kenelm Somerset." In *Dictionary of Falklands Biographies (Including South Georgia): From Discovery Up to 1981*, edited by David Tatham. Accessed June 30, 2019. falklandsbiographies.org /biographies/pierce-butler_kenelm.

Haward, Marcus. "Introduction: The Antarctic Treaty 1961–2011." *Polar Journal* 1, no. 1 (2011): 1–4.

Headland, R. "Historical Development of Antarctic Tourism." *Annals of Tourism Research* 21, no. 2 (1994): 269–280.

———. "Territory and Claims in the Antarctic Treaty Region: A Disquisition on Historical and Recent Developments." *Cartographic Journal* 57, no. 2 (2020): 160–174.

Heavens. Steve. "Brian Roberts and the Origins of the 1959 Antarctic Treaty." *Polar Record* 52, no. 267 (2016): 717–729.

Histarmar Foundation. *"Yapeyú."* Historia y arqueología, Maritima. 2020. Accessed June 10, 2020. histarmar.com.ar/Antartida/BuquesAntarticos /Yapeyu-.htm.

Hjorth-Sørensen, Odd. "Hortensgutten som ble amerikansk polarforsker." *Magasinet for alle,* November 28, 1953.

Hofstra, Warren R. "Richard E. Byrd and the Legacy of Polar Exploration." *Virginia Magazine of History and Biography* 110, no. 2 (2002): 137–152.

Houston-Post. "Ronne Expedition Sails for Antarctic Regions." January 26, 1947.

Hughes, Leonard. "Warming Up to the South Pole." *Washington Post,* June 24, 1993.

Iijima, G.C. "Our Most Remote Museum." *Odyssey* 3, no. 1 (1994): 42–43.

Jones, Beth. "Women Won't Like Working in Antarctica as There Are No Shops and Hairdressers." *Telegraph* (London), May 20, 2012. Accessed March 29, 2019. telegraph.co.uk/news/earth/environment/9260864/Women-wont-like -working-in-Antarctica-as-there-are-no-shops-and-hairdressers.html.

Jones, Virginia. "Jennie Darlington's Story of Honeymoon in the Antarctic." *Paducak Sun* (Paducak, KY), November 2, 1956.

Joyner, C.C. "United States Foreign Policy Interests in the Antarctic." *Polar Journal* 1, no. 1 (2011): 17–35.

Kay, Laura. "What It Takes to Get There: An Interview with Barbara Hillary." *Scholar and Feminist Online* 7, no. 1 (Fall 2008). sfonline.barnard.edu/ice/ hillary_01.htm.

Keeling, E.H., W.L.S. Fleming, and J.M. Wordie. "The Falkland Islands Dependencies Survey: Explorations of 1947–48: Discussion." *Geographical Journal* 115, nos. 4/6 (1950): 154–160.

Kirwan, L.P. "Lars Christensen." Obituary. *Geographical Journal* 132, no. 3 (1966): 446–447.

Kleinberg, Jay. "American Women in the Twentieth Century." In *America's Century: Perspectives on U.S. History Since 1900,* edited by Iwan W. Morgan and Nell A. Wynn, 214–246. New York: Holmes and Meier, 1993.

Klemesrud, Judy. "To These Women Geography Is Not Just Maps and Data." *New York Times,* October 12, 1975.

Knowles, Paul H. "Geology of Southern Palmer Peninsula, Antarctica." Reports of Scientific Results of the United States Antarctic Service Expedition, 1939–1941. *Proceedings of the American Philosophical Society* 89, no. 1 (April 30, 1945): 132–145.

Latady, William R. "Antarctic Interlude." *American Alpine Journal* 7, no. 3 (September 1949): 233–247.

———. "Report on Aerial Photography of the Ronne Expedition." *Photogrammetric Engineering and Remote Sensing* 14, no. 2 (1948): 202–222.

———. "A Year on the Antarctic Continent." *Appalachia* 27 (1949): 273–281.

Leane, Elizabeth. "Placing Women in the Antarctic Literary Landscape." *Signs* 34, no. 3 (2009): 509–514.

Lee, Gordon F. "Crimson Snows." *Boy's Life* 5 (January 1949): 18–19.

Legler, Gretchen. "The End of the Heroic Illusion: How Three Generations of Women Writers Have Changed the Literature of Antarctica." *Polar Journal* 1, no. 2 (2011): 207–224.

Lewander, Lisbeth. "Women and Civilisation on Ice." In *Cold Matters: Cultural Perceptions of Snow, Ice and Cold*, edited by Heidi Hansson and Cathrine Norberg, 89–104. Umea, Sweden: Umea University and the Royal Skyttean Society, 2009.

Lewandowski, Katherine. "Pioneers in Antarctic Research: Lois Jones and Her All-Woman Science Team Explore the Geochemistry of the Dry Valleys." In *Women and Geology: Who Are We, Where Have We Come from and Where Are We Going*, edited by Beth A. Johnson, 51–58. Boulder, CO: Geological Society of America, 2018.

Light, Richard U. "The Far-Off Hills." *Geographical Review* 38, no. 3 (1948): 352–354.

———. "The Geographical Society and the Explorer." *Geographical Review* 38, no. 3 (1948): 349–352.

Lim, Heidi. "At the Bottom of the World." *Scholar and Feminist Online* 7, no. 1 (Fall 2008). sfonline.barnard.edu/ice/print_lim.htm.

Lipps, Jere H. "East Base, Stonington Island, Antarctica." *Antarctica Journal of the United States* 13, no. 4 (1978): 231–232.

———. "The United States' 'East Base,' Antarctic Peninsula." *Antarctic Journal of the United States* 11, no. 4 (1976): 211–219.

Livezey, Emilie Tavel. "Admiral Byrd's Legacy in Limbo." *Christian Science Monitor*, March 6, 1980. Accessed May 11, 2019. csmonitor.com/1980/0306/030655.html.

Lüdecke, C., L. Tipton-Everett, and L. Lay, eds. "National and Trans-National Agendas in Antarctic Research from the 1950s and Beyond: Proceedings of the Third Workshop of the SCAR Action Group on the History of Antarctic Research." 2012. Byrd Polar Research Center, Columbus, OH.

Marson, Frank M., and Janet R. Terner. "United States IGY Bibliography 1953–1960." *IGY General Report* no. 18. 1963. National Academy of Sciences and National Research Council, Washington, D.C.

Mason, D.P. *Falkland Islands Dependencies Survey: Base E (Stonington Island) Survey Report.* 1949. ES2/EW 110/29. Falkland Islands Dependencies Survey Archives, British Antarctic Survey Archives, Cambridge, U.K.

———. "The Falkland Islands Dependencies Survey: Explorations of 1947–48." *Geographical Journal* 115, nos. 4/6 (1950): 145–154.

———. *F.I.D.S. Survey Report.* 1947. ES2/EW 110/29. Falkland Islands Dependencies Survey Archives, British Antarctic Survey Archives, Cambridge, U.K.

Mattuozzi, Robert N. "Richard Byrd, Polar Exploration and the Media." *Virginia Magazine of History and Biography* 10, no. 2 (2002): 208–236.

McMillin, Loyal. "Antarctic Explorers Reunite in Middleburg." *Fauquier Democrat* (Warrenton, VA), October 6, 1983.

Miller, Maynard M. "William Robertson Latady, 1918–1976." *American Alpine Journal* 22, no. 2 (1980): 694–697.

Millikan, Robert. "Love Lost in a Cold Climate: Sexual Harassment of Women Rife in Ice-Bound Antarctica." *Independent* (London), August 30, 1993.

Montgomery, Ruth. "Womanless Continent of Snow and Cold." *Lincoln Journal Star* (Lincoln, NB), November 2, 1958.

Morris, Jessica, and Jacqueline Weinstock. "Women in the Antarctic: Constructive Risk-Taking and Social Consequences." *Antarctic Journal of the United States* 29, no. 5 (1994): 379–382.

Mullin, Charles, and H.J.M. Connery. "Psychological Study at an Antarctic IGY Station." *Journal of American Psychiatry* 3 (March 10, 1959): 290–296.

Nash, Meredith, Hanne E.F. Nielsen, Justine Shaw, Matt King, Mary Anne Lea, and Narissa Bax. "'Antarctica Just Has This Hero Factor …': Gendered Barriers to Australian Antarctica Research and Remote Fieldwork." PLoS ONE 14, no. 1 (2019). doi.org/10.1371/journal.pone.0209983.

Nash, Meredith, and Robyn Moore. "An Evaluation of a Leadership Development Programme for Women in STEM in Antarctica." *Polar Journal* 8, no. 1 (2018): 110–125.

Naylor, S., M. Siegert, K. Dean, and S. Turchetti. "Science and the Geopolitics of Antarctica." *Nature Geoscience* 1, no. 3 (2008): 143–145.

Nelson, Paul D. *Human Adaptation to Antarctic Station Life.* Report no. 62-12. San Diego: U.S. Navy Medical Neuropsychiatric Research Unit, 1962.

Nichols, Robert L. "Dog Sledging in Antarctica." *Appalachia* 30, no. 12 (1964): 250–277.

———. "Memorial to Finn Ronne." *Antarctican Society Newsletter* 79/80, no. 4 (1980): 8–9.

Nielsen, H., and C. Jaksic. "Recruitment Advertising for Antarctic Personnel: Between Adventure and Routine." *Polar Record* 54, no. 274 (2018): 65–75.

Norman, F.I., J. Gibson, and J. Burgess. "Klarius Mikkelsen's 1935 Landing in the Vestfold Hills, East Antarctica: Some Fiction and Some Facts." *Polar Record* 34, no. 191 (1998): 293–304.

Office of the Quartermaster General. *Report of Quartermaster Equipment on the Ronne Antarctic Research Expedition.* Washington, D.C.: Military Planning Division Research and Development Branch, 1948.

Orelove, Eden. "Looking Back: The Columbian Women." GWToday, March 31, 2014. Accessed March 5, 2019. gwtoday.gwu.edu/looking-back-columbian-women.

Owen, Robert B. "The Life of Arthur Earl Owen 1927–2000." 2004. Accessed March 20, 2019. dstas.com/Media/Life_of_Arthur_Owen.doc.

Palinkas, L.A. *Health and Performance of Antarctic Winter-over Personnel: A Follow-Up Study.* Report no. 85-18. San Diego: Naval Health Research Center, 1985.

———. "Psychological Effects of Polar Expeditions." *Lancet* 371 (2008): 153–163.

Palm Beach Post (Palm Beach, FL). "Harry Darlington Obituary." November 13, 1996.

Parfit, Michael. "Reclaiming a Lost Antarctic Base." *National Geographic Magazine* 83, no. 3 (1993): 110–126.

Paterson, Billy. "Ex-Navy Pilot Tells of Survival Battle in the Antarctic." *Daily Record* (London), April 18, 2010. Accessed May 5, 2019. dailyrecord.co.uk/news /uk-world-news/ex-navy-pilot-tells-of-survival-battle-1056521.

Peterson, Harries-Clichy. "To All Hands and Feet." Letter dated February 4, 1948, and Found in the Snow by the British Team After the Departure of the Ronne Expedition Team (likely AD1/D1/4(9)). Falkland Islands Dependencies Survey Archives, British Antarctic Survey Archives, Cambridge, U.K.

Pierce-Butler, Kenelm. *F.I.D.S. Base Leader's Report for Year 1947–1948. Political. Visits by Foreign Shipping.* 1947. AD6/2E/1947/21. Falkland Islands Dependencies Survey Archives, British Antarctic Survey Archives, Cambridge, U.K.

———. *Falkland Islands Dependencies Survey Reports on the State of the U.S. Base on Stonington Island Before and After the Visit of the Chilean Frigate* Iquiqui. 1947. AD6/2E/1946/23. Falkland Islands Dependencies Survey Archives, British Antarctic Survey Archives, Cambridge, U.K.

———. *F.I.D.S. Report on the Visit of the Chilean Ships to Stonington Island, Marguerite Bay, Grahamland, 1947.* 1947. AD6/2E/1947/22. Falkland Islands Dependencies Survey Archives, British Antarctic Survey Archives, Cambridge, U.K.

———. "Marguerite Bay 1947 Base Journal." 1947. AD6/2E1947/B. Falkland Islands Dependencies Survey Archives, British Antarctic Survey Archives, Cambridge, U.K.

Pierce-Butler, Kenelm, and Finn Ronne. "Falkland Islands Dependencies Survey Exchange of Letters with Ronne Antarctic Research Expedition on Stonington Island, March 1947." 1947. AD6/2E/1946/22. Falkland Islands Dependencies Survey Archives, British Antarctic Survey Archives, Cambridge, U.K.

Polar Record. "Andrew A. Thompson." Obituary. 15, no. 97 (1971): 559.

Polar Record. "Argentine Antarctic Expeditions, 1942, 1943, 1947 and 1947–48." 6, no. 45 (1949): 656–662.

Polar Record. "Francis Dana Coman." Obituary. 6, no. 46 (1953): 839.

Polar Record. "Private Research Expedition to Antarctica, 1977–78." 19, no. 121 (1979): 378–379.

Polar Record. "Ronne Antarctic Research Expedition, 1946–48." 5, no. 39 (1950): 459–461.

Reich, R. "The Development of Antarctic Tourism." *Polar Record* 20, no. 126 (1980): 203–214.

Rejcek, Peter. "Long Time Coming: Women Fully Integrated into USAP Over Last 40 Years." USAP *Antarctic Sun.* November 13, 2009. Accessed Feb 11, 2018. antarcticsun.usap.gov/features/1951/.

Robarge, David S. "Richard Helms: The Intelligence Professional Personified in Memory and Appreciation." *Studies in Intelligence Studies* 46, no. 4 (2002): 35–43.

Roberts, Brian. "The Exploration of Antarctica." *Nature* 159 (March 22, 1947): 388–392.

Rohrer, J.H. *Human Adjustment to Antarctic Isolation.* Washington, D.C.: Office of Naval Research, Group Psychology Branch, 1960.

Ronne, Edith "Jackie." "From Heels to Mukluks." Ronne Family Antarctic Explorers. Accessed June 5, 2019. ronneantarcticexplorers.com/Edith_Jackie_Ronne.htm#FROM%20HEELS%20TO%20MUKLUKS.

———. "My Father-in-Law, Martin Rønne." Ronne Family Antarctic Explorers. Accessed June 5, 2019. ronneantarcticexplorers.com/Martin_Ronne.htm.

———. "Women in the Antarctic, or the Human Side of a Scientific Expedition." *Appalachia* 28 (1950): 1–15.

Ronne, Finn. "Antarctic Mapping and Aerial Photography." *Scientific Monthly* 71, no. 5 (1950): 287–293.

———. "Antarctica — One Continent." *Explorers Journal* 26, nos. 3/4 (1948): 1–16.

———. Draft notes by Finn Ronne about disciplinary problems with Harry Darlington. Found in the Snow by the British Team after the Departure of the Ronne Expedition. 1948. (likely AD1/D1/4(9)). British Antarctic Survey Archives, Cambridge, U.K.

———. "The Main Sledge Journey from East Base, Palmer Land, Antarctica." *Proceedings of the American Philosophical Society* 89, no. 1 (April 30, 1945): 13–22.

———. "Ronne Antarctic Research Expedition 1946–1948." *Geographical Review* 38, no. 3 (1948): 355–391.

———. "Ronne Antarctic Research Expedition, 1946–1948." *Photogrammetric Engineering* 14, no. 2 (1948): 197–205.

———. "Spitsbergen — Arctic Outpost." *Explorers Journal* 41, no. 2 (1963): 20–25.

———. "Third Sweeney African Expedition." *Explorers Journal* 28, no. 1 (1954): 11–12.

Ronne Antarctic Research Expedition. *Scientific Results of Ronne Antarctic Research Expedition.* Washington, D.C.: Office of Naval Research, Navy Department, 1948.

Roscoe, John H. "Exploring Antarctica Vicariously: A Survey of Recent Literature." *Geographical Review* 48, no. 3 (1958): 406–427.

Rosner, Victoria. "Gender and Polar Studies: Mapping the Terrain." *Signs* 34, no. 3 (2009): 489–494.

———. "Gender Degree Zero: Memoirs of Frozen Time in Antarctica." *Auto/ Biography Studies* 14, no. 1 (1999): 5–22. doi.org/10.1080/08989575.1999. 10846753.

———. "Where No Woman Has Gone Before." *Women's Review of Books* 25, no. 3 (May/June 2008): 21–23.

Rothblum, Esther D., Jessica Morris, and Jacqueline Weinstock. "Women in the Antarctic: Risk-Taking and Social Consequences." *World Psychology* 1, no. 1 (1995): 83–112.

Roura, R. "Monitoring the Transformation of Historic Features in Antarctica and Svalbard: Local Processes and Regional Contexts." *Polar Record* 46, no. 239 (2010): 289–311.

Routley, T.C. "Human Qualities and Polar Exploration." *Canadian Medical Association Journal* 82 (1960): 1128.

Rubin, Jeff. "Due South: A RARE Reunion." *Polar Times* 3, no. 6 (2005): 6.

Rush, Elizabeth. "These Women are Changing the Landscape of Antarctic Research." *National Geographic*, March 7, 2019. Accessed June 4, 2019. nationalgeographic.com.au/nature/these-women-are-changing-the-landscape-of-antarctic-research.aspx.

Sarris, Aspa. "Antarctic Station Life: The First 15 Years of Mixed Expeditions to the Antarctic." *Acta Aeronautica* 131 (2017): 50–54.

———. "Behavioral Norms and Expectations on Antarctic Stations." *Environment and Behavior* 39, no. 5 (2007): 706–723.

Sataloff, Robert. "In Memory of Ralph E. Becker." *Journal of Voice* 9, no. 1 (1995): 1–2.

Satchell, Michael. "Women Who Conquer the South Pole." *Parade Magazine*, June 5, 1983.

Schmidt, Lacey L., JoAnna Wood, and Desmond J. Lugg. "Gender Differences in Leader and Follower Perceptions of Social Support in Antarctica." *Acta Astronautica* 56 (2005): 923–931.

Science News-Letter. "Data for Polar Explorers." 51, no. 8 (1947): 116.

Seag, Morgan. "Equal Opportunities on Ice: Examining Gender and Institutional Change at the British Antarctic Survey, 1975–1996." Ph.D. diss., Scott Polar Research Institute/Department of Geography, University of Cambridge, 2015.

———. "The Trouble with Heroism." *Chemistry World*, September 3, 2017. Accessed May 27, 2019. chemistryworld.com/opinion/when-antarctica-stopped-being-only-for-men/3007778.article.

———. "Women in Polar Research: A Brief History." Arctic Institute Center for Circumpolar Security Studies. Accessed March 19, 2019. thearcticinstitute.org/women-polar-research-brief-history/.

———. "Women Need Not Apply: Gendered Institutional Change in Antarctica and Outer Space." *Polar Journal* 7, no. 2 (2017): 319–335.

Secretariat of the Antarctic Treaty. Visitor Site Guidelines. "23. Stonington Island." Secretariat of the Antarctic Treaty. 2018. Accessed May 23, 2019. ats.aq/devAS/Ats/Guideline/efd2788f-5bdc-44f4-8ed0-9649d56261be.

Seyferth, Mimi. "Edith (Jackie) Ronne: First Lady of Antarctica." *Knitting Traditions*, Spring 2015.

Shortis, Emma. "In the Interest of All Mankind: Women and the Environmental Protection of Antarctica." In *Feminist Ecologies: Changing Environments in the Anthropocene*, edited by Lara Stevens et al., 247–261. London: Palgrave Macmillan, 2018.

Siple, Paul A. "Carl R. Eklund." Obituary. *Arctic* 16, no. 2 (1963): 147–148.

Sladen, W.J.L., and W.L.N. Tickell. "Antarctic Bird-Banding by the Falkland Islands Dependencies Survey, 1945–1957." *Bird-Banding* 29, no. 1 (January 1958): 1–26.

Smith, William M. "Scientific Personnel in Antarctica: Their Recruitment, Selection and Performance." *Psychological Reports* 9 (1961): 163–182.

Society of Endocrinology. "Women More Resilient to Extreme Physical Activity than Previously Reported." Science Daily, November 19, 2018. Accessed December 13, 2018. sciencedaily.com/releases/2018/11/181119064145 .htm.

Spude, Catherine Holder, and Robert L. Spude. *East Base Historic Monument Stonington Island, Antarctic Peninsula: Part I: A Guide for Management; Part II: Description of the Cultural Resource and Recommendations.* Denver Service Center: United States Department of the Interior, 1993.

Starkweather, S., M. Seag, O. Lee, and A. Pope. "Revisiting Perceptions and Evolving Culture: A Community Dialogue on Women in Polar Research." *Polar Research* 37, nos. 1–4 (2018). Accessed May 19, 2019. polarresearch .net/index.php/polar/article/view/2639.

Stephenson, A. "*Antarctic Conquest* by Finn Ronne: A Review." *Geographical Journal* 115, no. 4/6 (1950): 233–235.

———. "Surveying in the Falkland Islands Dependencies." *Polar Record* 6, no. 41 (1951): 28–44.

Stone, H.W. *Falkland Islands Dependencies Survey: A Report of Survey Carried Out on the U.S. "City of Beaumont" at Marguerite Bay on the 4th of April 1947.* 1947. AD6/2/1947/R. Falkland Islands Dependencies Survey Archives, British Antarctic Survey Archives, Cambridge, U.K.

Strange, R.E., and S.A. Youngman. "Emotional Aspects of Wintering Over." *Antarctic Journal* 6, no. 6 (1971): 255–257.

Tanner, Virginia. "B & O Man's Daughter Visits Antarctic." *B & O Railroad Magazine,* February 1958.

Taylor, A.J.W., and I.A. McCormick. "Reactions of Family Partners of Antarctic Expeditioners." *Polar Record* 23, no. 147 (1987): 691–700.

Telegraph (London). "Richard Butson, GC." Obituary. March 24, 2015.

Thompson, Andrew. "Establishment of a Seismological Station." *Science* 115, no. 2977 (1952): 65–69.

United Kingdom Antarctic Heritage Trust. *East Base Emergency Repairs Report.* 2018. Unpublished. British Antarctic Survey Archives, Cambridge, U.K.

U.S. Department of Labor. *Women in the Federal Service, 1923–1947: Part 1: Trends in Employment.* Washington, D.C.: U.S. Department of Labor/ Women's Bureau, 1949.

Various. *Capt. Finn Ronne's Tourist Cruise to Antarctica.* 1965–69. FO 371/179736. National Archives, London, U.K.

———. "Finn Ronne's Photography: American Falkland Islands." n.d. OD 6/894. National Archives, London, U.K.

———. "Recruitment, Sex Discrimination Act, Antarctic Bases" files. 1970. AD3/2/234/255/01. British Antarctic Survey Archives, Cambridge, U.K.

———. "Survey — Ronne (Air Photos)." 1951–1961. AS/183/6/A. British Antarctic Survey Archives, Cambridge, U.K.

Verbitsky, Jane. "Antarctica as a Community." In *Identity, Culture and the Politics of Community Development,* edited by Stacey-Ann Wilson, 46–64. Newcastle-upon-Tyne, U.K.: Cambridge Scholars, 2015.

Wade, F. A. "An Introduction to the Symposium on Scientific Results of the United States Antarctic Service Expedition, 1939–41." *Proceedings of the American Philosophical Society* 89, no. 1 (1945): 1–3.

Walton, Kevin. *Marguerite Bay 1947 Report on Two Journeys in Support of R.A.R.E.* 1947. F.I.D.S.S.B. No. 78/48. Copy No. 2. AD6/2E/1947/K4. Falkland Islands Dependencies Survey Archives, British Antarctic Survey Archives, Cambridge, U.K.

———. *Report on American Equipment, Clothing and Sledging Methods as Used by the Ronne Antarctic Research Expedition in 1947.* 1947. AD6/2E/1947/K7. Falkland Islands Dependencies Survey Archives, British Antarctic Survey Archives, Cambridge, U.K.

———. *Report on Ten-Day Journey by Dr. Butson and Lt. E Walton in Support of R.A.R.E.* 1947. Falkland Islands Dependencies Survey Archives, British Antarctic Survey Archives, Cambridge, U.K.

———. "William Robertson Latady." *Polar Record* 20, no. 124 (1980): 83–84.

Walton, Myra. "Dr. Bernard Stonehouse." Obituary. *Antarctic* 33, no. 1 (2015): 10–11.

Warga, Mary E. "Irvine C. Gardner." Obituary. *Physics Today* 26, no. 9 (1973): 73.

White, Sidney E. "Memorial to Robert L. Nichols." *Geological Society of America* 34 (1995): 11–13.

Wood, J., D. Lugge, S. Hysong, and D. Harm. "Psychological Changes in Hundred-Day Remote Antarctic Field Groups." *Environment and Behavior* 31, no. 3 (1999): 299–337.

Ziegler, Frank. "A Private Hero." *Explorers Journal* 32, nos. 1–2 (1969): 264–266.

Zimmer, M., J.C.C.R. Cabral, F.C. Borges, K.G. Coco, and B. Hameister. "Psychological Changes Arising from an Antarctic Stay: Systematic Overview." *Estudos de Psicologia Campinas* 30, no. 3 (2013): 415–423.

BOOKS

American Geographical Society. *Problems of Polar Research.* Special Publication No. 7. New York: American Geographical Society, 1928.

Anonymous. *Operation Deep Freeze III: The Story of Task Force 43 Third Phase 1957–1958.* Paoli, PA: Dorville Corporation, 1958.

Aston, Felicity. *Alone in Antarctica.* London: Counterpoint, 2013.

———. *Call of the White: Taking the World to the South Pole.* London: Summersdale, 2011.

Barr, Susan, and Paul Chaplin. *Cultural Heritage in the Arctic and Antarctic Regions.* Oslo: International Polar Heritage Committee of ICOMOS, 2004.

Bart, Sheldon. *Race to the Top of the World: Richard Byrd and the First Flight to the North Pole.* Washington, D.C.: Regnery History, 2013.

Beaglehole, J.C., ed. *The Journals of Captain James Cook II.* Vol. 2, *The Voyage of the* Resolution *and* Adventure, *1772–1775.* Cambridge: Cambridge University Press, 1969.

Behrendt, John. *Innocents on the Ice: A Memoir of Antarctic Exploration, 1957.* Niwot: University Press of Colorado, 1998.

Belanger, Dian Olson. *Deep Freeze: The United States, the International Geophysical Year, and the Origins of Antarctica's Age of Science.* Niwot: University Press of Colorado, 2010.

Bertrand, Kenneth J. *Americans in Antarctica, 1775–1948.* Special Publication No. 39. New York: American Geographical Society, 1971.

Blackadder, Jesse. *Chasing the Light.* Sydney: Fourth Estate, 2013.

Bloom, Lisa. *Gender on Ice: American Ideologies of Polar Expeditions.* Minneapolis: University of Minnesota Press, 1993.

Boothe, Joan. *The Storied Ice*. Berkeley, CA: Regent Press, 2011.

Braxton, Dorothy. *The Abominable Snow-Women*. Melbourne: A.H. and A.W Reed, 1969.

Burns, Robin. *Just Tell Them I Survived!: Women in Antarctica*. Crows Nest, Australia: Allen & Unwin, 2001.

Butson, A.R.C. *Young Men in the Antarctic: A Doctor's Illustrated Diary (1946–48)*. Eugenia, ON: Battered Silicon Dispatch Box, 2010.

Byrd, Richard E. *Discovery: The Story of the Second Byrd Antarctic Expedition*. New York: G.P. Putnam's Sons, 1935.

———. *Little America*. New York: G.P. Putnam's Sons, 1930.

Chafe, William H. *The Paradox of Change: American Women in the Twentieth Century*. New York: Oxford University Press, 1992.

Chipman, Elizabeth. *Women on the Ice: A History of Women in the Far South*. Melbourne: Melbourne University Press, 1986.

Christensen, Lars. *Such Is the Antarctic*. London: Hodder and Stoughton, 1935.

Cochrane, Rexmond. *Measures for Progress: A History of the National Bureau of Standards*. Washington, D.C.: NBS/U.S. Department of Commerce, 1966.

Coontz, Stephanie. *A Strange Stirring: The Feminine Mystique and American Women at the Dawn of the 1960s*. Philadelphia: Basic Books, 2011.

Darlington, Jennie, with Jane McIlvaine. *My Antarctic Honeymoon: A Year at the Bottom of the World*. London: Frederick Muller, 1957.

Day, David. *Antarctica: A Biography*. New York: Oxford University Press, 2013.

Devine, Carol, and Wendy Trusler. *The Antarctic Book of Cooking and Cleaning*. Toronto: HarperCollins, 2015.

Dodds, Klaus, Alan D. Hemmings, and Peder Roberts, eds. *Handbook on the Politics of Antarctica*. Cheltenham, U.K.: Edward Elgar, 2017.

Druett, Joan. *Petticoat Wives: Whaling Wives at Sea, 1820–1920*. Lebanon, NH: University Press of New England, 2001.

Dudeney, John, and John Sheail. *Claiming the Ice: Britain and the Antarctic 1900–1950*. Newcastle-upon-Tyne, U.K.: Cambridge Scholars, 2019.

Fiennes, Ranulph. *Shackleton: A Biography*. London: Michael Joseph, 2021.

Fogg, G.E. *A History of Antarctic Science*. Cambridge: Cambridge University Press, 1992.

Fox, Adrian J., ed. *Antarctic Peninsula: A Visitor's Guide*. London: Natural History Museum, 2012.

Fuchs, Sir Vivian. *Of Ice and Men: The Story of the British Antarctic Survey 1943–73*. Oswestry, U.K.: Anthony Nelson, 1982.

Glasberg, Elena. *Antarctica As Cultural Critique: The Gendered Politics of Scientific Exploration and Climate Change*. New York: Palgrave Macmillan, 2012.

Glines, Carroll V. *Bernt Balchen: Polar Aviator*. Washington, D.C.: Smithsonian Institution Press, 1999.

Goodrich, Peggy. *Ike's Travels*. Neptune, NJ: Township of Neptune, 1974.

Grierson, John. *Challenge to the Poles: Highlights of Arctic and Antarctic Aviation*. London: G.T. Foulis, 1964.

Griffiths, Tom. *Slicing the Silence: Voyaging to Antarctica*. Cambridge, MA: Harvard University Press, 2007.

Hattersley-Smith, G. *A History of Place-Names in the British Antarctic Territory*. Scientific Report no. 113. Cambridge: British Antarctic Survey, 1991.

Headland, R.K. *Chronological List of Antarctic Expeditions and Related Historical Events*. Cambridge: Cambridge University Press, 1989.

Healy, Joseph D. Diary of Joseph D. Healy. Second South Pole Expedition. Sept. 10, 1940–Jan. 23, 1941. Accessed May 13, 2019. islandstars.com /Healy/_Antarctic/Diary.pdf.

Herbert, Kari. *Polar Wives: The Remarkable Women Behind the World's Most Daring Explorers*. Vancouver: Greystone, 2012.

Howes, Ruth H., and Caroline L. Herzenberg. *After the War: Women in Physics in the United States*. San Rafael, CA: Morgan & Claypool, 2015.

Huntford, Roland. *The Last Place on Earth: Scott and Amundsen's Race to the South Pole*. New York: Modern Library, 1999.

———. *Shackleton*. London: Hodder and Stoughton, 1985.

Jaburg, Conrad J. *Con Trails: A Memoir from a Flying Dutchman*. Palm Beach, FL: Casa de Gatos, 2012.

Joyner, C.C., and Ethel R. Theis. *Eagle Over the Ice: The U.S. in the Antarctic*. Lebanon, NH: University Press of New England, 1997.

Krehbiel, Jane Alexandra. *Lawrence DeWolfe Kelsey: The Life of the Explorer*. Charlottesville, VA: Woodwind Realm, 2017.

Land, Barbara. *The New Explorers: Women in Antarctica*. New York: Dodd, Mead, 1981.

Leane, Elizabeth. *Antarctica in Fiction: Imaginative Narratives of the Far South*. Cambridge: Cambridge University Press, 2012.

Legler, Gretchen. *On Ice: An Intimate Portrait of Life at McMurdo Station, Antarctica*. Minneapolis: Milkwood Editions, 2005.

Lindblad, Lars-Eric. *Passport to Anywhere: The Story of Lars-Eric Lindblad*. New York: Times Books, 1983.

Macmillan, Miriam. *I Married an Explorer*. London: Travel Book Club, 1952.

Map House of London. *The Mapping of Antarctica*. London: Map House of London, 2012.

Mott, Peter. *Wings Over Ice: The Falkland Islands and Dependencies Aerial Survey Expedition*. Long Sutton, U.K.: Peter Mott, 1986.

Paine, M.L., ed. *Footsteps on the Ice: The Antarctic Diaries of Stuart D. Paine, Second Byrd Expedition*. Columbia: University of Missouri Press, 2007.

Passel, Charles F. *Ice: The Antarctic Diary of Charles F. Passel*. Lubbock: Texas Tech University Press, 1995.

Patterson, Diana. *The Ice Beneath My Feet: My Year in Antarctica*. Sydney: HarperCollins, 2012.

Peary, Josephine. *My Arctic Journal: A Year Among Ice-Fields and Eskimos*. New York: Contemporary Publishing, 1894.

Polk, R.L. *Baltimore City Directory 1918–1919*. Baltimore: R.L. Polk, 1919.

Riffenburgh, Beau. *The Myth of the Explorer: The Press, Sensationalism and Geographical Discovery*. Oxford: Oxford University Press, 1994.

Roberts, June, and Steve Heavens. *Penguin Diplomacy: Brian Roberts Polar Explorer, Treaty Maker and Conservationist*. Cirencester, U.K.: Mereo, 2020.

Ronne, Edith M. "Jackie." *Antarctica's First Lady: Memoirs of the First American Woman to Set Foot on the Antarctic Continent and Winter-Over*. Beaumont, TX: Clifton Steamboat Museum, 2004.

Ronne, Finn. *Antarctic Command*. New York: Bobbs-Merrill, 1961.

———. *Antarctic Conquest: The Story of the Ronne Expedition 1946–48*. New York: G.P. Putnam's Sons, 1949.

———. *Antarctica, My Destiny: A Personal History by the Last of the Great Polar Explorers*. New York: Hastings House, 1979.

Ronne, Finn, with Howard Liss. *The Ronne Expedition to Antarctica*. New York: Julian Messner, 1971.

Rose, Lisle A. *Explorer: The Life of Richard E. Byrd*. Columbia: University of Missouri Press, 2008.

Rosenberg, Rosalind. *Divided Lives: American Women in the Twentieth Century*. London: Penguin, 1993.

Rothblum, Esther D., Jacqueline S. Weinstock, and Jessica F. Morris, eds. *Women in the Antarctic*. Binghampton, NY: Harrington Park, 1998.

Sandler, Gilbert. *Jewish Baltimore: A Family Album*. Baltimore, MD: Johns Hopkins University Press, 2000.

Siple, Paul. *A Boy Scout with Byrd*. New York: G.P. Putnam's Sons, 1931.

Sörlin, Sverker, ed. *Science, Geopolitics and Culture in the Polar Region*. Norden Beyond Borders. Farnham, U.K.: Ashgate Publishing, 2013.

Stam, David H. *What Happened to Me: My Life with Books, Research Libraries, and Performing Arts*. Bloomington, IN: AuthorHouse, 2014.

Stam, David H., and Deidre C. Stam. *Books on Ice: British and American Literature of Polar Exploration*. New York: Grolier Club, 2005.

Thomas, Lowell. *Sir Hubert Wilkins: His World of Adventure*. Toronto: McGraw-Hill, 1961.

Thomson, W. Tommy. *The Life of a Swordfish Flyer*. Isle of Arran, U.K.: Banton Press, 2011.

Walton, Kevin. *Two Years in the Antarctic*. Colwall, U.K.: Knell Press, 1982.

ORAL HISTORIES

Aughenbaugh, Nolan. Interview by Brian Shoemaker and Dian Belanger. April 12, 2001. Accessed through the Byrd Polar Research Archival Program, Byrd Polar and Climate Research Center, Ohio State University, Columbus, Ohio.

Behrendt, John C. Interview by Brian Shoemaker. March 14, 2000. Accessed through the Byrd Polar Research Archival Program, Byrd Polar and Climate Research Center, Ohio State University, Columbus, Ohio.

Black, Richard Blackburn. Interview by William J. Cromie. February 1962. Accessed through the Oral History Research Office, Columbia University, New York, New York.

Bull, Colin. Interview by Brian Shoemaker. August 20, 2000. Accessed through the Byrd Polar Research Archival Program, Byrd Polar and Climate Research Center, Ohio State University, Columbus, Ohio.

Chipman, Elizabeth. Interview by Ros Bowden. 1987. Accessed through the Australian Antarctic Division Oral History Collection, National Library of Australia, Sydney, Australia.

Dalrymple, Paul C. Interview by Dian O. Belanger. June 1987. Accessed through the Byrd Polar Research Archival Program, Byrd Polar and Climate Research Center, Ohio State University, Columbus, Ohio.

DenHartog, Stephen. Interview by Brian Shoemaker. October 22, 2002. Accessed through the Byrd Polar Research Archival Program, Byrd Polar and Climate Research Center, Ohio State University, Columbus, Ohio.

Dodson, Robert. Interview by Chris Eldon Lee. February 2000. Accessed through the British Antarctic Survey, Cambridge, England.

———. Interview by Brian Shoemaker. July 24, 2000. Accessed through the Byrd Polar Research Archival Program, Byrd Polar and Climate Research Center, Ohio State University, Columbus, Ohio.

Fiske, Clarence O. Interview by Evelyn M. Cherpak. September 11, 1975. Accessed through the Naval War College, Newport, Rhode Island.

Fountain, Gordon. Interview by Brian Shoemaker. October 19, 1996. Accessed through the Byrd Polar Research Archival Program, Byrd Polar and Climate Research Center, Ohio State University, Columbus, Ohio.

Jaburg, Conrad J. *Ice Eagles: An Account of American Aviation in Antarctica.* By Thomas Henderson. Graceful Willow Productions, n.d. YouTube video. March 29, 2015. youtube.com/watch?v=7txtTap43Nw.

———. Interview by Dian O. Belanger. May 8, 1998. Accessed through the Byrd Polar Research Archival Program, Byrd Polar and Climate Research Center, Ohio State University, Columbus, Ohio.

Kirwan, John. Interview by Chris Eldon Lee. June 17, 2011. Accessed through the British Antarctic Survey, Cambridge, England.

Malville, McKim. Interview by Brian Shoemaker. October 3, 2000. Accessed through the Byrd Polar Research Archival Program, Byrd Polar and Climate Research Center, Ohio State University, Columbus, Ohio.

McCormack, William S. Interview by Laura Kissel. March 8, 2000. Accessed through the Byrd Polar Research Archival Program, Byrd Polar and Climate Research Center, Ohio State University, Columbus, Ohio.

McLean, Donald. Interview by Brian Shoemaker. April 27, 1997. Accessed through the Byrd Polar Research Archival Program, Byrd Polar and Climate Research Center, Ohio State University, Columbus, Ohio.

Neidle, Alan. Interview by Brian Shoemaker. July 19, 2000. Accessed through the Byrd Polar Research Archival Program, Byrd Polar and Climate Research Center, Ohio State University, Columbus, Ohio.

Passel, Charles. Interview by Gary McCaleb. February 4, 1988. Accessed through the University of North Texas Libraries, The Portal to Texas History, Abilene, Texas.

———. Interview by Raimund E. Goerler. February 13–14, 2000. Accessed through the Byrd Polar Research Archival Program, Byrd Polar and Climate Research Center, Ohio State University, Columbus, Ohio.

Patterson, Diana. Interview by Tim Bowden. March 16, 1996. Accessed through the Australian Antarctic Division Oral History Collection, National Library of Australia, Sydney, Australia.

Peden, Irene. Interview by Brian Shoemaker. May 8, 2002. Accessed through the Byrd Polar Research Archival Program, Byrd Polar and Climate Research Center, Ohio State University, Columbus, Ohio.

Peterson, Harries-Clichy. Interview by Brian Shoemaker. May 8, 2000. Accessed through the Byrd Polar Research Archival Program, Byrd Polar and Climate Research Center, Ohio State University, Columbus, Ohio.

Pugh, Marion Stirling. Interview by C.D.B. Bryan. 1987. Accessed through the Society of Woman Geographers, Washington, D.C.

Reed, Dale R. Interview by Brian Shoemaker. May 6, 2002. Accessed through the Byrd Polar Research Archival Program, Byrd Polar and Climate Research Center, Ohio State University, Columbus, Ohio.

Reimer, John David. Interview by Brian Shoemaker. May 6, 2000. Accessed through the Byrd Polar Research Archival Program, Byrd Polar and Climate Research Center, Ohio State University, Columbus, Ohio.

Revelle, Roger Randall Dougan. Interview by Sarah L. Sharp. 1984. Accessed through the Regional Oral History Office, Bancroft Library, University of California, Berkeley, California.

Ronne, Finn. *Antarctic Show*. By Mark Evans. 1961. Austad Collection MS 107-A. Ambassador Mark Evans Austad Collection Addendum. Stewart Library, Special Collections, Weber State University, Ogden, Utah.

Ronne, Jackie. Interview by Fauno Cordes. October 22, 1993. Accessed through the Society of Woman Geographers, Washington, D.C.

———. Interview by Brian Shoemaker. July 20, 2000. Accessed through the Byrd Polar Research Archival Program, Byrd Polar and Climate Research Center, Ohio State University, Columbus, Ohio.

———. Interview by Elizabeth Smith Brownstein. 2002. Accessed through the Society of Woman Geographers, Washington, D.C.

Roscoe, John H. Interview by Brian Shoemaker. September 18, 2002. Accessed through the Byrd Polar Research Archival Program, Byrd Polar and Climate Research Center, Ohio State University, Columbus, Ohio.

Schlossbach, Isaac "Ike." Interview by John T. Mason Jr. June 17 and June 25, 1969. Accessed through the U.S. Naval Institute, Annapolis, Maryland.

Shapley, Alan. Interview by Brian Shoemaker. January 31, 1997. Accessed through the Byrd Polar Research Archival Program, Byrd Polar and Climate Research Center, Ohio State University, Columbus, Ohio.

Steeves, John M. Interview by Dennis O'Brien. June 17, 1970. Accessed through the John F. Kennedy Presidential Library and Museum, Boston, Massachusetts.

———. Interview by Charles Stuart Kennedy and Thomas Stern. March 27, 1991. Accessed through the Association for Diplomatic Studies and Training Foreign Affairs Oral History Project, Georgetown University, Washington, D.C.

Stonehouse, Bernard. Interview by Chris Eldon Lee. December 12, 2011, and February 7, 2012. Accessed through the British Antarctic Survey Archives, Cambridge, England.

Sweeney, Catherine "Kay" Hauberg. Interview by Georgia Trasker. December 20, 1993, and February 16 and February 23, 1994. Accessed through the Society of Woman Geographers, Washington, D.C.

Swithinbank, Charles. Interview by Paul Merchant. December 12, 2009–February 16, 2010. Accessed through British Library National Life Stories Series, London, England.

Thompson, Tommy. Interview by Chris Eldon Lee. October 1, 2009. Accessed through the British Antarctic Survey, Cambridge, England.

IMAGE CREDITS

American Geographical Society. Courtesy of Karen Ronne Tupek: 116

Author, courtesy of: 7, 67, 148, 206 (top)

Byrd Polar and Climate Research Center, Ohio State University, courtesy of: 135

Clarence O. "Larry" Fiske Collection, Accession # 9458, American Heritage Center, University of Wyoming, courtesy of: 88, 100

Curtis, Leland. Courtesy of Karen Ronne Tupek: 59

DeAtley, Thelma. Courtesy of Karen Ronne Tupek: 139

DeAtley, Thelma. Courtesy of the Navy Art Collection, U.S. Naval History and Heritage Command, Washington, D.C.: 129

Devine, Carol (map) and Aidan Meighan (illustration) for the journal *Ernest.* Courtesy of Carol Devine and Aidan Meighan: 214–15

Eggvin, Jens. Courtesy of the Norwegian Polar Institute, NP002093: 8

Harris & Ewing. Wikimedia Commons: 150

Hondius, Hendrik. digitalcollections.lib. washington.edu/digital/collection/maps/id/80/: 4

Latady, William. Courtesy of the Latady family: 64–66, 75, 80, 104, 114

McSaveney, Eileen, courtesy of. pri.org/stories/2019-05-20/hi-i-want-job-antarctica-meet-first-female-researchers-blaze-path: 191 (top)

Mittelholzer, Walter. ETH-Bibliothek, Zürich. Public domain: 160

Norwegian Polar Institute, NP037157, courtesy of: 9

Payne, Duncan, courtesy of: 42, 61

Penguin Random House, courtesy of: 155

Price, D.I. Courtesy of Karen Ronne Tupek: 32 (bottom)

Ronne Tupek, Karen, courtesy of: 16 (top & bottom), 22, 23, 26, 30, 32 (top), 35, 36, 38, 44, 47, 56, 69, 73, 76, 82, 86, 89, 93–95, 97, 107, 113, 124, 125, 133, 138, 144, 151, 153, 158, 165, 168, 169, 171, 176, 178, 179, 183, 187, 197, 200, 204, 206 (bottom), 213

Smithsonian Institution Archives, Acc. 90-105-Science Service, Records, 1920s–1970s: 191 (bottom)

Star. Courtesy of Karen Ronne Tupek: 161

Times. discerninghistory.com: 210

U.S. Naval History and Heritage Command, Curator Branch, Washington, D.C., courtesy of: 119

Underwood & Underwood. Wikimedia Commons: 50

Wikimedia Commons: 170, 201

INDEX

International Association of Antarctic
Tour Operators (IAATO), 198
International Geophysical Year (IGY),
157, 162–63, 165–66, 195, 245–46,
249

Japanese West Antarctica Expedition,
182
Jones, Dr. Lois, 186, 190–91, 228

Kasco Dog Food Company, 135
Kelly, Ruth, 175, 228
Kelsey, Lawrence "Larry," 55, 99, 101
Ketchum, Commodore Gerald, 117
Klenova, Maria, 175, 228
Kon Tiki Expedition, 52–53

Lapataia, 180–81
Lassiter, James "Jim," 67, 100, 112–13,
117, 124, 137
Latady, William "Bill," 3, 55, 77, 79, 86,
93, 99, 104–5, 115, 124, 224, 242
LeMay, General Curtis, 51, 135
Light, Richard, 48, 133, 136
Lindblad, Lars-Eric, 180–81, 247

Marguerite Bay, 10, 77, 85, 91, 117–18,
120, 199
Marie Byrd Land, 3, 164, 214, 234
Maslin, Charles Jackson, 15–19, 235
Maslin, Edith Pratt, 18, 24
Maslin, Merriel Pratt (later Gardner), 16,
18–19, 21–25, 37–38, 72, 127, 185
Maslin, Samuel Jackson, 18, 24
Mawson, Sir Douglas, 6, 126, 211
McClary, Jane McIlvaine, 156
McClary, Nelson, 67, 77, 90–94, 99, 117,
124, 204
McLean, Donald, 55, 73, 90, 92–93, 99,
101, 108, 118, 124
McWhinnie, Mary Alice, 190–91, 229
Mikkelsen, Caroline, 9–10, 211, 227
Mikkelsen, Klarius, 9

Morgan, Elizabeth, 8
Morrell, Abby Jane, 7
Mount Vinson, 182, 230

National American Woman Suffrage
Association, 20
National Bureau of Standards (NBS), 18,
21, 24, 29–30, 236
National Geographic Society (NGS),
23–27, 136, 195, 197
National Woman's Party, 20
Nef, Evelyn Stefansson, 149, 193
Nichols, Robert "Bob," 54, 70, 90, 100,
124, 132
Nineteenth Amendment, 20
North American Newspaper Alliance
(NANA), 52, 71, 87, 109
Norway, 5, 35, 37, 52, 137, 164, 177–78,
180

Operation Tabarin, 78
Owen, Arthur "Art," 67, 100, 105, 124
Owen, Russell, 134, 150

Parlett, Daniel, 18
Parlett, Elizabeth, 15–21
Pennsylvania Shipyards, 63, 68
Peterson, Harries-Clichy "Harcly," 55,
99, 105–7, 124, 130, 140, 241
Phi Mu, 24–25, 31, 73, 235
Pierce-Butler, Kenelm "Ken," 79–80,
105–6, 109
Pope Sr., Robert, 118–19
Port of Beaumont, 56, 69, 73, 75–77,
81–82, 86, 92–93, 117–21, 124, 132,
139, 203, 238
Pugh, Marion Stirling, 26–27
Punta Arenas, Chile, 74–75, 120–21

Rachlew, Ingebjørg Lillemor, 9–10, 227
Roberts, Brian, 181, 247
Robertson, James "Jimmy," 67, 86, 90–91,
105, 124

ABOUT THE AUTHOR

Photo by Hannele Kafarowski-Payne.

JOANNA KAFAROWSKI IS a Canadian independent scholar and geographer and holds a Doctor of Philosophy degree in Natural Resources and Environmental Studies. She has worked on gender issues in the polar regions for over two decades and participated in a Last Degree North Pole Expedition. She is a Fellow of the Royal Geographical Society, a Fellow of the Explorers Club, and a Member of the Society of Woman Geographers.